ALICE Programming

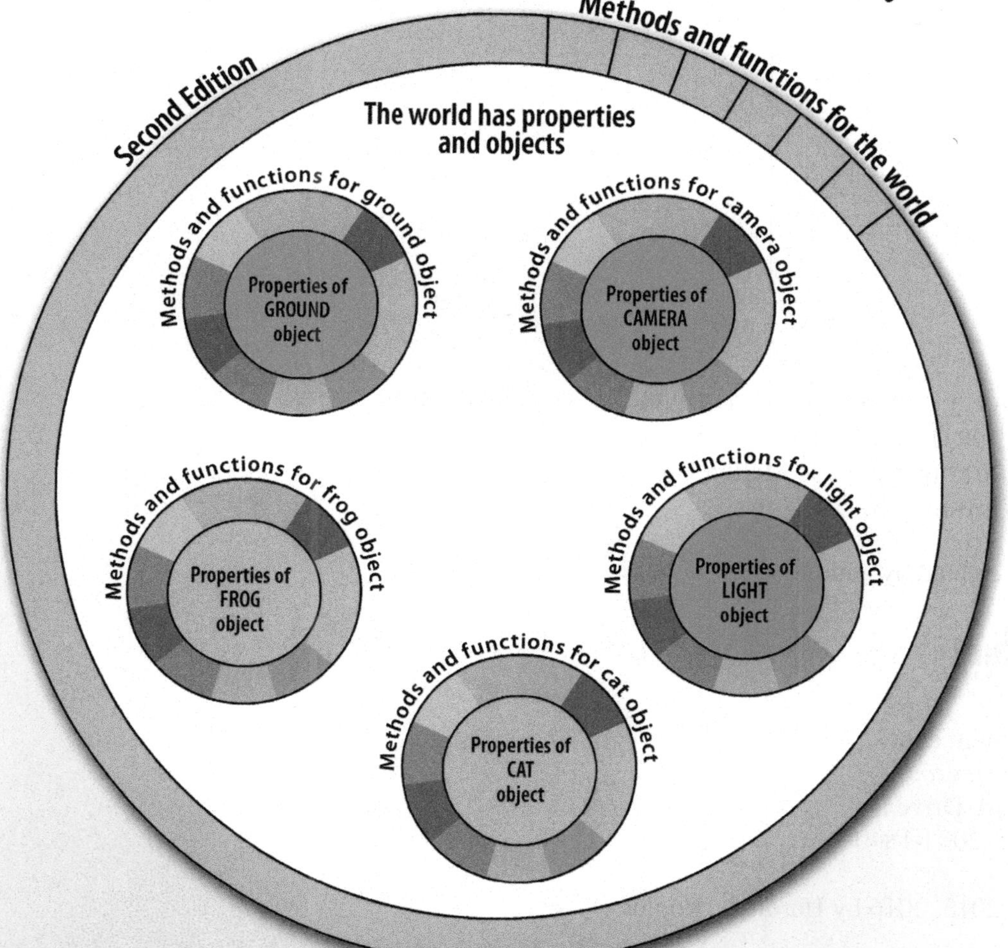

HAROLD L. ROGLER, PH.D.

Kendall Hunt
publishing company

Kendall Hunt
publishing company

www.kendallhunt.com
Send all inquiries to:
4050 Westmark Drive
Dubuque, IA 52004-1840

ISBN 978-1-4652-8980-3

Printed in the United States of America

Table of CONTENTS

CHAPTER 4. METHODS AND FUNCTIONS

CHAPTER 5. CONTROL STRUCTURES

Preface and ACKNOWLEDGMENTS

Several texts on Alice programming have been written that are thorough, accurate, and obviously reflect the authors' great experience and breadth of knowledge in computer programming. However, if a text is intended to introduce programming and not animation in about 20 classroom hours, as done in many schools that include Alice in an introduction to computer science course, a shorter text is warranted that focuses on programming elements. Because properly documenting a program with pseudocode so the author and others can follow the logic is so important, shouldn't that be stressed? (And by the way, shouldn't the example programs supplied to the students be good examples?) Programming uses expressions (arithmetic, Boolean, and string concatenations), so in the limited class time available, shouldn't those be stressed?

With these issues in mind, I kept the book length to under 150 pages, and I separated the material on programming with Alice into a separate text from the remaining content of the course Introduction to Computer Systems, so that the Alice programming text could be replaced with another text if a language other than Alice is used.

Auxiliary materials include over 40 computer programs, each focused on one or a few elements of programming, and projects to practice programming.

A lecture-by-lecture outline is available to guide instructors while teaching Alice.

Some sections of chapters are marked *optional*. Such material is included because students' interests and time available to study vary considerably. In the classes I teach, students are not responsible in projects and on exams to have studied the optional materials.

I acknowledge many stimulating discussions with my colleagues in the Computer Science & Information Systems Department at Santa Monica College over the last decade.

Thank you, students, for your stimulating questions, curiosity, and hard work on your many Alice projects.

Folders and Programs Using Alice to Illustrate Programming Features

Stored at \Acshare\busdata\ROGLER_HAROLD\CS3 Introduction to Computer Systems\CS3 Alice examples

- Demonstrate comments, user story, pseudocode, top-down design
  - Demonstrates multi-level top-down design.a2w
  - Demonstrates user story and outline with frog and cat after coding.a2w
  - Demonstrates user story and outline with frog and cat before coding.a2w
  - Scenario and pseudocode example.txt (text file)
- Demonstrate dummy objects
  - Demonstrates use of dummy objects for camera POVs.a2w
- Demonstrate events
  - Demonstrates event to open and close castle door.a2w
  - Demonstrates events that set property values for opacities.a2w
  - Demonstrates events with helicopter.a2w
- Demonstrate good or interesting Alice projects
  - Changing seasons by Lauren Gifford.a2w
  - Demonstrates parameters with underhanded throwing of ball.a2w
  - Demonstrates parameters with underhanded throwing of ball_B.a2w
  - Squares Game by Seth Wax
  - TOP_N00B.a2w
- Demonstrate If control structure
  - Demonstrates If controlled by a Boolean expression comparing strings.a2w
  - Demonstrates If controlled by question using dragon.a2w
  - Demonstrates parameters with four types of data with somersaults and IF.a2w
- Demonstrate loops
  - Demonstrates For loop with five ways a number can be supplied.a2w
  - Demonstrates While loop with woman chasing a man.a2w
- Demonstrate user-generated world- and object-level methods
  - Demonstrates methods generated by user object-level and world-level.a2w
  - Demonstrates object- and world-level methods.a2w
  - Demonstrates object-level method for dragon to flap wings.a2w
  - Demonstrates object-level method for stepping soldier.a2w
  - Demonstrates object-level method user-generated with pterodactyl flying.a2w
  - SteppingToySoldier.a2c
- Demonstrate parameters
  - Demonstrates hypotenuse function with parameters.a2w
  - Demonstrates method with object parameters using moveTo.a2w
  - Demonstrates parameter and method for toySoldier to march.a2w
  - Demonstrates parameter number based on Christian_Mary.a2w
  - Demonstrates parameter number for walking.a2w
  - Demonstrates parameters string and object.a2w
  - Demonstrates parameters string with Old MacDonald had a farm.a2w
  - Demonstrates parameters with four types of data with somersaults.a2w
  - Demonstrates parameters with pterodactyl flying.a2w
  - Demonstrates stepMany with parameter.a2w
- Demonstrate translations and rotations of airplane
  - Demonstrates point of view with airplane that translates and rotates.a2w
- Demonstrate user-generated function
  - Demonstrates user-generated function for frog volume.a2w
- Demonstrate variables
  - Demonstrates variables and expressions.a2w
  - Demonstrates variables number and interactive inputs.a2w
  - Demonstrates variables string and interactive inputs.a2w
- Miscellaneous
  - DefendingNaptime.a2w
  - Demonstration of method using moveTo.a2w
  - IceSkater.a2w

Chapter 1 INTRODUCTION TO ALICE

Contents

INTRODUCTION

What is Alice?

Alice is an object-oriented computer language that allows you to create animations with three-dimensional **objects** such as animals, people, buildings, cars, airplanes, and hundreds of others. You can see most objects on your screen. These objects are created (instantiated) from **classes** (blueprints, recipes, or templates for the objects). The classes are stored in easily accessible Alice libraries stored on your computer when you install Alice or available from the Internet. At least for elementary programming, classes are not created by the programmer, but rather many hundreds of built-in classes are used to create objects.

Alice has many built-in programs called methods and func.tions, and you can create your own. Alice has expressions (arithmetic, Boolean, and string), comments to document your code, variables, parameters, events, and arrays. The programmer can create local variables within user-created methods and functions. The programmer also can create property variables (variables that store values for new properties of an object or the world). These property variables have a global scope. Sounds as MP3 and wav files can be imported and played. It's almost impossible to have a syntax error because the coding is done by dragging tiles into the editing area, and syntax errors are not allowed even in an unfinished program or an incomplete statement.

Behind Alice is the Java language (a powerful and widely used object-oriented language), and you can see your code in Java style or a simpler (Alice) style if you like. When running Alice programs, they're interpreted (not compiled).

Because Alice uses objects, it's especially useful to introduce programming concepts without, at the same time, also facing syntax errors. **Syntax errors** arise when you violate the rules of the language, rules such as spelling key words and punctuation.

Alice introduces **multi-threaded or concurrent programming** through its *doTogether* statement, which means that Alice can execute several programs at the same time, which is an amazing capability for a beginning programmer. It also has other control structures such as an *If/else* structure so you can execute different statements under different conditions, several repetition structures (loops) so you can repeatedly execute some statement, and the *doInOrder* or sequential structure.

Like videos and movies, an allusion of motion is created on the screen by rapidly displaying separate frames. From the program, Alice creates the separate frames and transfers them to the computer screen.

100% opaque, solid hare.
This object has 16 body parts.

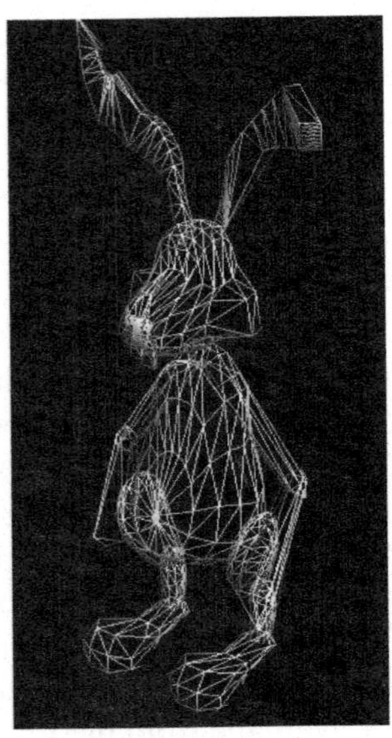

Wire frame composed of 1,730 polygons provides the outer shape of the 3D hare.

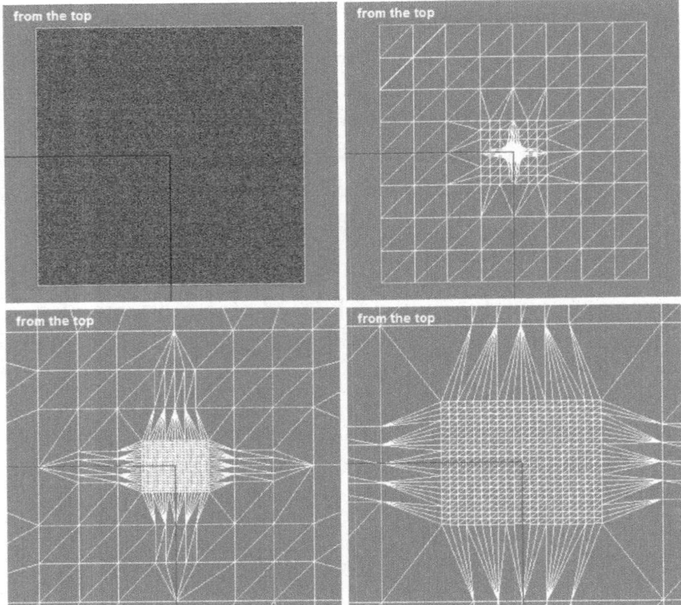

If you look straight down on the grassy ground and zoom very far out, you'll see the ground is composed of a square patch. Will you fall into the abyss if you step over the edge? ☺ Also shown at several magnifications are the 1,152 polygons that make up the ground.

A 12-minute video that introduces Alice: http://www.alice.org/index.php?page=what_is_alice/what_is_alice

On-line tutorials for Alice programming by Dick Baldwin: http://www.dickbaldwin.com/tocalice.htm

Ways to learn computer programming

- Write code (including short programs as experiments just to see how statements and other features work). It's better for you to be running Alice and trying little experiments while you study Alice. It's also more fun. Good reference materials are essential while learning a computer programming language, but you'll learn to program by programming.
- Study programming languages by enrolling in programming courses, listening to and studying lectures, completing Alice's four built-in tutorials, and studying this book and other books.
- Study code to see how other programmers have handled various tasks. Look at the example worlds in Alice. Dozens of Alice programs are in the folder \\Acshare\busdata\ROGLER_HAROLD\CS3 Introduction to Computer Systems\Alice examples.

If your classroom has computers, you may also follow a lecture and code the examples described by your professor.

Installing Alice on your home or office computer (optional)

At your home or office where you can permanently store files, the Alice folder need only be stored once unless files become corrupted or deleted.

If you have an Internet link, download Alice from www.Alice.Org in compressed form, after which you must "unzip" it or uncompress it. From that website, you can choose Windows, Macintosh OS X, or Linux versions of Alice.

No formal installation is required to install Alice (no entries are made into the system registry and there's no special folder or place where Alice's program and libraries of files are stored), although keep the entire Alice folder intact.

Conversely, to remove Alice from your computer, you can drag the entire Alice folder to the trash. Unlike many application programs that require formal installs and de-installs, no formal de-install of Alice is necessary.

You can even run Alice from your USB flash drive without copying it to your internal hard drive, although it'll run slower because the transfer rate from the USB device to the computer's primary memory (its RAM) is slower than from the internal hard drive to the RAM.

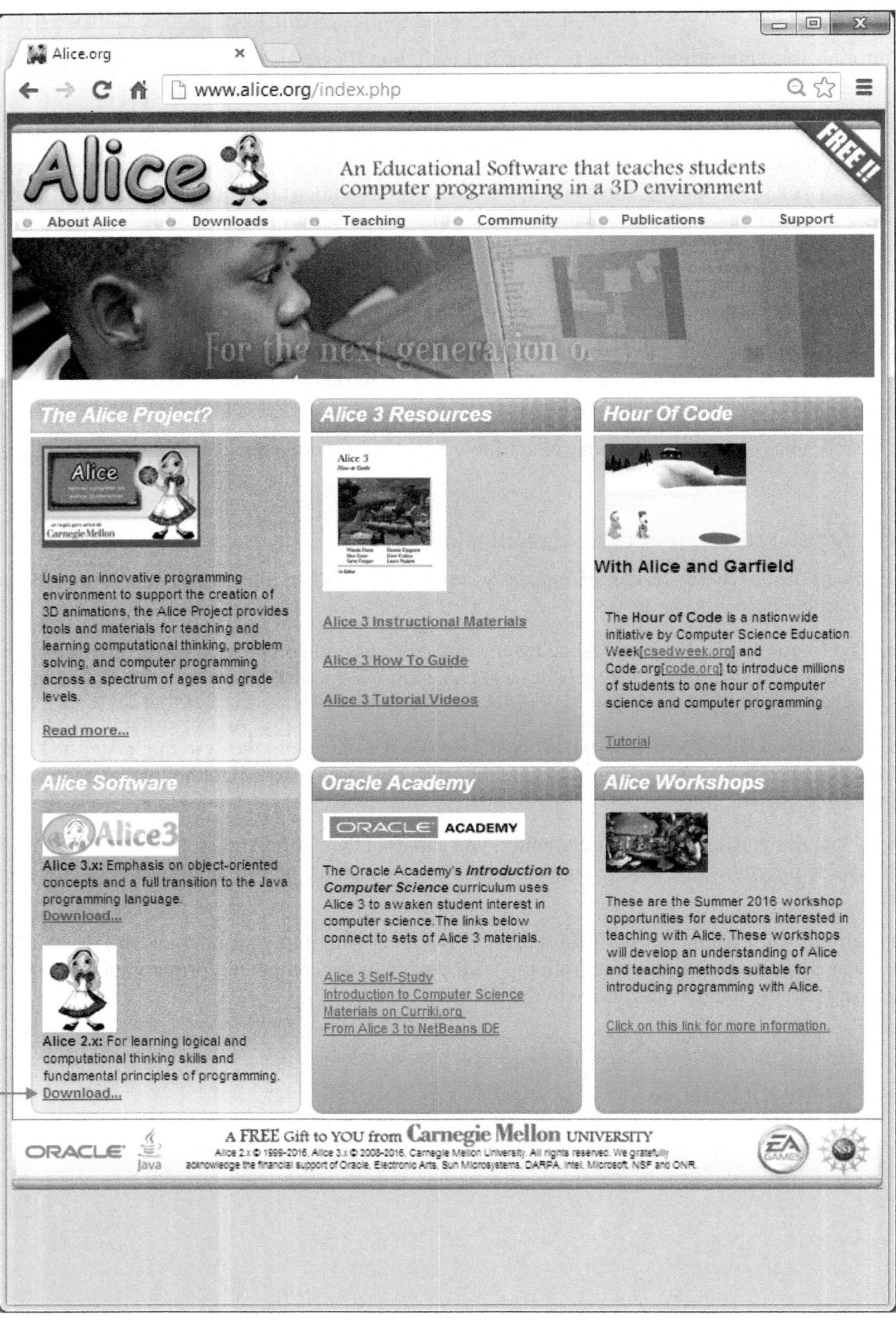

First screen of the Alice.org website. Under Alice 2.x on the lower left, click on Download… Note that another Download for version 3.x appears just above. For a version of Alice compatible with this textbook and the example programs supplied, download the latest version of 2.x, not 3.x.

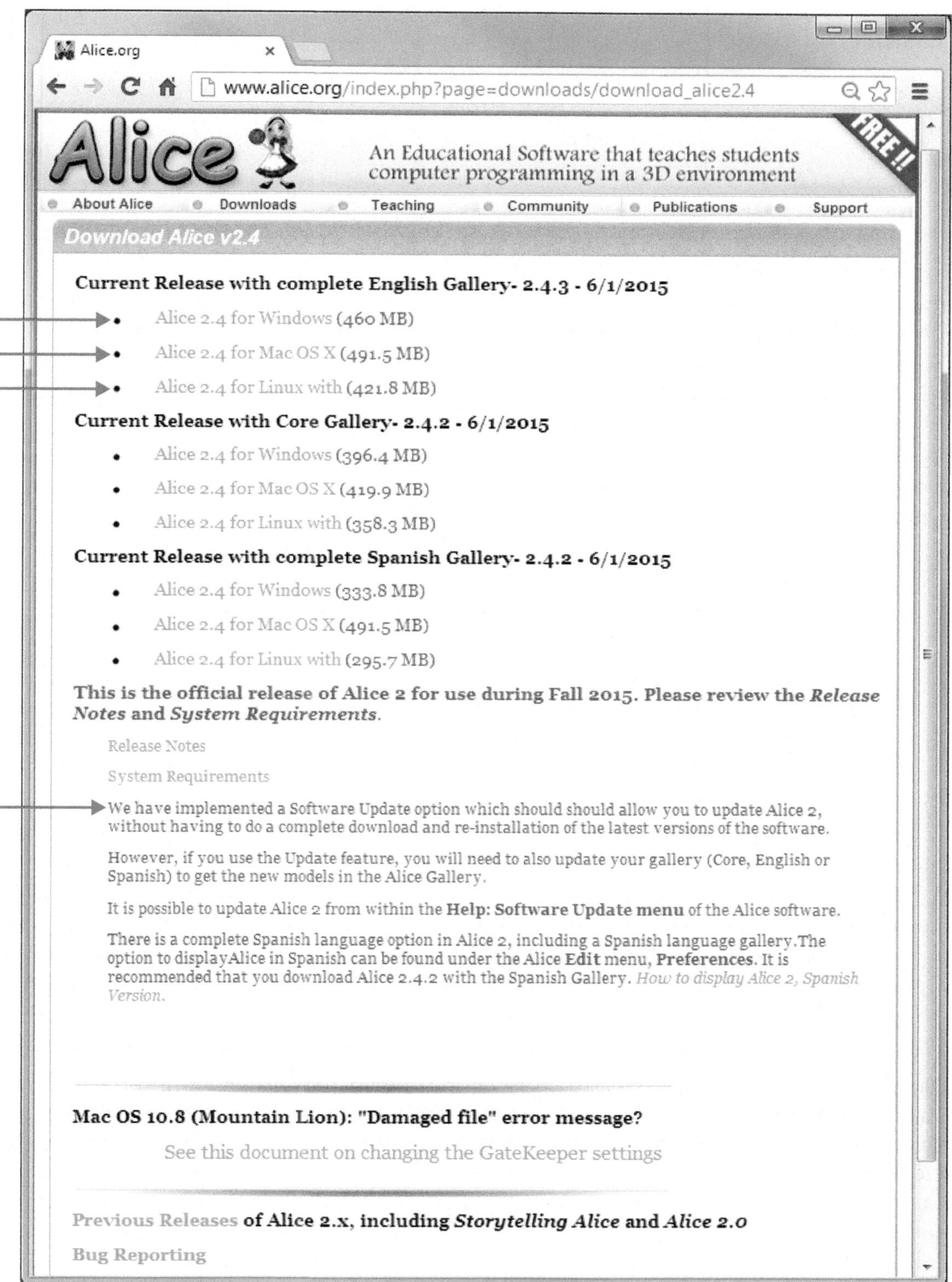

This screen of the Alice.org website lists downloads for version 2.x available for Windows, Mac OS X, and Linux operating systems. Before downloading, click on System Requirements and check to see if your personal computer can run Alice.

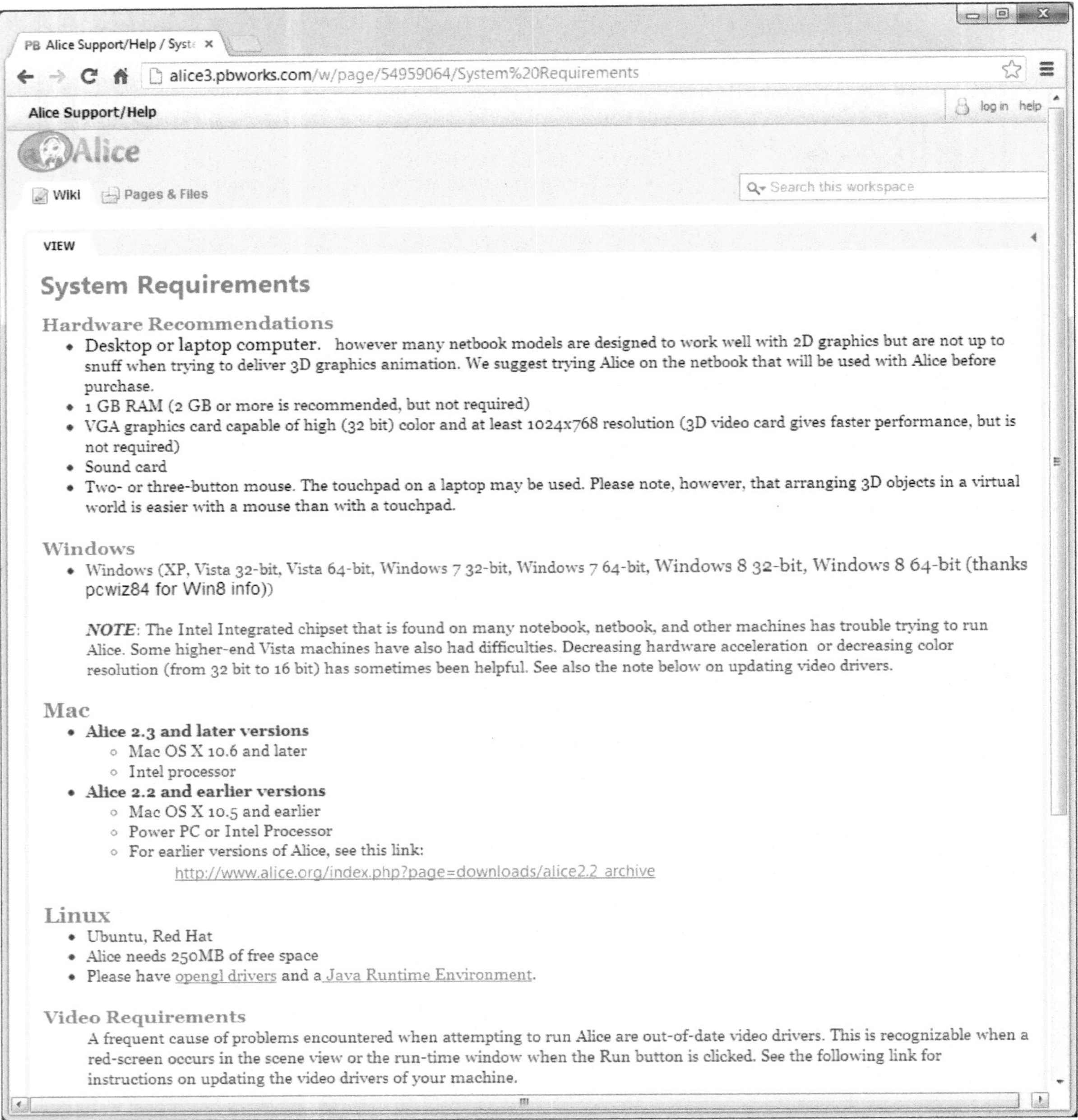

Check these system requirements for Alice 2.x to run successfully on your operating system and hardware. If your system meets these requirements, then return to the previous webpage and download the latest version of Alice 2.x. If you have problems later, you also can return to this webpage. Once you've downloaded the Alice version, you'll need to unzip or decompress the compressed file that you've received.

Diagrams illustrating Alice's world, objects, properties, and their intimately bound methods and functions

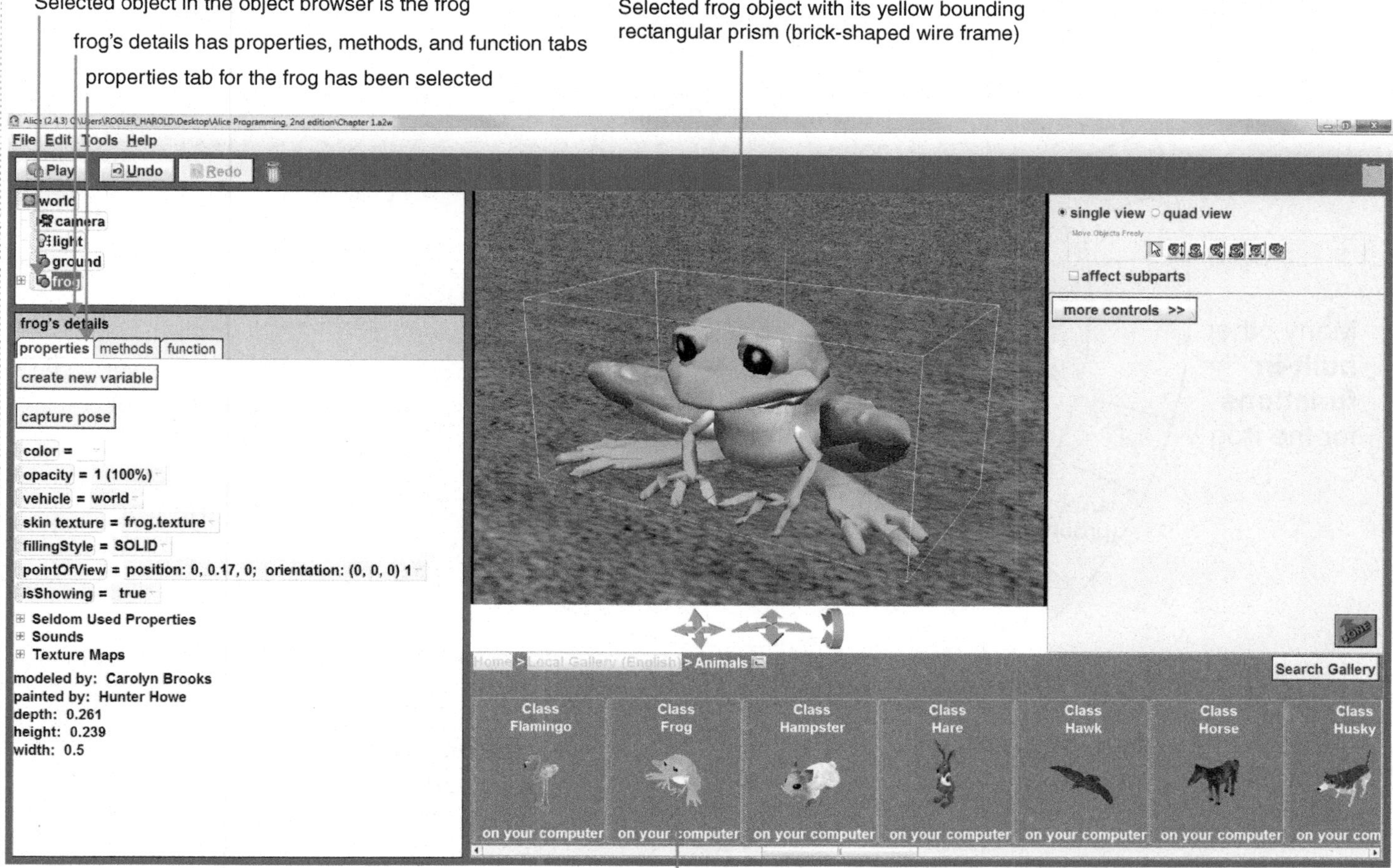

Above is Alice's **integrated development environment (IDE)**, where you create and execute (play or run) Alice programs. You also can load and execute Alice programs created by others, such as those in Alice's example worlds. On the upper left appears the object tree, which lists the world and objects in it. Some of these objects (camera, light, and ground) automatically appear in a new (pristine) world, whereas other objects are added to the world by creating an instance of the class. Object-oriented programmers refer to this process of creating an instance of a class as **instantiating the class**. A **class** is a blueprint, template, or recipe for the object. The distinction between a class and an object instantiated from that class is analogous to the blueprint for a house and the house built according to those blueprints. Of course, the frog object in Alice is virtual. The Frog class is just one of hundreds of classes that you can choose to create objects in your world.

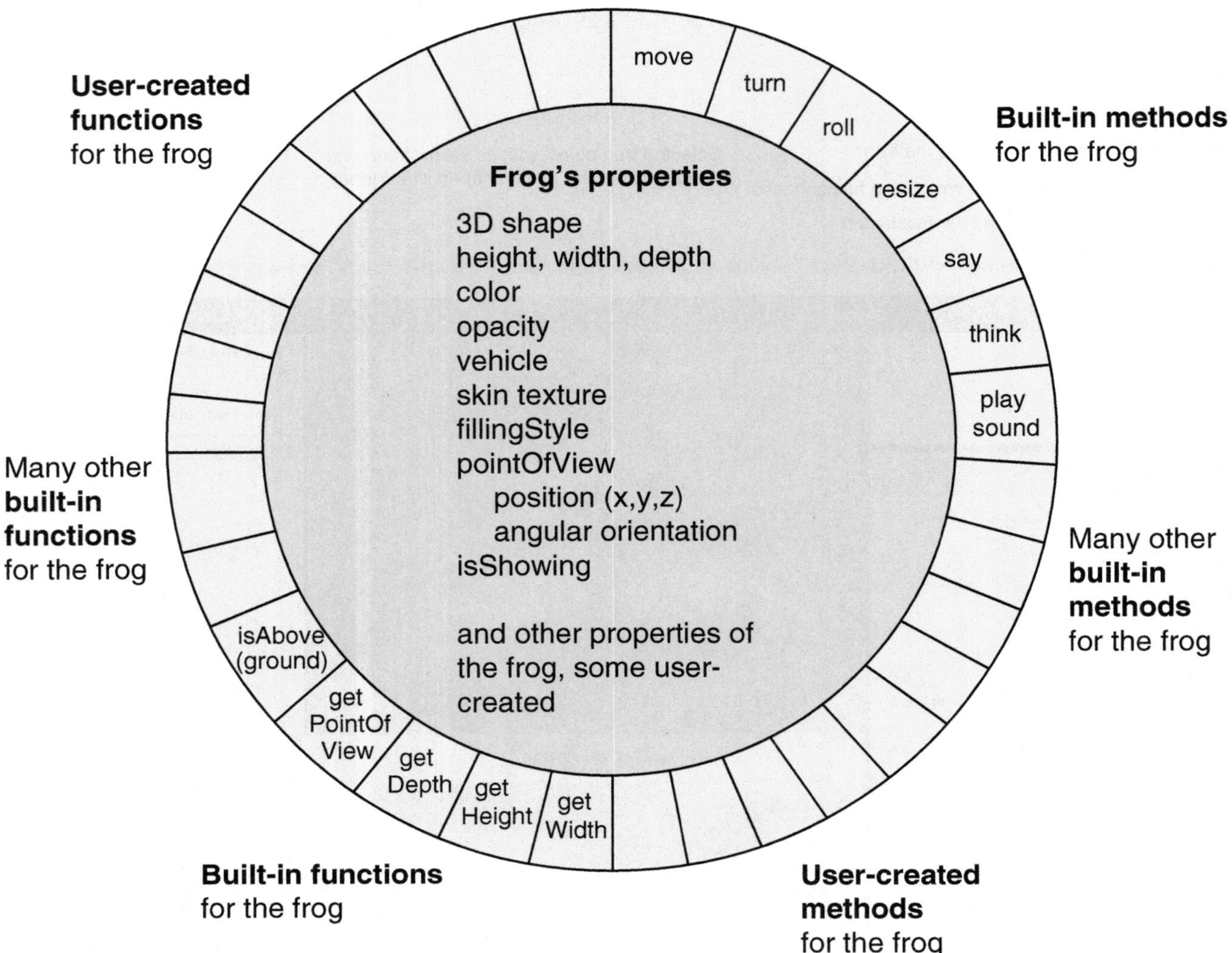

An object's **methods** act to change the properties of the object. For example, the method *move* changes the object's position (the x, y, z coordinates of the object's center relative to the World's coordinate system). These coordinates are displayed under the object's properties as the three *position* coordinates of the object's pointOfView. The methods *turn* and *roll* change the frog's angular orientation; they cause the frog to pitch, yaw, and roll. An object's angular orientation is displayed following the word *orientation* of the object's pointOfView. However, the angular orientation in the pointOfView is not expressed as angles in fractions of a revolution or degrees. Rather, they're trigonometic functions of the angles, with details not important in this book. The combination of an object's position and orientation is called its **quaternion**.

The **functions** answer questions about the object (for example, what is the frog's height or what is the frog's distance from another object). The methods and functions for the frog are shown in a ring around the properties because the methods and functions are intimately associated with a specific object (here, the frog).

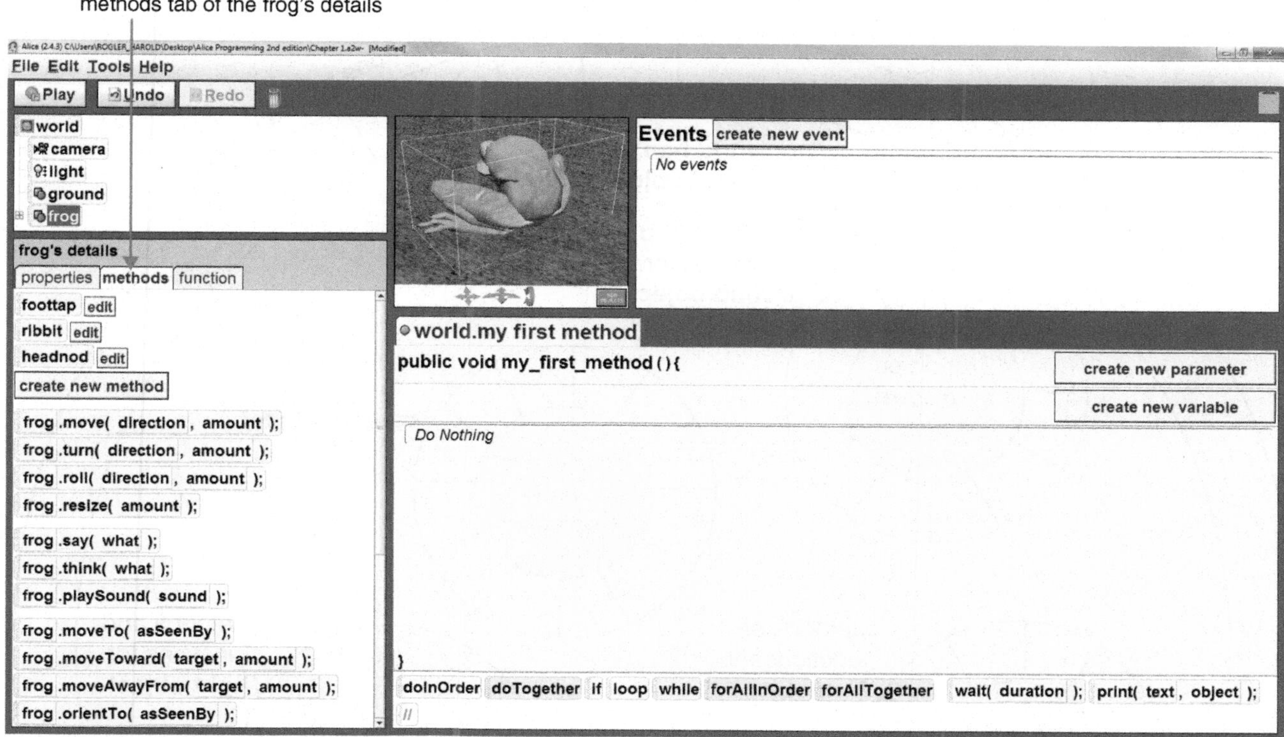

In the details window for the frog, here the methods tab has been selected. On the left are the **built-in (or intrinsic) methods** for the frog. Different objects can have the same or different methods. Above the *create new method* button are three methods that are built in but for which you can view and edit the code. You also can create new methods for the frog, which will also be listed above the *create new method* button.

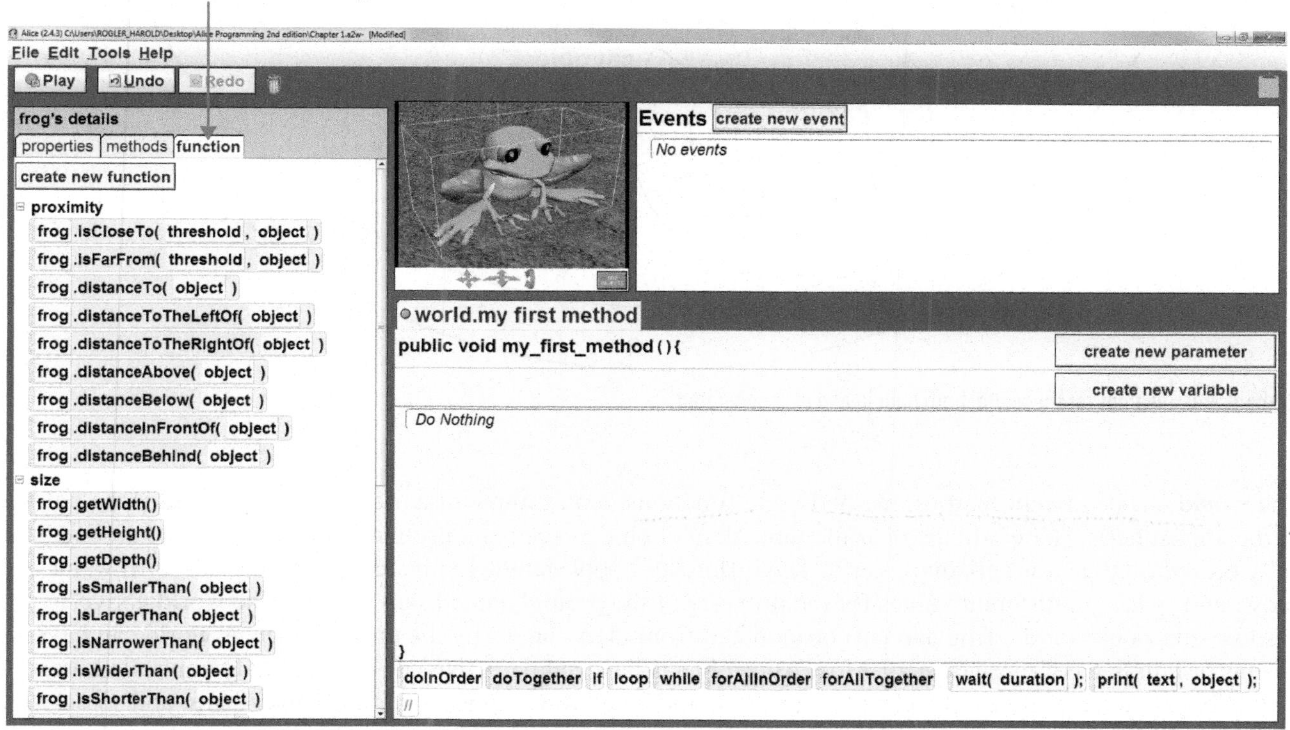

The frog's built-in functions are listed under the functions tab of the frog's details. Functions of an object are intimately linked to that object, and different objects can have the same or different functions. Functions can be built-in or user-created (user-generated or user-coded). Functions don't change the values of properties. Instead, they return values for the properties of an object or several objects. For example, a function could tell you the height of an object, or tell you the distance between two objects.

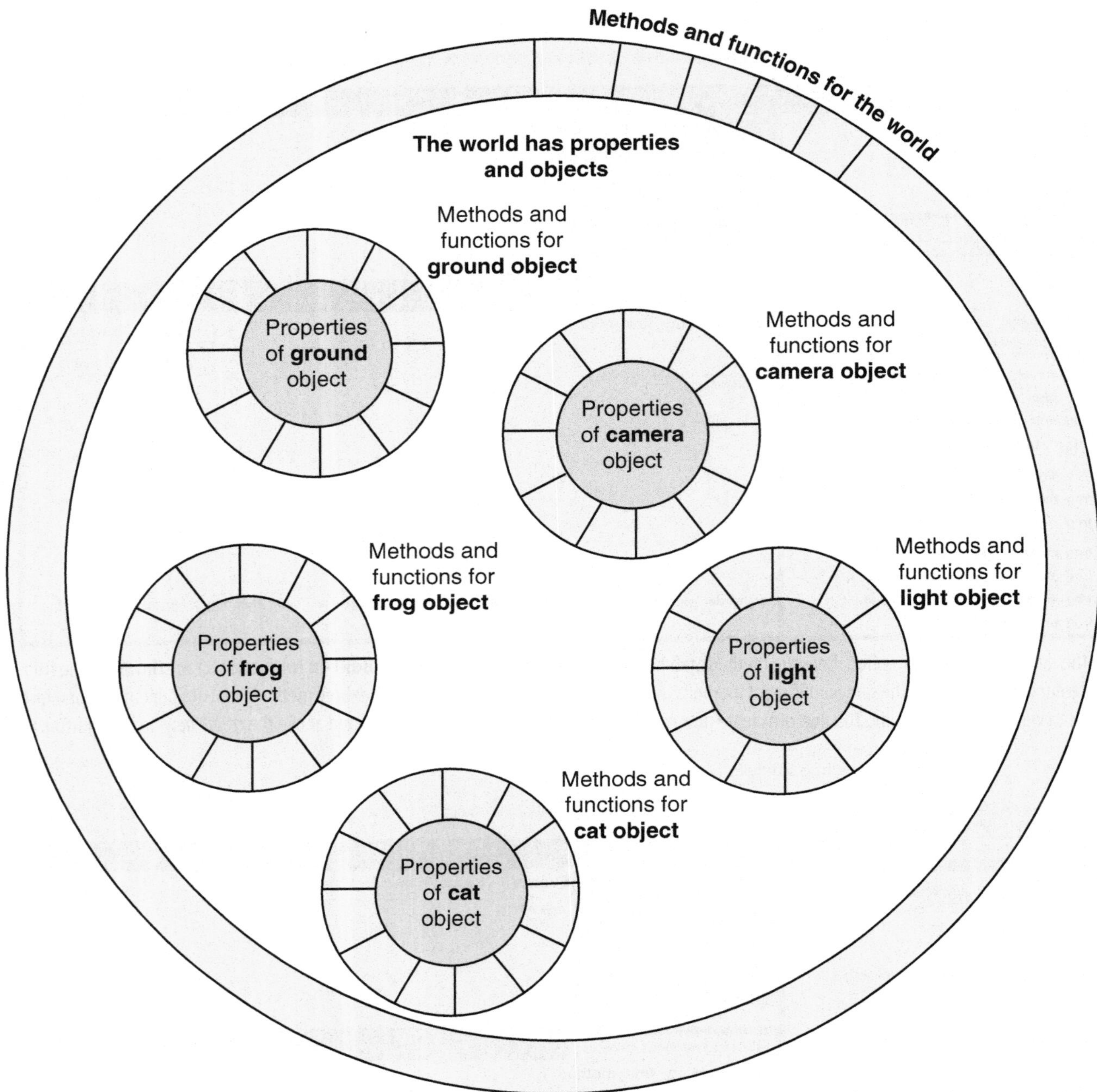

Methods and functions for the world, both built in and user generated.

The **world** has its own properties, methods, and functions. An example of a property of the world is the color of the atmosphere. The world also has the three default objects (camera, ground, and light) that are automatically brought into a new (pristine) world. The differences between the templates for sand, grass, dirt, water, snow, and space are different values for the property of the ground named *skin texture*. The world above has two other objects (the frog and cat) instantiated from their classes by the programmer. A world can have dozens or hundreds of these objects. Most Alice objects have subparts that can be separately controlled. For example, people objects have heads, necks, torsos, upper and lower legs, upper and lower arms, and so on (although different objects can have differently named subparts and different numbers of subparts).

Windows in Alice's programming interface

In Alice's IDE, as shown on page 7, are these windows:

- **World** displays the objects (the instantiations from classes), such as the frog object, as you program or build your animation. You also see the objects move when you run your program.
- **Object tree** lists the objects in your world, some of which can be expanded in a hierarchy to show parts of the object, such as the upper legs, lower legs, and so on. Three objects are automatically created in a new world that you create: camera, light, and ground. These three and others that you instantiate are listed in the object tree. To keep your objects organized, you can right click in the object tree and *create new group* to create folders to store your people, animals, furniture, vehicles, and other categories.
- **World's details** or, for example, the **frog's details,** show details about the world or about whatever object has been selected in the object tree. These details appear under three tabs:

  properties of an object, such as its position (the coordinates x, y, z of the "center" of the object), orientation (the pitch, yaw, and roll angles), color, and others. Not all properties of an object are listed. Some unlisted properties, such as an object's height, can be found by using programs called functions. These properties can be changed in several ways. Other properties such as the geometrical shape of the frog can be seen on the screen, but except for affecting the orientation and position of body parts (e.g., stretching legs) cannot be altered except by Alice's developers.

  methods or programs that change properties of an object. For example, the *move* method changes the position of the object. Other methods change the height, orientation, color, and the many other properties of an object.

  functions are programs that can answer questions about properties, such as

  What is the height of an object?
  How far apart are two objects?
  Is one object taller than another object?

  Functions can return (tell you) the value of a property or some combination of properties (such as the distance between two objects), but functions cannot change the values of those properties.

  Besides the many 2D and 3D objects that you can see on the screen, Alice has a math object, which is not visible in the world view like the many other objects. Associated with this math object are math functions such as square root and trigonometric functions that can return a value. A math function returns a value also.

- **Editor area** where you create new programs (as methods or functions) by dragging and dropping tiles for statements for an object to move, turn, talk, and many others. When creating a program in the Alice language, you need not type these statements. You drag them into the editing area from the methods and functions tabs, or from other places that you'll learn about. The statements are the instructions that tell the computer what to do.

  In this editor area also appear comments that describe your code so you can follow its logic later and so other programmers can understand it. These comments are non-executable, but they're still important because people must read the instructions that tell the computer what to do.

  How the statements appear in the editing area and the events area can be the standard Alice format or Java format, the format used by the powerful and popular object-oriented language.

- **Events area** is where you program **when** to do certain things. It's where you specify what happens when you click the *Play* button (which triggers the event *When the world starts*) and what happens when the user interactively controls the program with arrow keys and other key presses and mouse clicks.

Choices from Alice's menu bar

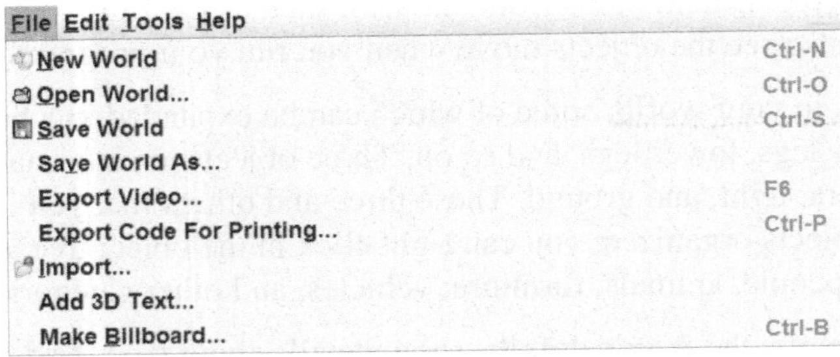

The menu **File** allows you to create a new world, open existing programs, save a world, export a world as a Web page, and others.

The menu **Edit** links to the **Preferences** window below.

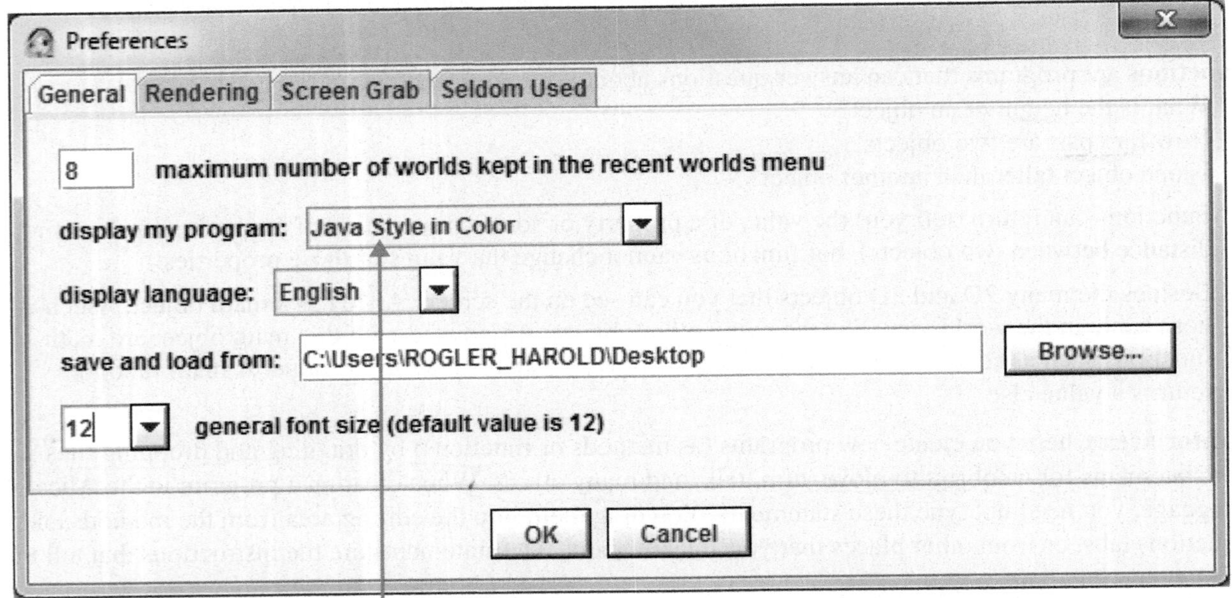

The choice to display your program as *Java Style in Color* is recommended for computer science students. Compared with the choice *Alice Style* for the display, *Java Style* will show Java code and Java syntax. If you change any of these settings, you'll have to restart Alice.

Preferences window.

The menu **Tools** leads to **World Statistics** (shown below), Text Output, and the Error Console.

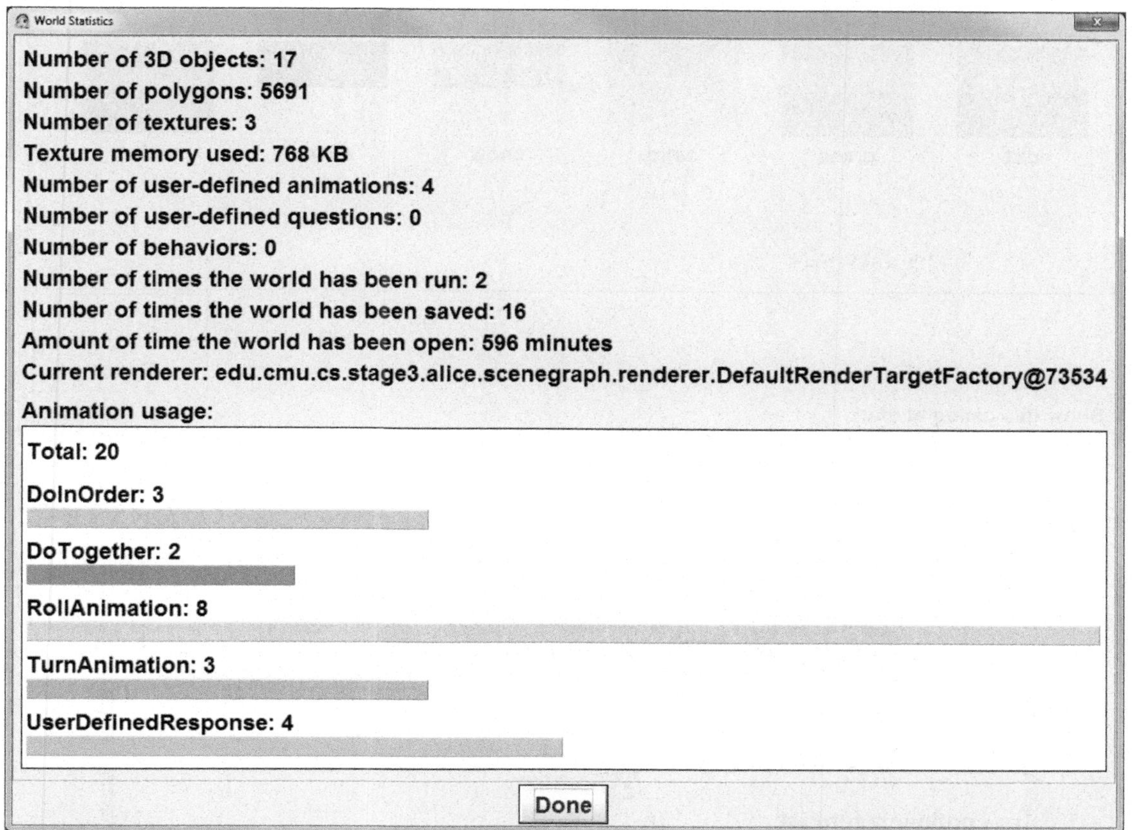

World Statistics.

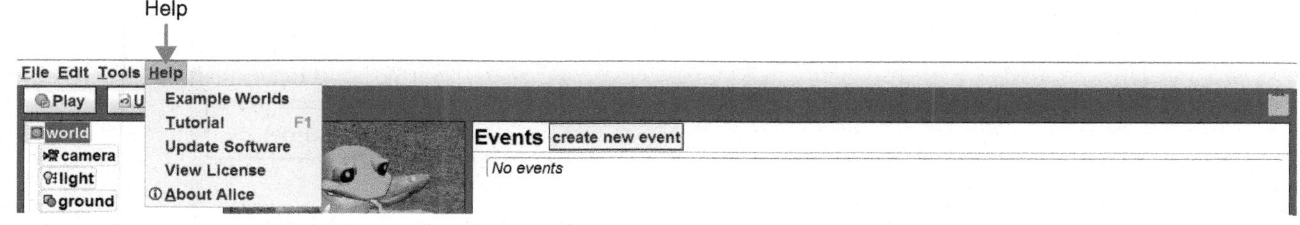

Help links to the Example Worlds, the Tutorials, and Update Software, View License, About Alice.

Opening a new or existing Alice world

Double-click on the Alice 2.4.3 (or a later version you installed) executable file, Alice.exe, and either the following window will appear or the choice of templates under the Templates tab will appear.

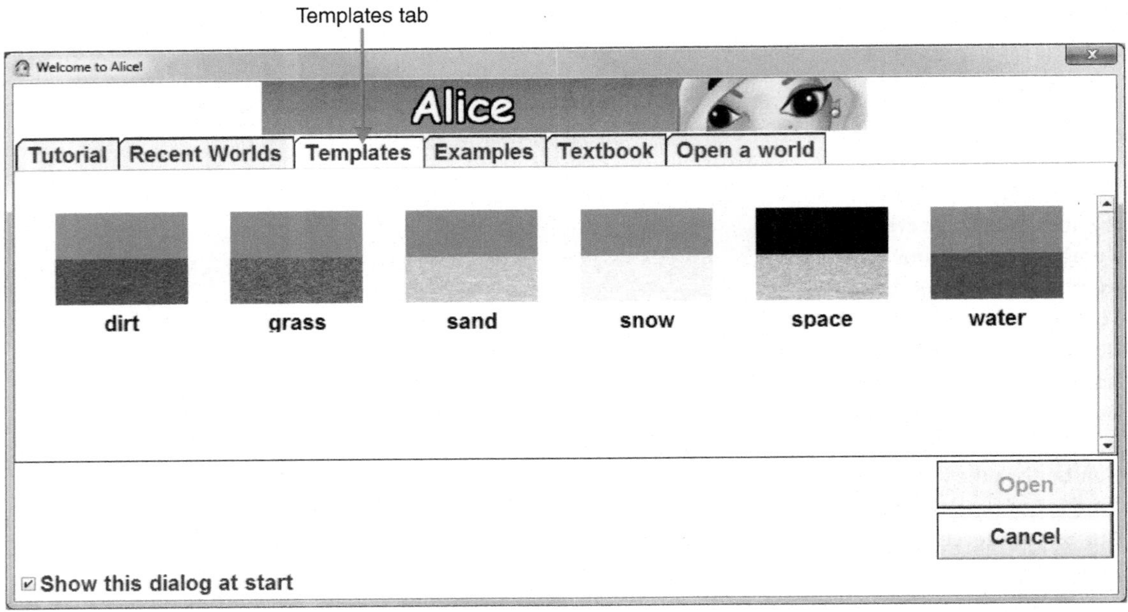

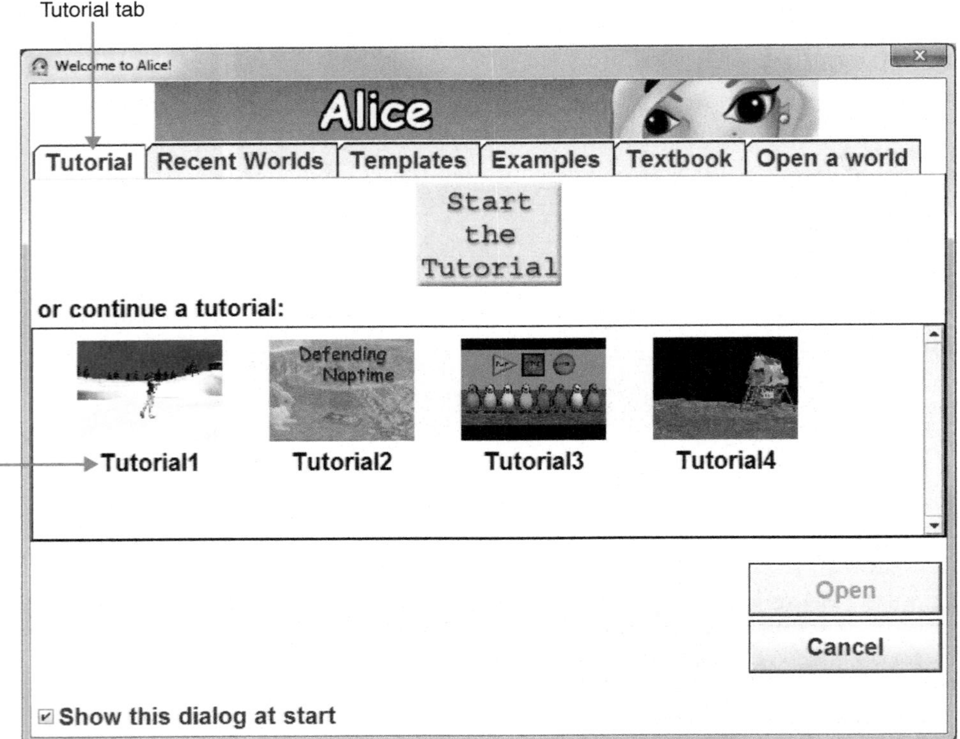

The built-in tutorials can be accessed from the Tutorial tab. Click on Tutorial1 to begin.

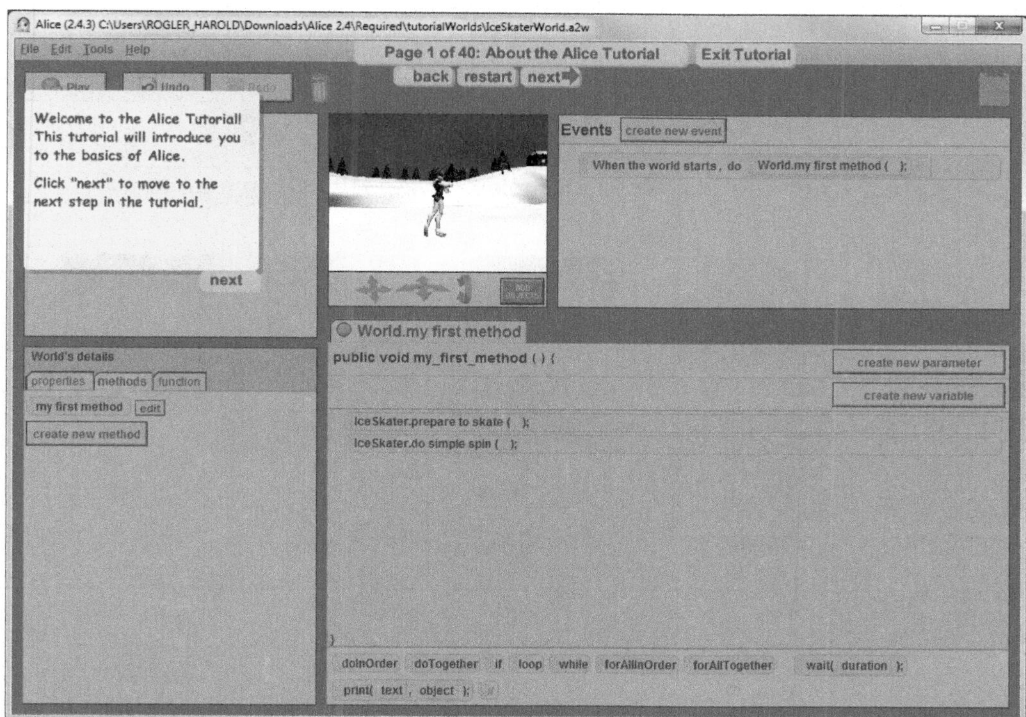

Here's the first screen of the first tutorial with a blue film covering all but what the authors want you to focus on. If you can't finish a tutorial at one sitting, then later open it again and quickly click to the page where you stopped. Alice has four good tutorials that you should finish. I'll now exit the tutorial and move to the next tab.

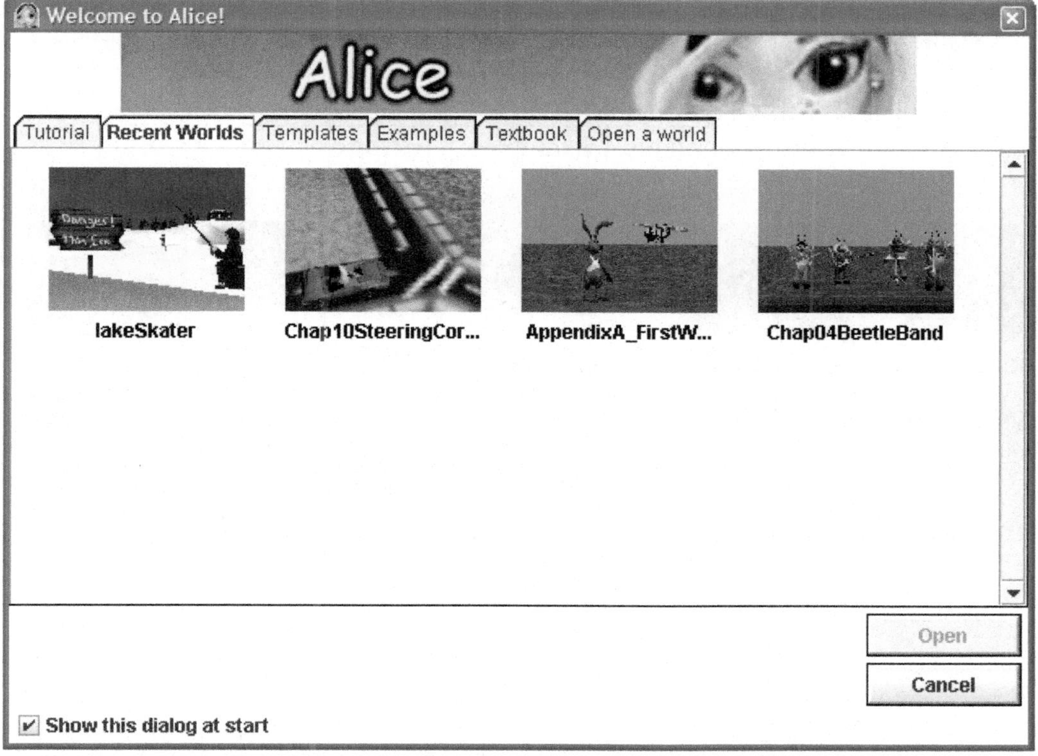

Alice worlds that have been recently opened can be accessed from the Recent Worlds tab.

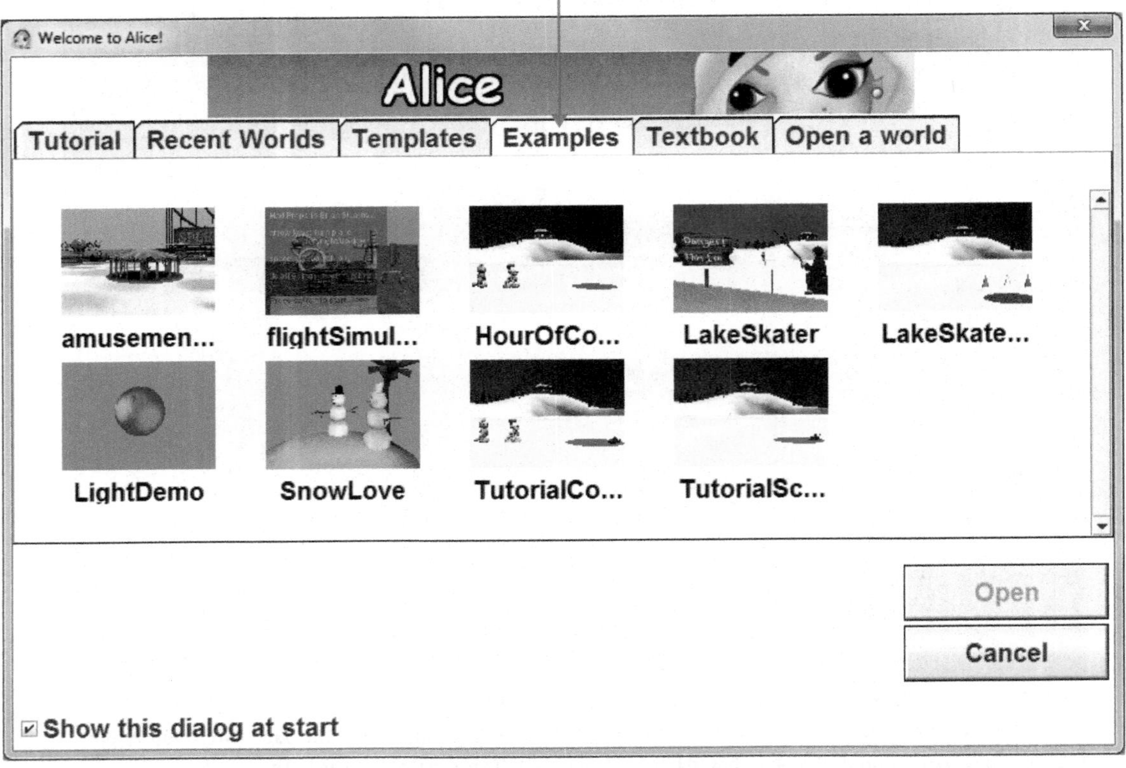

Example worlds can be accessed from the Examples tab. Other Alice programs to demonstrate programming features are stored at Acshare\busdata\ROGLER_HAROLD\CS3 Introduction to Computer Systems\CS3 Alice examples.

Textbook tab

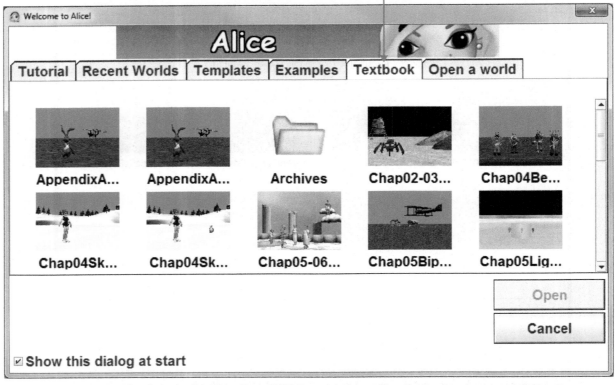

Alice files directly associated with the textbook from Carnegie Mellon can be opened by selecting the program and clicking *Open*.

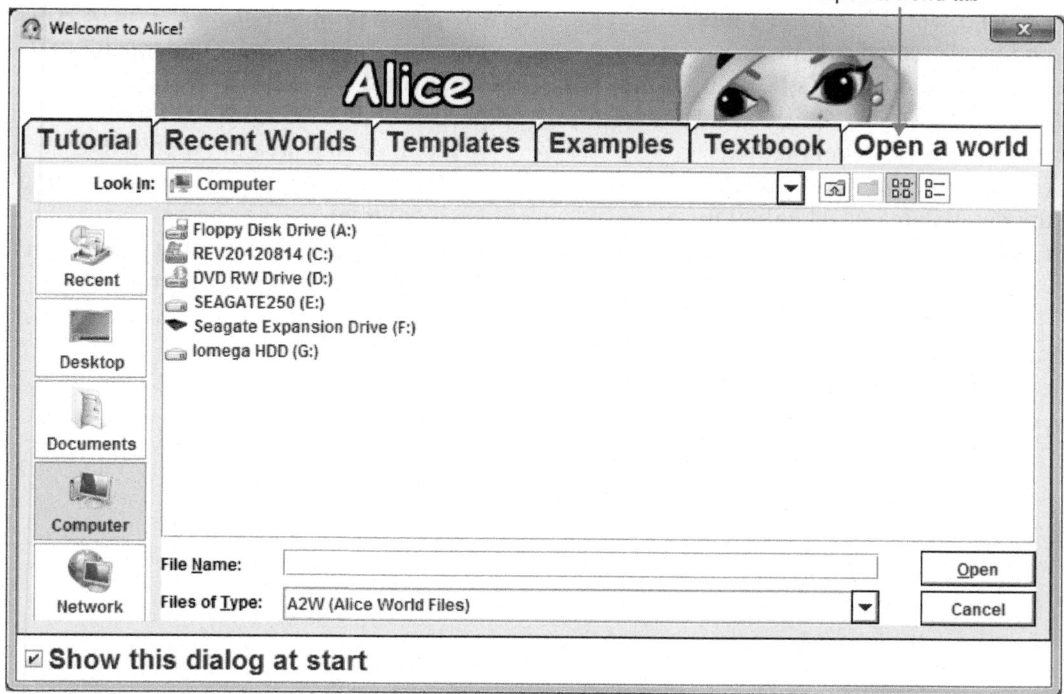

From the *Open a world* tab and then *My Computer*, you can open Alice.a2w files on your USB device and elsewhere on yourcomputer. For Alice to recognize your USB device, it must be connected before you run Alice.

EXERCISES

1.1 Download and "install" Alice on your home or laptop computer.
1.2 Complete the four Alice tutorials.
1.3 Run the example worlds under the Examples tab when you open a new world.
1.4 Describe Alice's IDE: (a) What's listed in the Object browser? (b) Where are the properties of the world or an object listed in the IDE? (c) Where are functions of the world or an object listed? (d) Where are methods for the world or an object listed?
1.5 What's meant by an object's *Point of View* (POV)? Where are POV values listed?

KEY WORDS FOR THE CHAPTER

Alice programming language
Alice's integrated development environment (IDE)
- object tree
- details of the world or an object
  - properties pane
  - functions pane
  - methods pane
- editing or coding area
- events area
- world window

bounding box or rectangular prism for an object
classes
- instantiation of a class (creating an instance of a class)
- libraries of classes

clipboard, Alice
comments
errors while programming or while running a program:
- syntax, logical, and runtime

events

functions
- object-level and world-level functions
- built-in and user-created functions
- pane in details area of Alice's IDE

methods
- object-level and world-level methods
- built-in (or intrinsic) and user-created methods
- pane in the details area of Alice's IDE

object-oriented programming languages

object tree

objects
- listed in the object tree
- properties, methods, and functions of an object
- subparts of

preferences (settings)
- display a program in Java style or Alice style
- number of clipboards (under seldom used)

pristine world

properties of an object or the world
- pane in details area of Alice's IDE
- changing a property value while running a program

running a program or executing a program

system requirements for a program

Chapter 2 CLASSES, OBJECTS, AND POSITIONING OBJECTS

Contents

INTRODUCTION TO CLASSES AND OBJECTS

Classes are the recipes or blueprints to create objects. Objects have properties, and objects also have intimately bound programs called methods and functions. In Alice, the classes are provided in libraries either stored on your computer or accessible through the Internet. In other object-oriented languages such as Java or C# (C Sharp), the programmer would either code the class from scratch or import a class from those available and either use it as it is or, usually, extend the class through a process called inheritance. Objects in Alice are 3D virtual objects that you can see on your screen.

CREATING AN OBJECT IN YOUR WORLD (I.E., CREATING AN INSTANCE OF A CLASS)

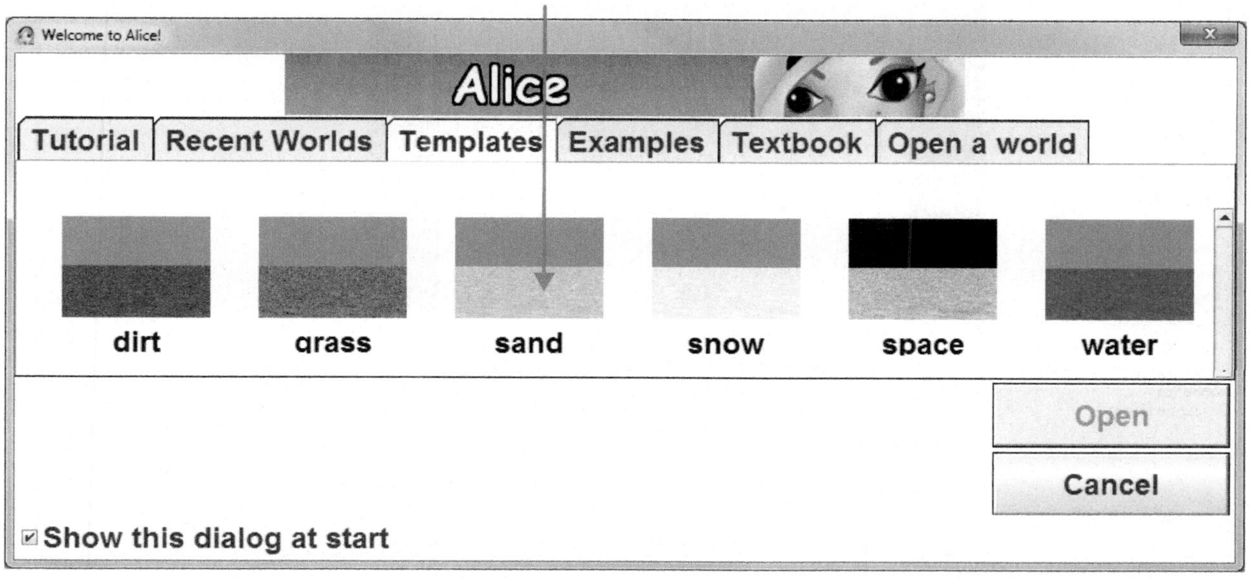

Opening a new Alice world will display the templates tab. Choose one of the templates for the ground. For the example below, I've chosen *sand*.

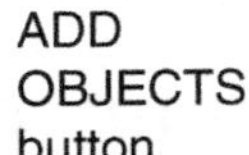

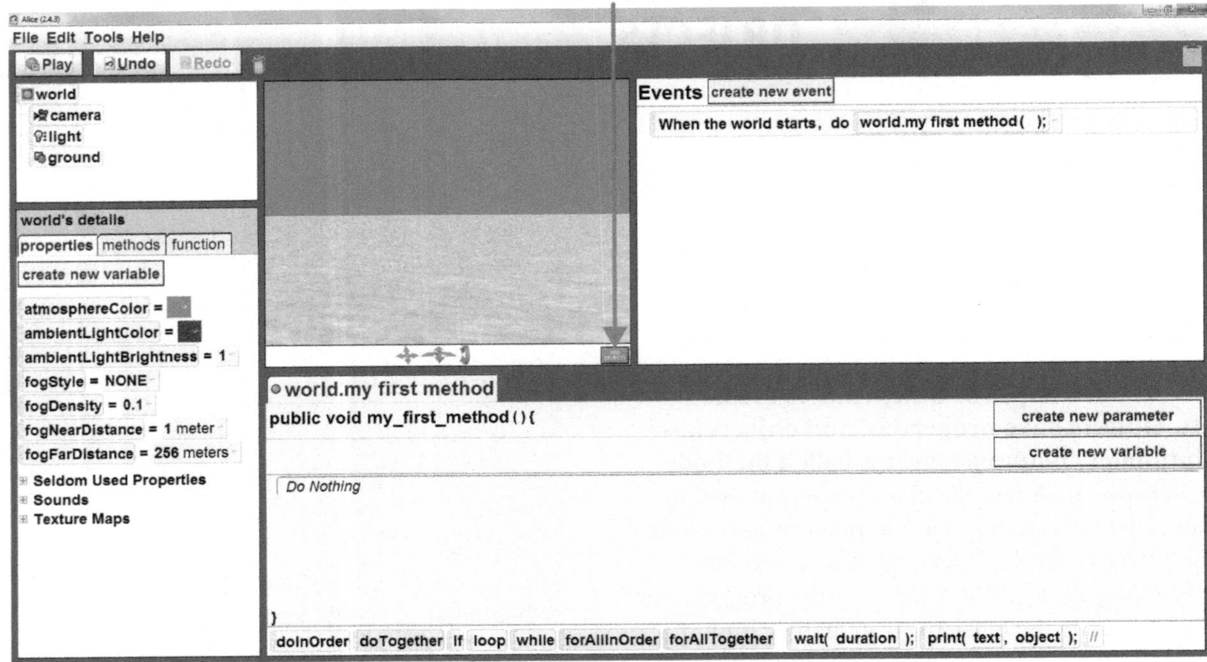

The Alice integrated development environment (IDE) displays the world, object browser, details area, events area, and editing area described in Chapter 1. This is a (new) pristine world with only a camera, light, and the ground. Except for the one event (When the world starts) and the method *my first method* that it causes to execute, this pristine world has no other coding. Click the *ADD OBJECTS* button to add one or more objects or position objects.

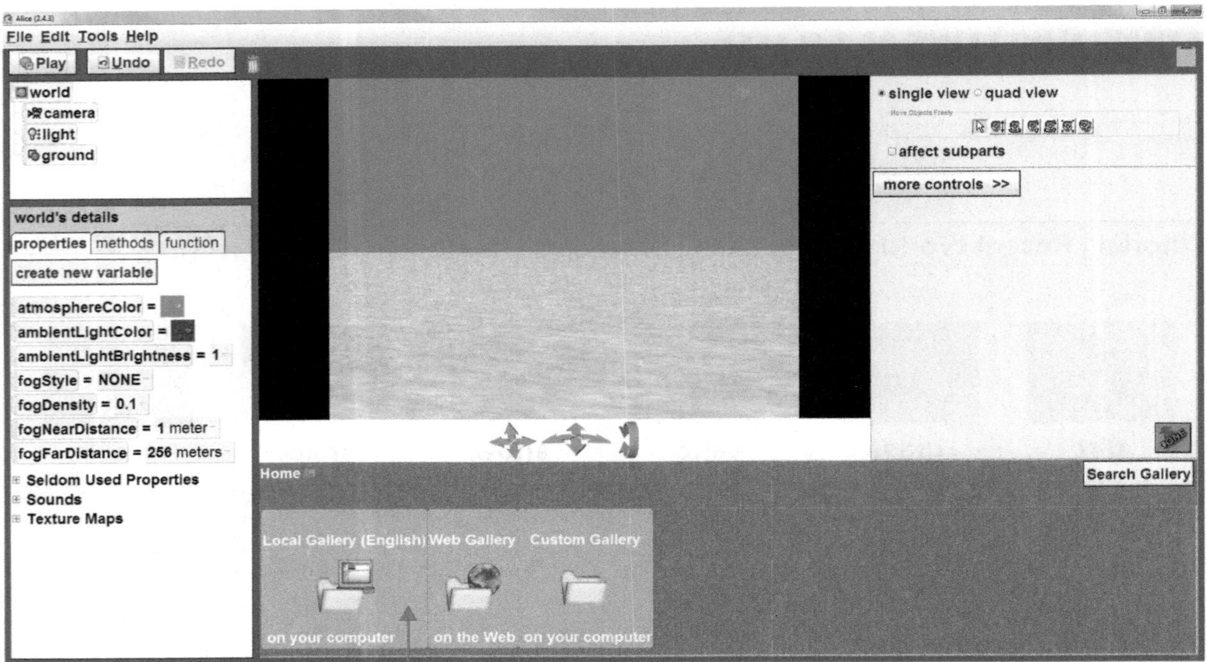

Clicking *ADD OBJECTS* displays two libraries of classes (used to create objects): the Local Gallery stored on your computer when you installed Alice, and the Web Gallery that allows you to access classes on the Internet.

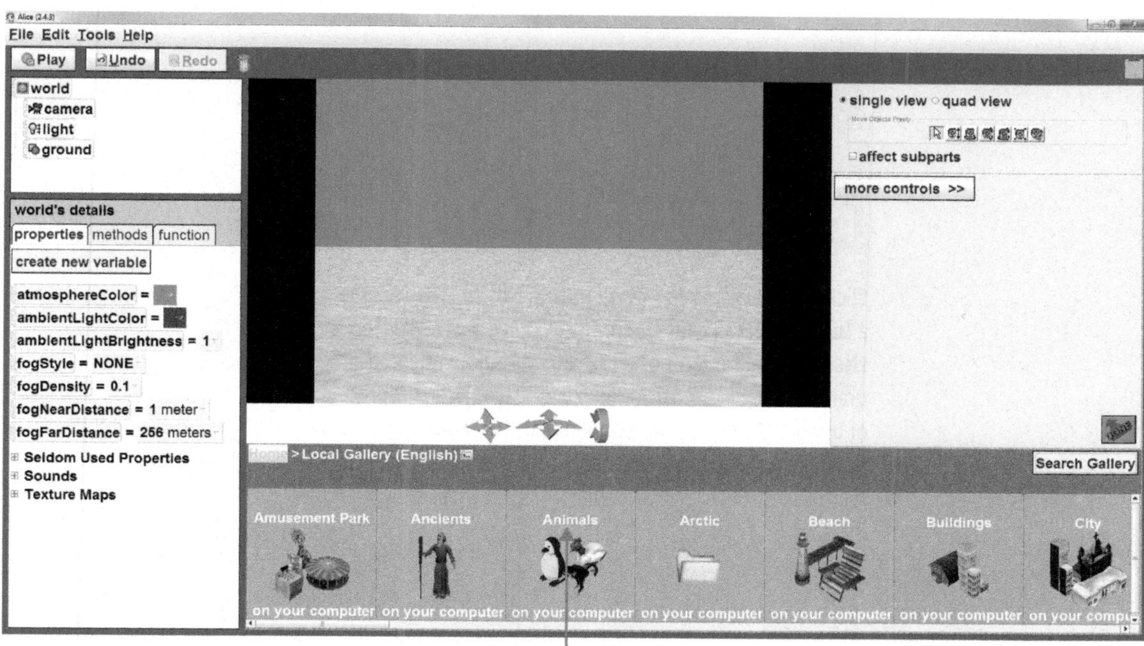

The Local Gallery has been expanded. Classes are listed alphabetically. Select *Animals*.

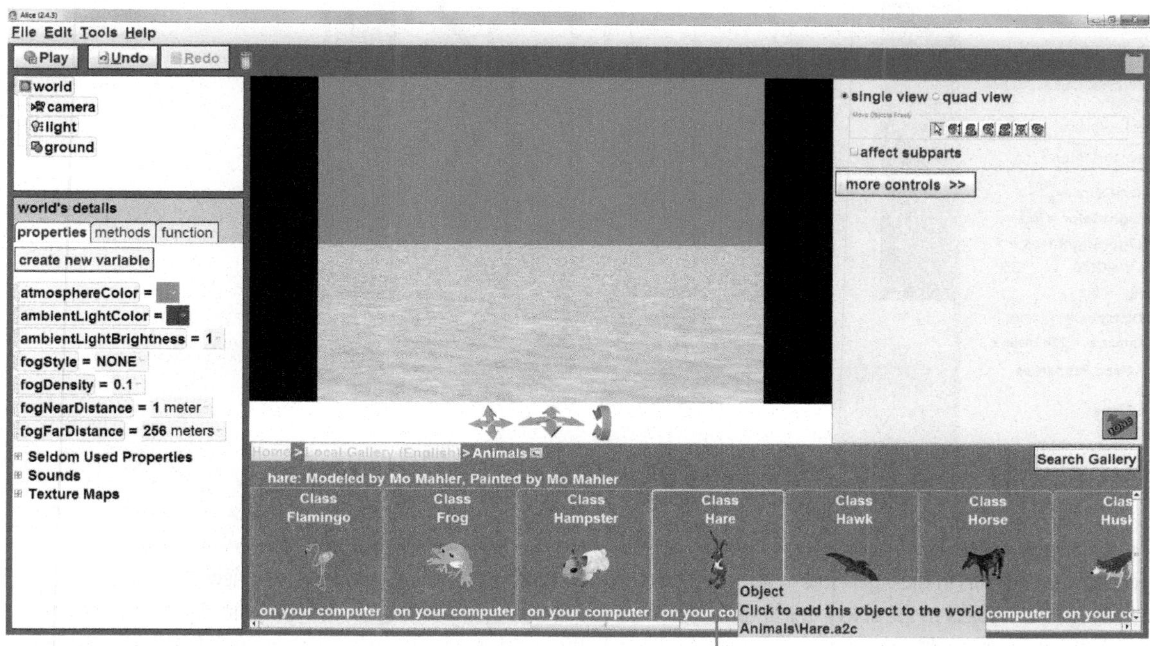

Selecting *Class Hare* opens the dialog box as shown on the next page.

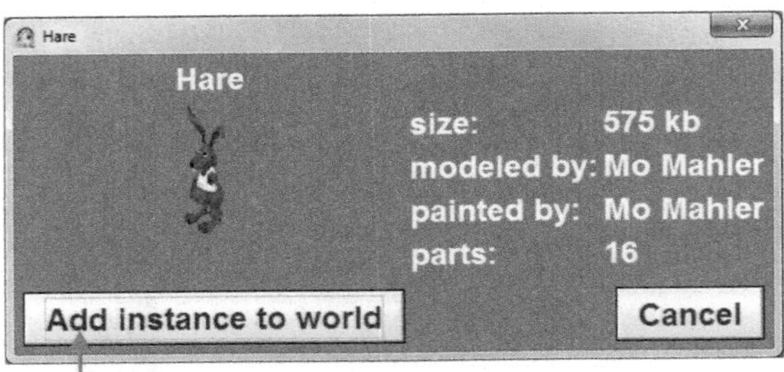

Clicking *Add instance to world* uses the **Hare class** to create a **hare object** in your world. This is called **instantiation of the class**. Although not all objects in object-oriented programming (OOP) are 3D or even 2D virtual objects, the process of using a class as a recipe or blueprint to create an object is used throughout object-oriented programming.

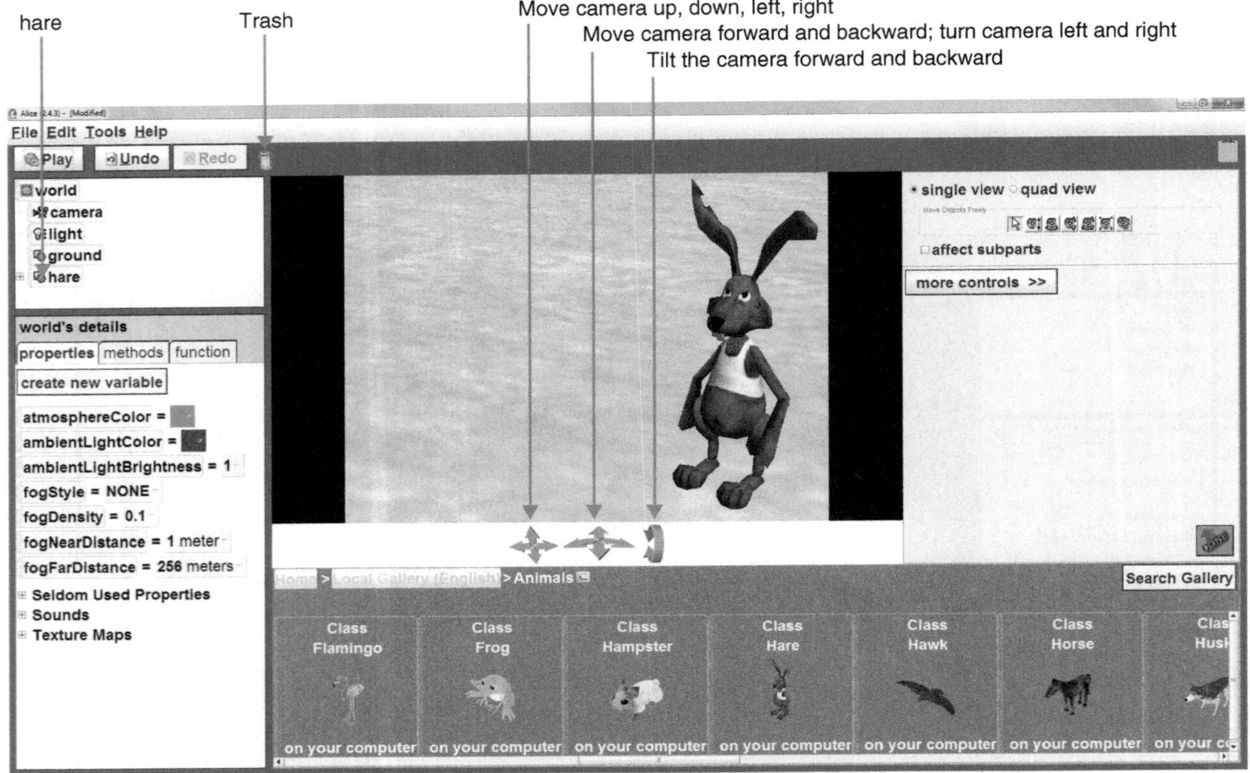

The object *hare* now appears in the object tree in the upper left and the virtual 3D hare appears in the world view. You can delete an object by right-clicking on the object in the object tree or directly in the world and selecting *delete*, or dragging the object from the object tree into the trash. When finished with adding objects, click *DONE*. Beneath the world are the manual camera controls described at the top of the page. To the right of the world window are controls that are described below. These controls only appear while you're adding objects and you're in *single view*.

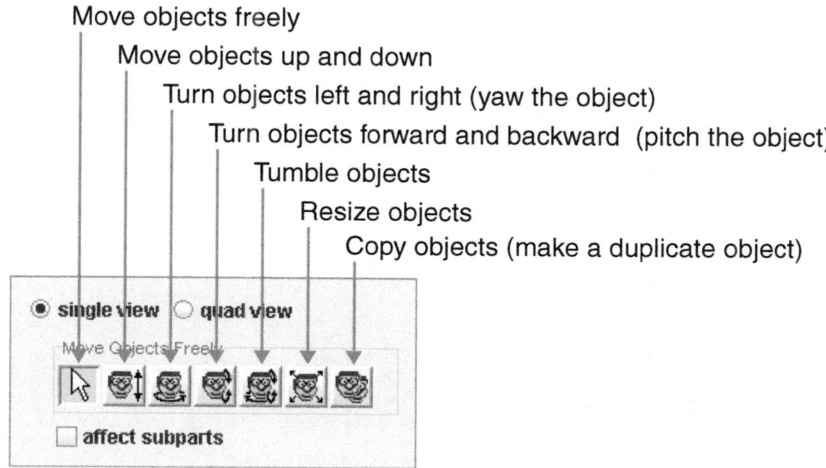

These controls allow you to position and orient a selected object with your mouse. The best way to learn about these controls is to try them while running Alice.

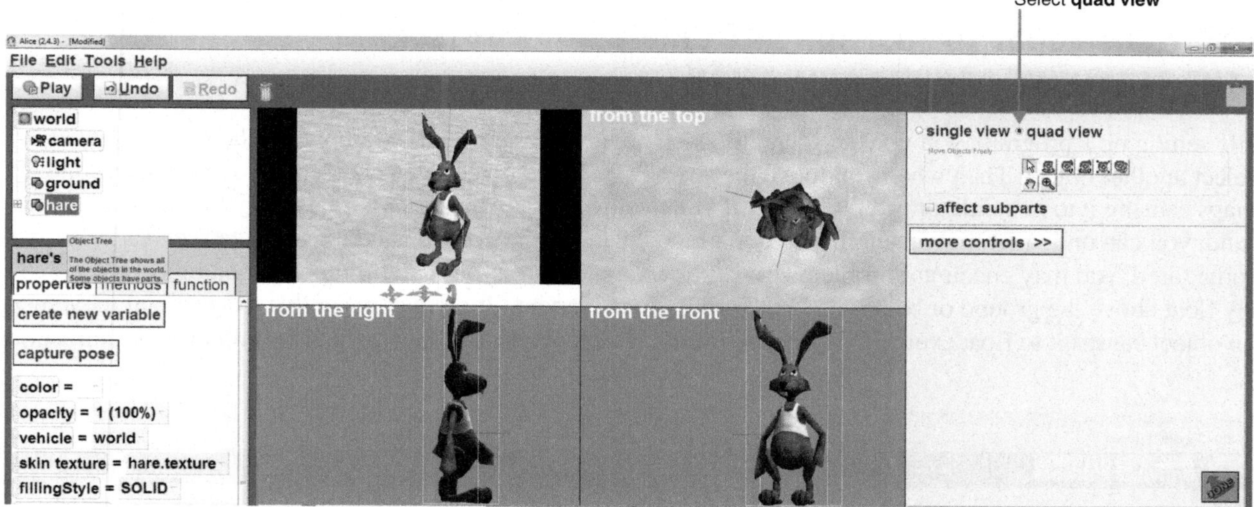

Selecting **quad view** provides views from the top, right, and front as well as the world view. The hare has been selected, either by clicking on the hare in the object tree or by clicking on the hare in the world view. Surrounding the selected object is a yellow bounding box (or rectangular prism) with sides that just touch the front and back, left and right, and top and bottom of the object.

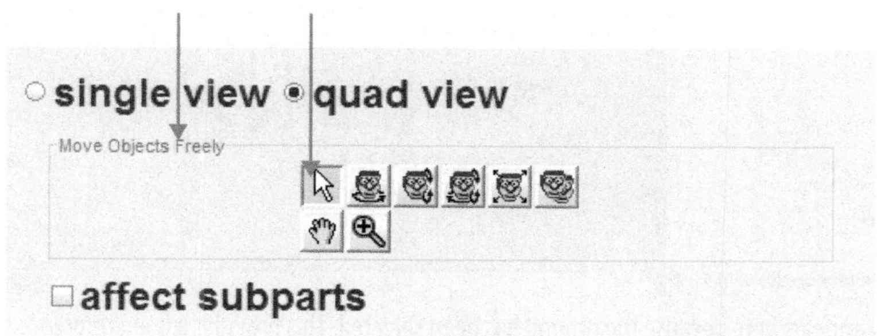

When you're in quad view, a description of the tool appears when your cursor touches the tool and when you select the tool with a mouse click.

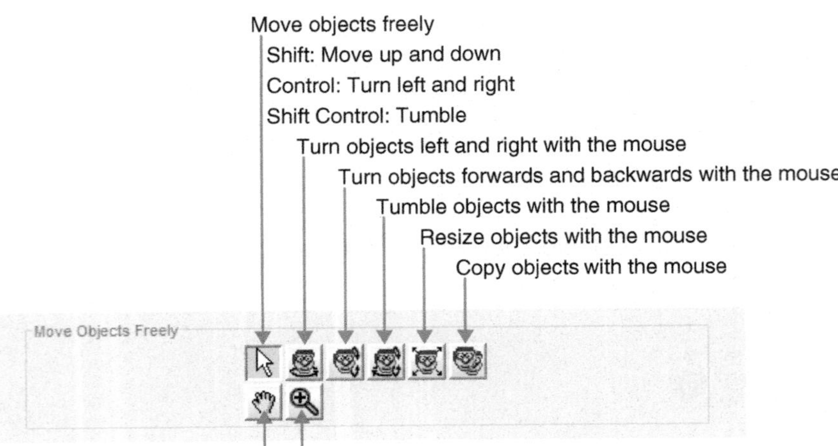

USING YOUR MOUSE TO POSITION AND ORIENT YOUR OBJECTS AT THE BEGINNING OF YOUR ANIMATION

While setting up a program, you may accidentally click on the ground (or other template) when you intended to select another object. Then when you move the wrongly selected object, you accidentally move the ground, perhaps causing it to rise, fall, or tilt. Of course, if you then recognize that you've mistakenly moved or tilted the ground, you can undo that movement. If you don't recognize that the ground is no longer at zero elevation or has become tilted, you may encounter problems later. For example, all of your carefully positioned objects may suddenly float above the ground or be buried in the ground. Inadvertent tilting may mean that a horizontal movement of an object causes it to float ever-higher or bury itself ever-deeper as it moves in the downhill or uphill directions.

The ground's coordinate system appears here because the ground has been selected. This provides a good reference for adjusting the elevations of objects that sit on the ground. Notice on the left that the ground's pointOfView in the ground's properties has a position (0, 0, 0) and orientation (0, 0, 0). This ground's coordinate system is perfectly aligned with the world's; this ground is neither elevated nor lower than the world and is not tilted or rotated.

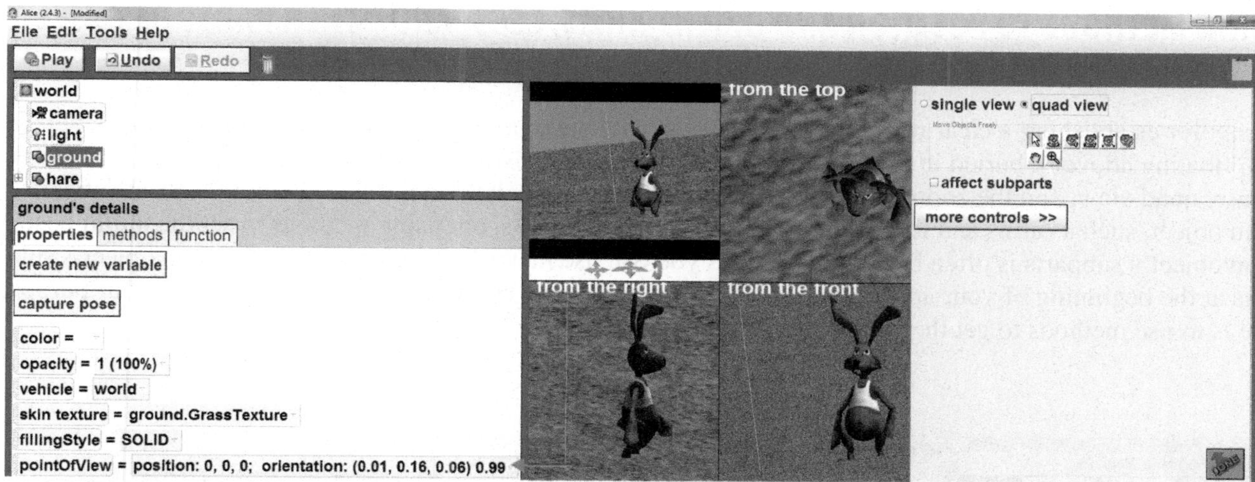

Here I've tilted the ground significantly (the orientation is 9.01, 0.16, 0.06). If you recognize a mistaken tilting but too late to undo it, right-click after the orientation values in the ground's pointOfView and select the "untilted" choice, as shown in the next figure.

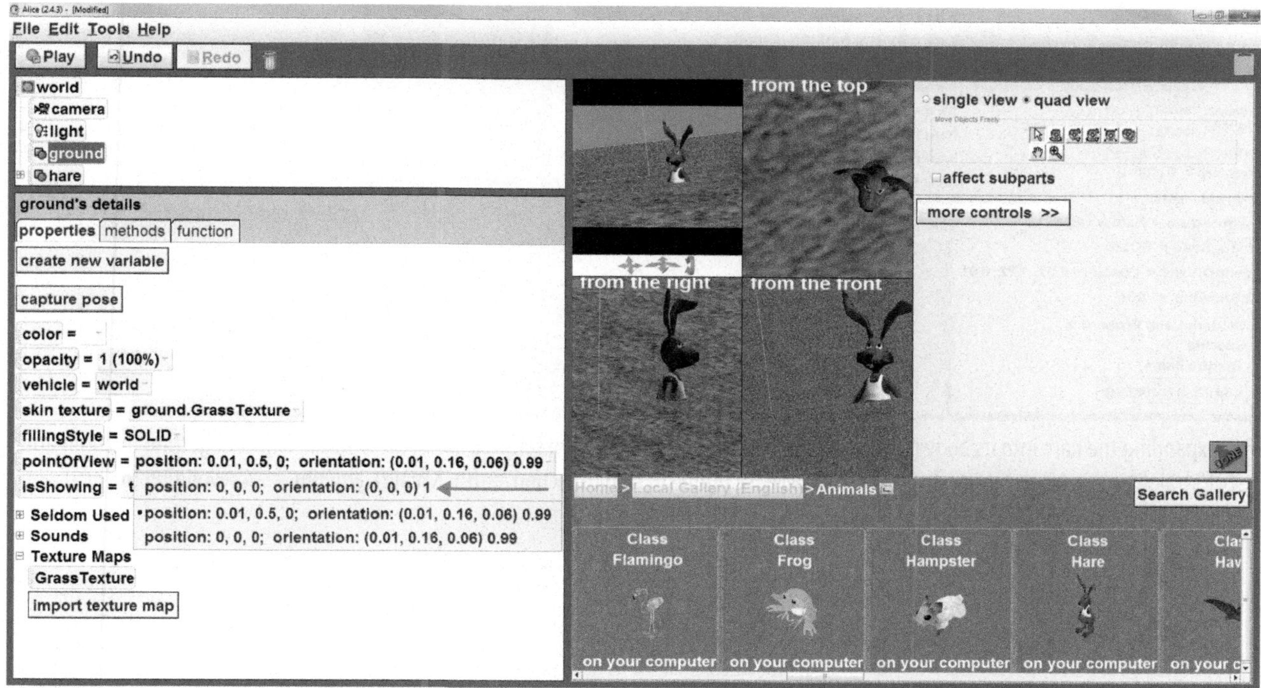

The ground has been accidentally moved up a half-meter along with the tilting (the position is 0.01, 0.5, 0) and the poor hare is half buried. By clicking after the orientation values, you can reset the ground's coordinate system to coincide with the world's.

USING METHODS TO POSITION AND ORIENT ARMS, LEGS, AND OTHER PARTS OF OBJECTS AT THE BEGINNING OF YOUR ANIMATION

Except for establishing a clear reference line so objects that belong on the ground are on the ground rather than floating above or buried in the ground, you can accurately position and orient most objects using your mouse, quad view, and the zoom tool to magnify your view. You also can use your mouse to orient subparts of an object, such as arms and legs on animals and doors on houses, but using methods to set the initial pose of an object's subparts is often better. This means you can use methods to orient and position an object's subparts at the beginning of your animation as well as use methods when you execute your program. Our purpose here is to use methods to get the initial pose of an object right.

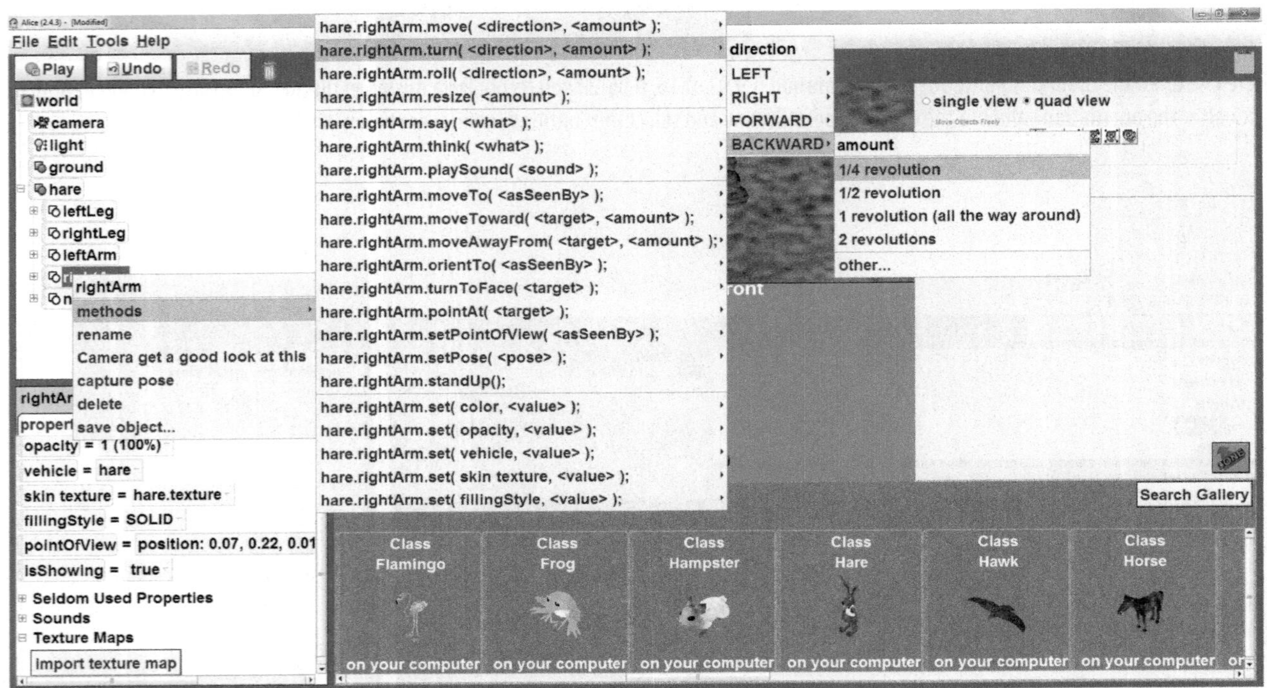

After expanding the hare into its body parts, I right-clicked on the right arm and selected *methods*. With the object of getting the right arm to stick straight out in front, I chose (by trial and error) hare.rightArm.turn (direction = BACKWARD, amount = ¼ revolution [or 90°]).

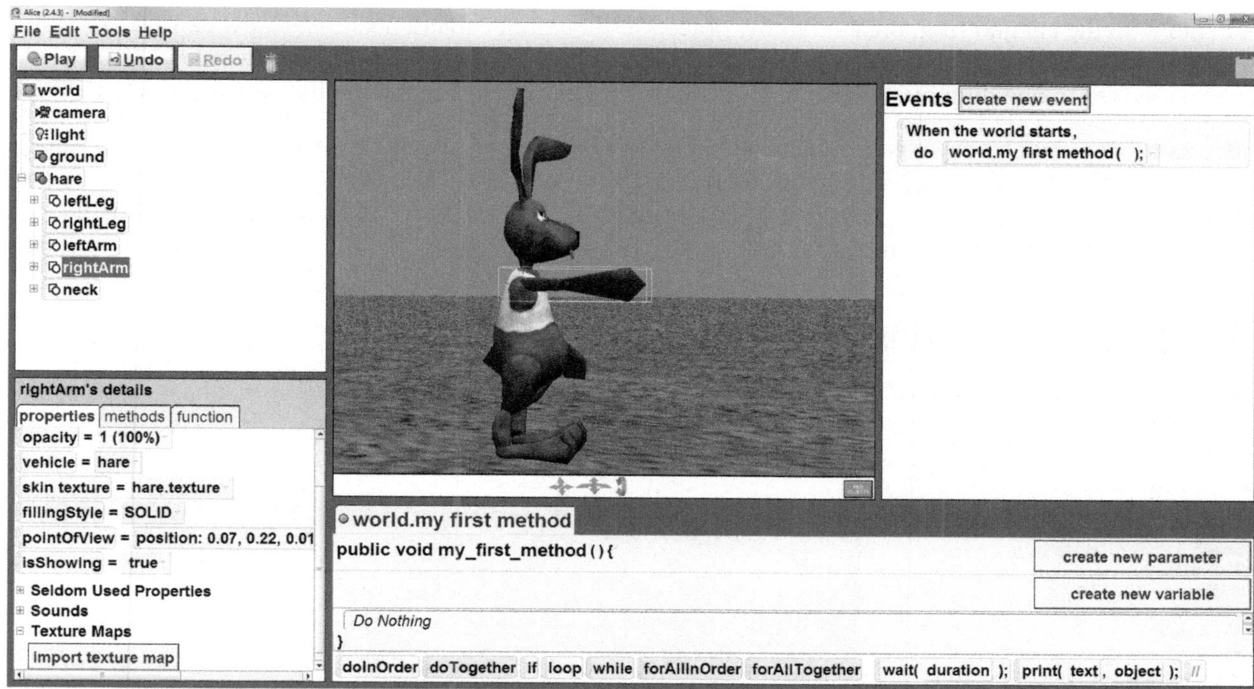

The result is that this turn method caused the arm to rotate as shown. Angles are specified as fractions of a revolution. If you're not sure whether to use a *turn* or *roll* and whether to choose one direction or another, just try it, be ready to click *Undo,* and don't cry! ☺

You also can use your mouse to orient body parts by selecting *affect subparts*, selecting the body part, and using the buttons here or under quad view to move/orient the part. Using a method may give you the precision necessary, but turning arms and legs using the mouse is OK.

DUMMY OBJECTS AND THEIR USE TO CONTROL THE CAMERA'S POINT OF VIEW

The **point of view (POV) of any object, including the camera, is its position (the x, y, z coordinates) and orientation (three angular coordinates for the roll, pitch, and yaw).** It may be useful while a program is running to change a camera's POV in a scene by moving from the current POV to another POV that has been previously specified (stored). For example, in a scene with two people talking, you may want to alternate between two or more camera POVs, say (1) a wide POV showing both people, and (2) a close-up view of one, and (3) close-up view of another. If the POVs are stored, each would be called a **dummy**. They're objects listed in the dummy folder in the object tree. They act like invisible vectors, each with a position and orientation.

Procedure to create and use dummy objects: click the *Add objects* button. Click *More controls*, then click *Drop dummy at camera* (this will record in a dummy object the present POV of the camera).

Then in the object tree, **name the dummy object so its name suggests the POV it stores**. For example, maybe you'd name several dummies as *POV at the program beginning*, *POV close-up to frog*, *POV close-up to cheshireCat*. Or maybe you'd name them *scene 1 shot 1*, *scene 1 shot 2*, *scene 1 shot 3*, and so on (where a different shot is a different camera POV). This naming of objects (and later your naming of methods, variables, and other things) is part of a programmer's job to internally document a program by naming things descriptively.

As a demo with the cat and frog, create dummy objects at the initial camera position, a new camera position closer to both the cat and frog, close to the frog, and close to the cat. Then in the editing window, place tiles for camera moves to one dummy object, then another, and a third by using the method *camera.setPOV*.

Besides using dummy objects to control a camera's point of view, you can use them to control the POV of other objects. With a similar procedure, you can record the current POV of any object in a dummy, then name it descriptively in the object tree. Later, you can move and orient that object to that position by setting its POV to be that you've stored in the dummy.

EXAMPLE PROGRAM THAT USES DUMMY OBJECTS

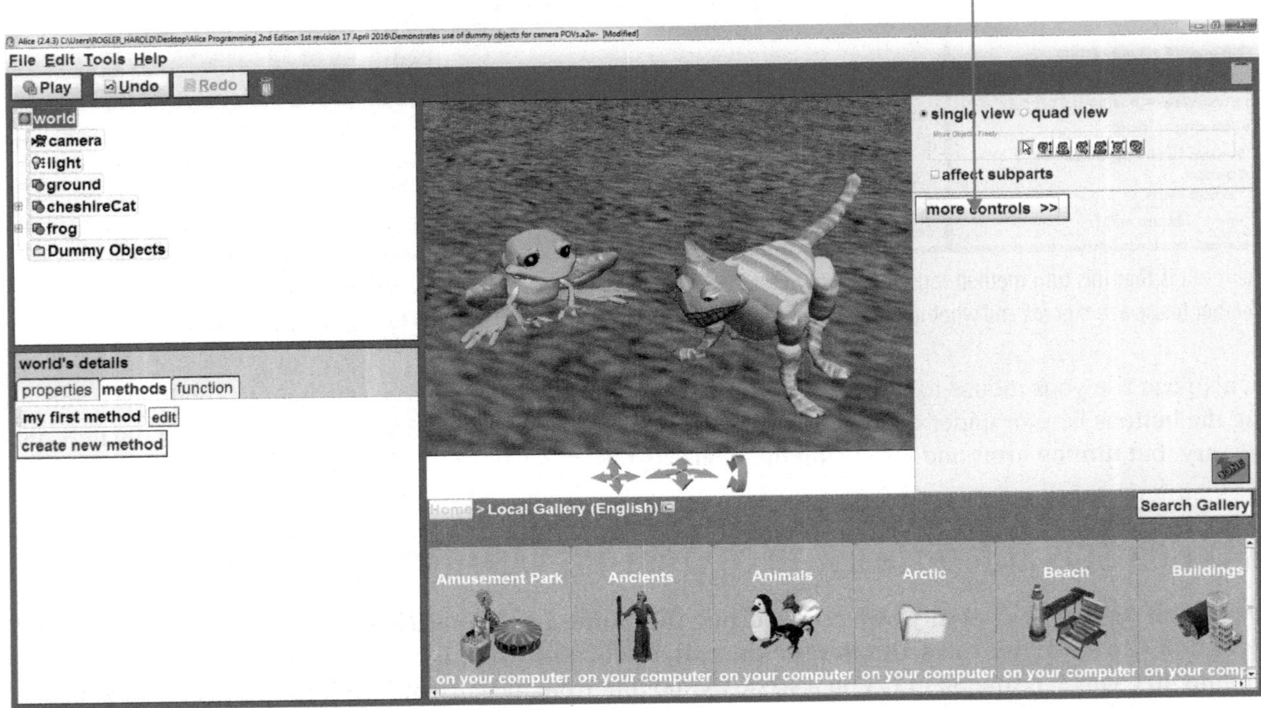

In a pristine world, we've added a frog and cheshireCat, enlarged the frog, and manually moved the camera by using the controls. Clicking *more controls* displays the controls to create dummy objects, shown in the next figure.

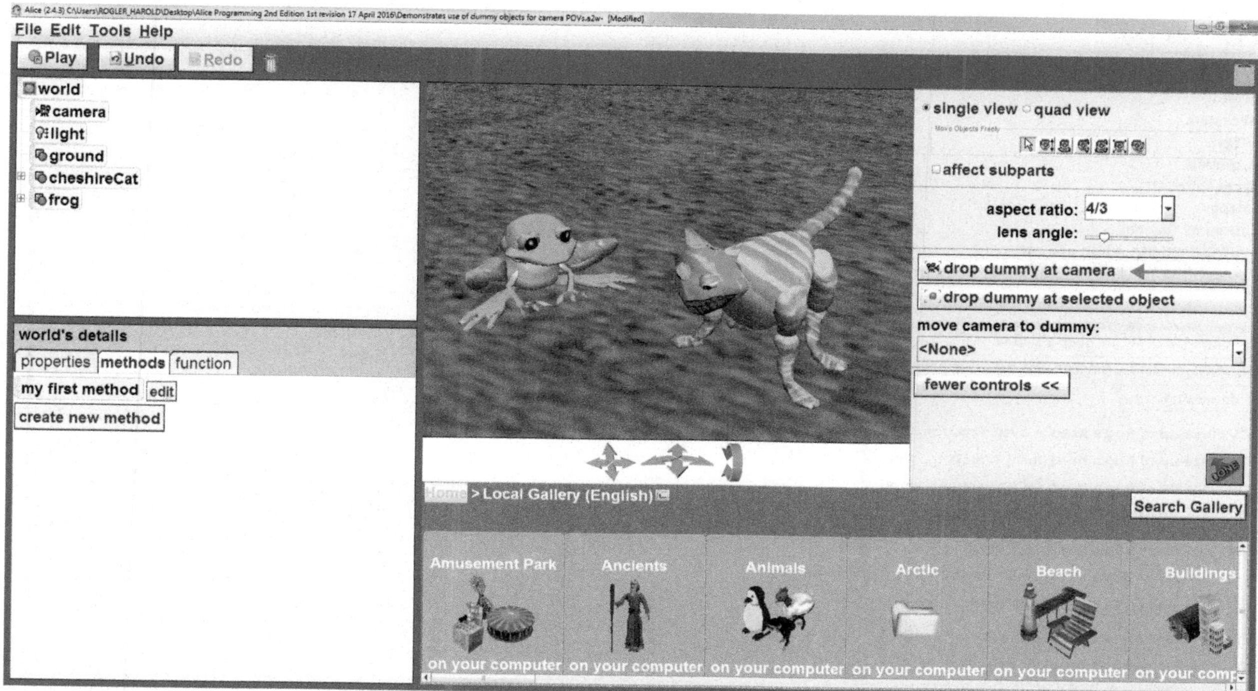

This is a view of the frog and cat that we'd like to use several times. Click *drop dummy at camera* to store the camera's POV (the camera's position and orientation).

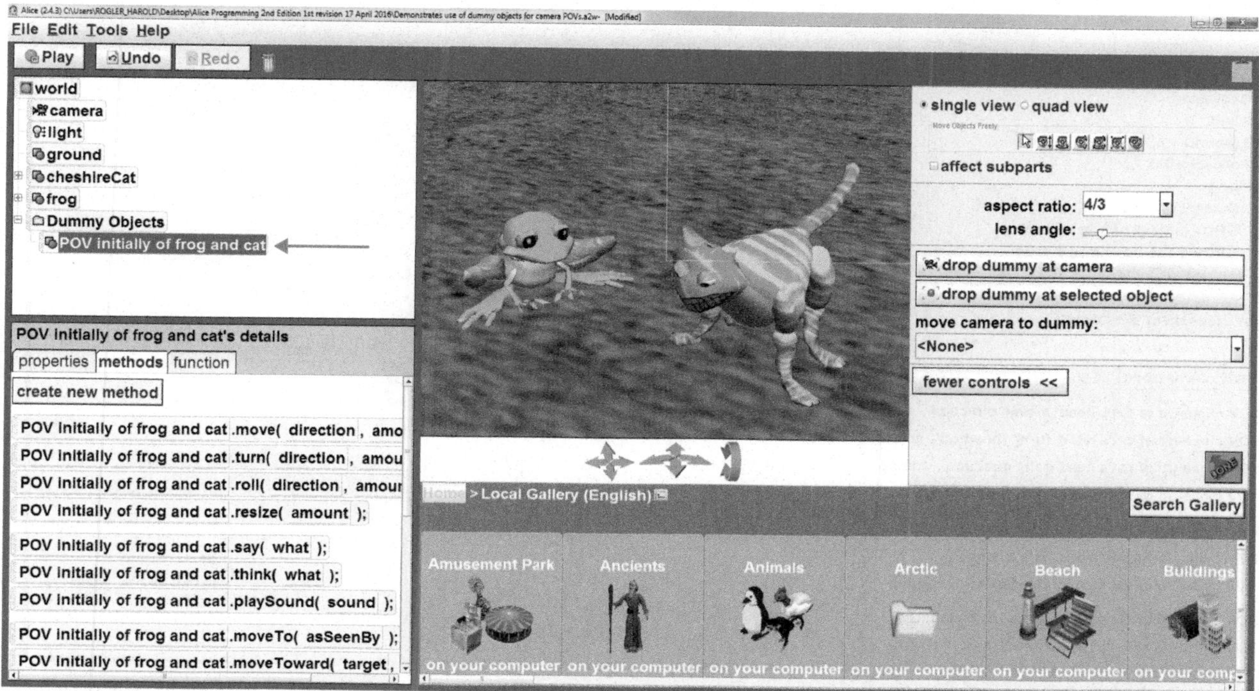

In the object tree at the top left, a folder appears that I've opened, then renamed the dummy object to the more descriptive *POV initially of frog and cat*. Descriptively name your dummy objects so you can keep them straight.

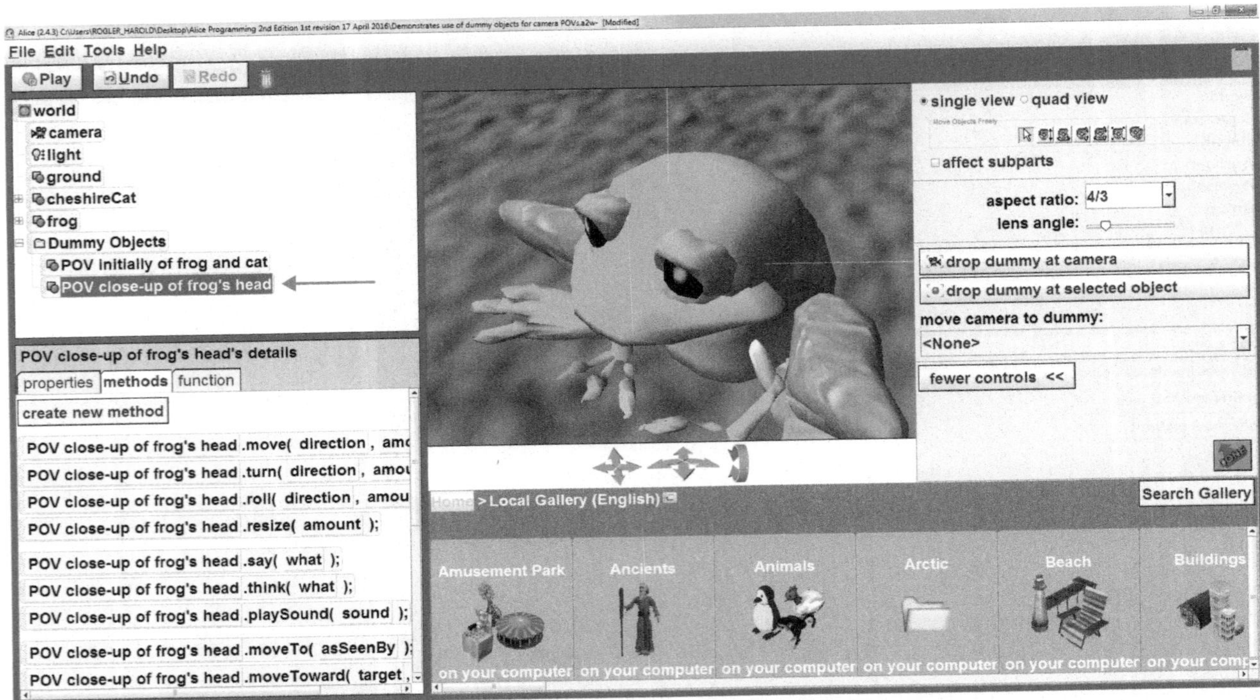

Now I've moved the camera close-up to the frog's head (a POV for the camera that I want to store), then clicked *drop dummy at camera,* and in the object tree at the top left, renamed it descriptively to be *POV close-up of frog's head.*

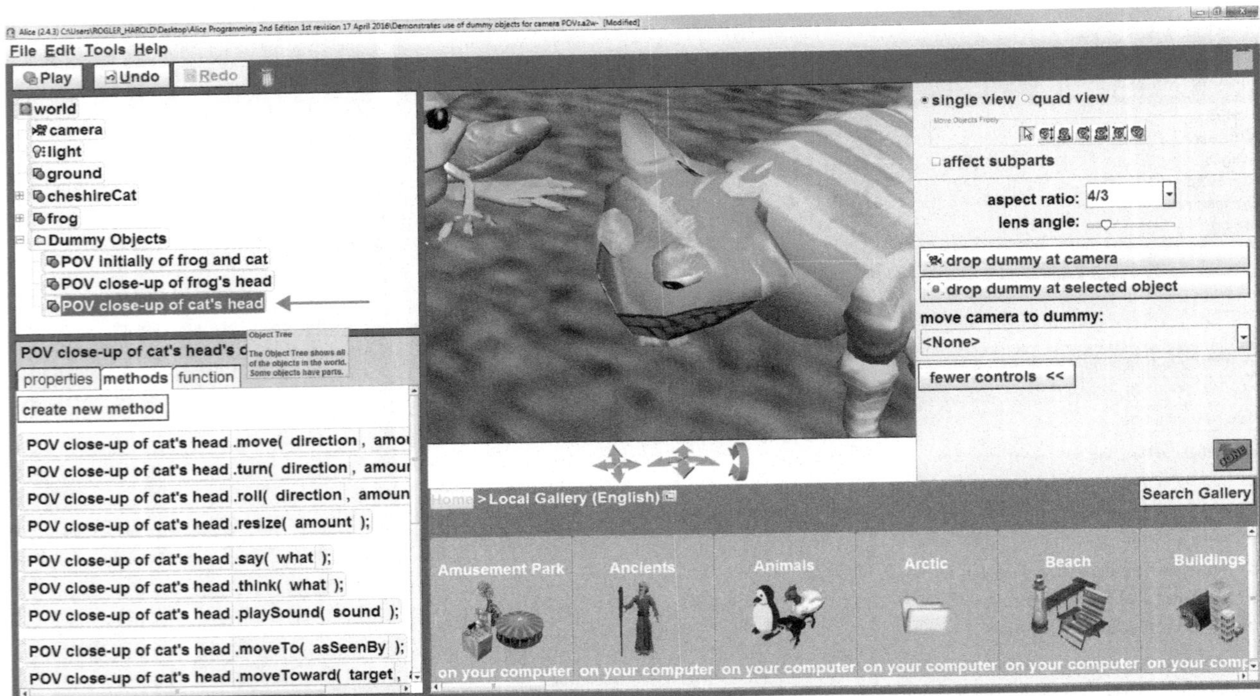

Now I moved the camera to a POV close-up to the cat's head, clicked *drop dummy at camera,* and renamed the dummy object as *POV close-up of cat's head.*

Now we have three dummy objects that store the three positions of the camera that we plan to use. Next, let's use the first POV (the one named *POV initially of frog and cat*) as the camera's POV at the start of our program.

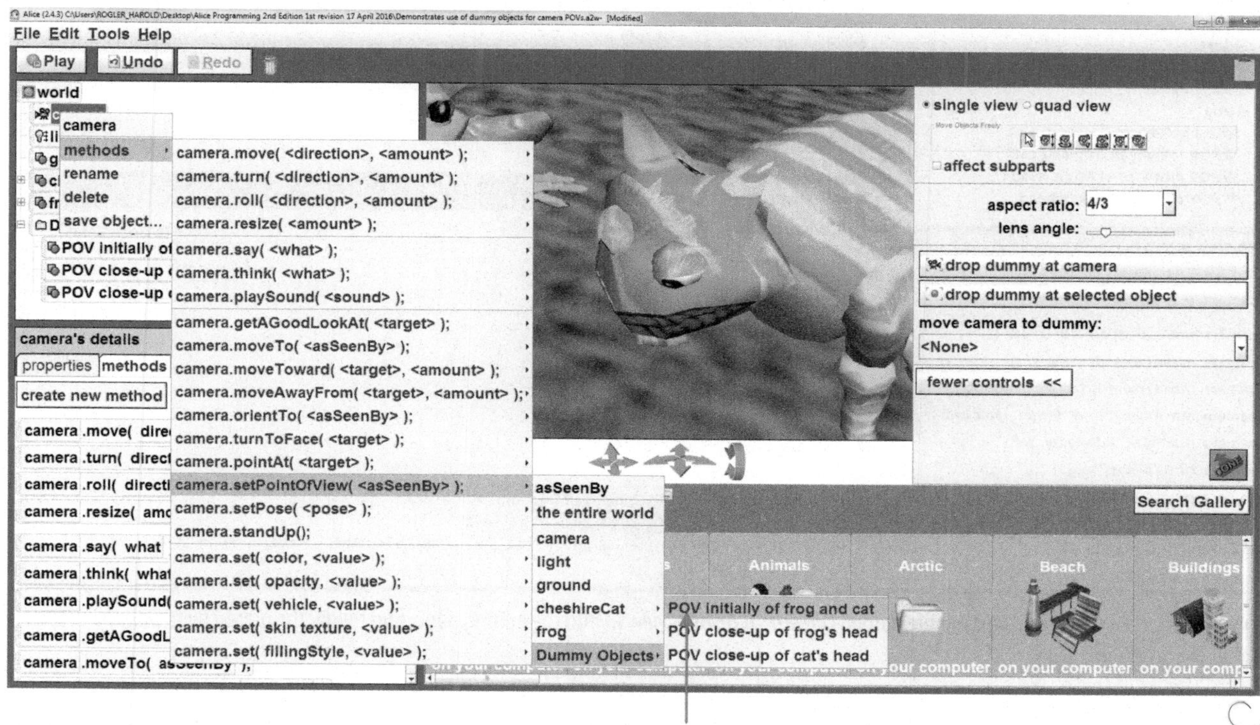

Right-click on the camera's object, and select *methods* | *camera set point of view to* | *asSeenBy: Dummy Objects* | *POV initially of frog and cat.* You also could change the camera's POV by using the control on the right called *move camera to dummy* and choosing in the drop-down list the dummy *POV initially of frog and cat.*

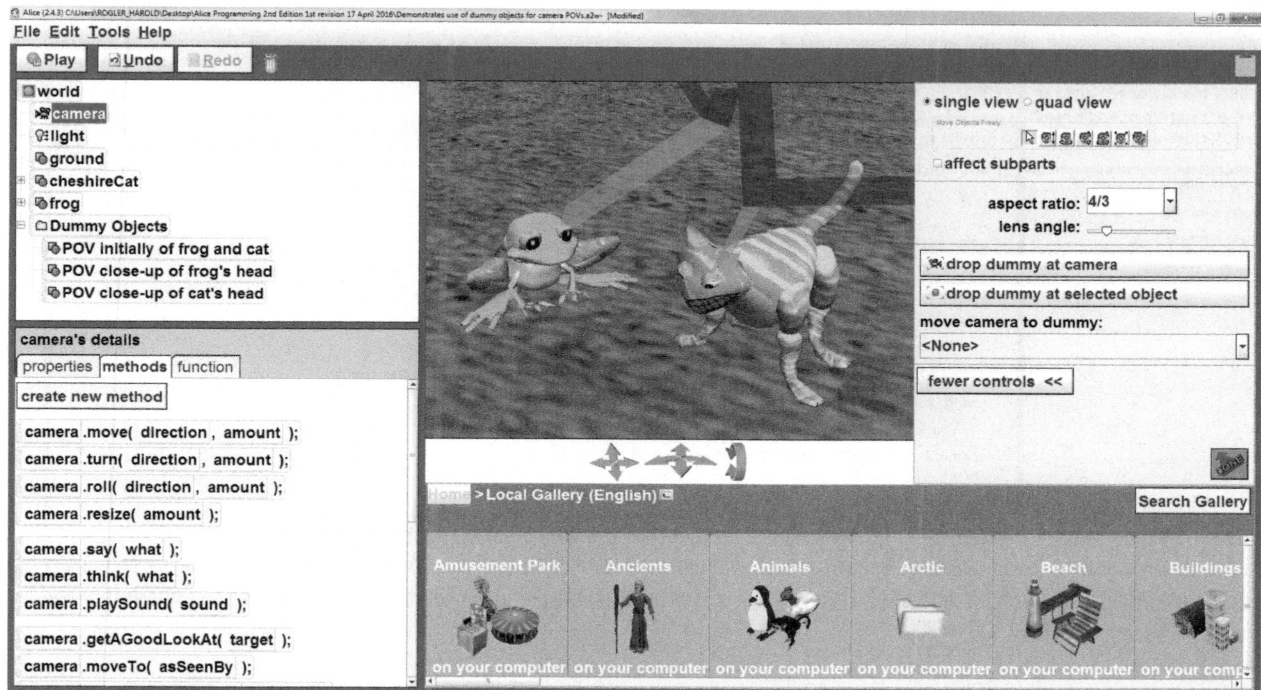

Now we're back at the initial camera position to begin our program. Click *DONE.*

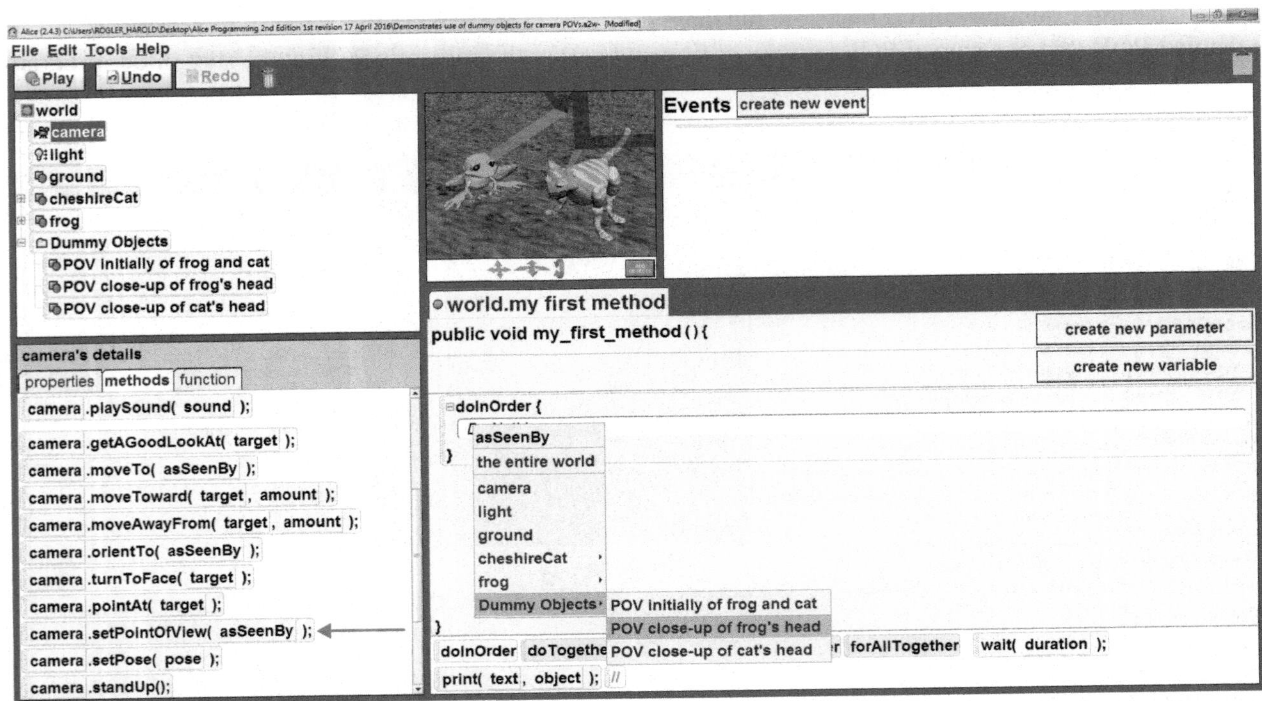

From the camera's methods, drag the tile named *camera set point of view to* into the editing pane, and follow the hierarchy to *Dummy Objects: POV close-up of frog's head.*

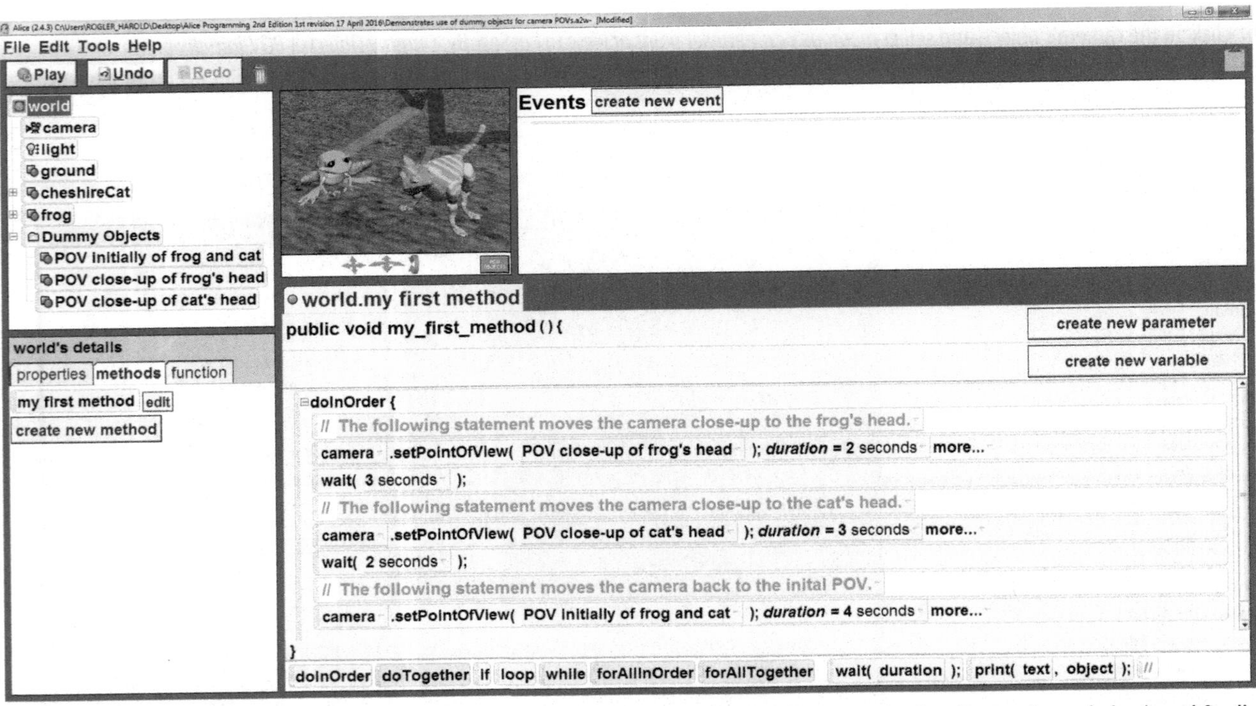

I've added three comments, two more moves of the camera, and two wait statements (so I can take the pictures shown below), and finally ended with the POV that shows both the frog and cat. I clicked *more* to adjust the duration of each method. The duration controls the time in seconds to execute a method.

When you click *Play*, the camera sequentially moves close up to the frog, close up to the cat, and back to the initial POV:

This program named *Demonstrates use of dummy objects for camera POV* is in folder *Demonstrates dummy objects* in *Alice examples*.

SAVING YOUR ALICE PROGRAMS, AND THE AUTOMATICALLY SAVED BACKUP FILES AND FOLDER

As you create your Alice Programs, protect them by frequently saving them to your hard drive, solid-state drive, USB flash memory, or other secondary storage. A professional programmer is aware of the many ways that programs can be corrupted, lost, or damaged, and aware of the time lost to re-create the programs. The amateur programmer, however, assumes that everything will work perfectly. It's amazing how much we learn in the few seconds after you realize that we've lost hours of work—or much worse—from some mistake or failure, a loss that could have been avoided or reduced had if you'd backed up your work regularly.

Shortly after beginning a new project, save it. This will create a default path to where you're saving your file, and it tests whether you can save it there. Take the time to name your file descriptively and store it where you have plenty of storage space—not just any old place. Indeed, you might encounter problems, but it's better to solve those problems when you have only a minute's worth of work on your project than find out later.

The professional programmer has learned to value reliable software and software, protects against power outages and voltage spikes through uninterruptible power supplies, tests to see if the computer functions properly, and saves regularly.

While you're working on an Alice program, a portion of your operating system, the Alice executable file, and your program all are stored in the primary memory—the Random Access Memory (RAM)—of your computer as shown below.

What happens when you first save your file? Assume that you select the path and save your file with the name MyProgram. Alice writes that file as shown below, but also sets up a folder named Backups of MyProgram and saves the file again except with a date and time appended to your filename. For this example, I assumed the date was October 5, 2016 and the time was 8:34:27 AM for the first save. After this save, you have two copies of your program only differing in their filenames with the date and time appended to the backup file.

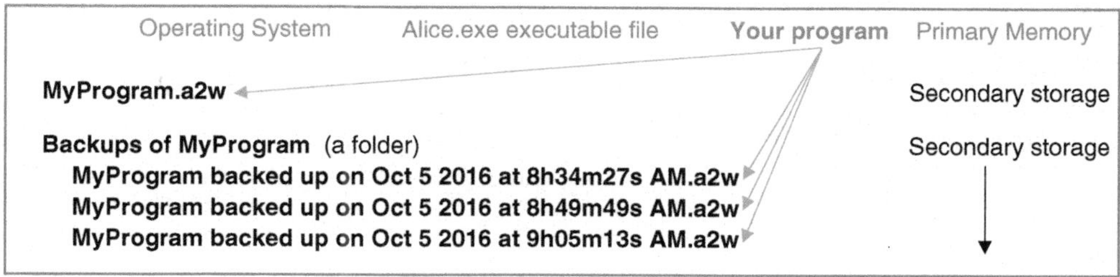

About 15 minutes later you save your file again. Maybe you added objects or positioned them or drug tiles into your program. What happens now? This 2nd save overwrites the earlier MyProgram.a2w file. Into the backup folder is added another file with the new time appended. After this 2nd save, you have two identical files.

About 15 minutes later, you save again. Again the earlier MyProgram file is overwritten and another backup file with the later time is saved into your backup folder. This process is repeated as many times as you save your file. You can limit how many backup versions you keep in Menu | Preferences | Seldom Used.

You normally have two versions of your latest file. If MyProgram becomes corrupted or some problem occurs while you're coding that you cannot recover from, you can use your backup files. Begin with the latest. If you continued programming after your last save, then your most recent changes won't be stored in the latest backup, but starting with the backup should be much better than starting over from scratch.

The file and backup folder are stored on one drive. If that drive fails or your computer is lost or stolen, you'd lose all of your files. Store your files in two different places, such as to another USB flash drive or some internet storage or as an attachment to an email to yourself if the size is less than the email attachment limit of 10MB. Copy the file and backup folder to another computer if you have access to another.

In summary, save your files every 15 minutes or so, save your files to more than one place, and save your file to a purposeable path, a path perhaps of folder and other folders in a hierarchy to keep your work organized. When you save your file, two copies are saved. The backup files can save you much time when a problem arises.

By saving regularly and keeping your files organized, you're on your way to becoming a professional.

EXERCISES

2.1 Using the procedure described in the section *Dummy objects and their use . . .*, into a pristine world add two objects of your choice that are visible in the World pane. Store the pointOfView (POV) for the camera by clicking on the *drop dummy at camera* button, finding the dummy in the object browser in the *Dummy Objects* folder, and renaming it descriptively. Move the camera either by using the manual controls beneath the World pane or by using a method to move the camera so the camera has a close-up view of your first object. And store the camera's POV, followed by naming it descriptively. Finally, again move the camera to show a close-up view of your second object, drop a dummy for the camera POV, and rename it.

2.2 Move between your three dummies by selecting each, one at a time, from the drop-down list beneath *move camera to dummy*. Good names for the dummies will help to choose the one you want.

2.3 Choose the method *camera.set point of view to*, found under the *camera's details: methods*, drag that tile into the coding pane, and set its point of view to be one of the three dummies that you created in Exercise 2.1. Drag another tile for that method into the coding pane, and set its POV to be a second dummy that you stored. Finally, drag a third such tile and set its POV to be the third dummy. Click *Play* to execute your program that moves the camera between the three POVs for the camera.

KEY WORDS FOR THE CHAPTER

bounding box of an object
camera movements and positioning
classes
  instantiation of a class (creating an instance of a class)
  libraries of classes
comments are not executable
dummy objects
  folder in the object tree
  more controls button allows you to create dummy objects
inheritance
objects
  listed in the objects tree
  process to create an object from a class
quad view and single view

CHAPTER 2 PROJECT: CREATING THE INITIAL SETUP OF AN ALICE WORLD

Due ______________________________

Before beginning this project, study Chapters 1 and 2. Connect your USB flash memory **before** running Alice, so Alice will recognize your USB device. Unless your professor instructs you to use an Alice 3 version, use the latest version of Alice 2. An Alice program created with Alice version 2 cannot be opened in Alice 3, and a program created with Alice 3 cannot be opened with Alice 2.

Run Alice, and immediately after choosing the background as you begin your project, use *Save As*... and save your Alice file as *CourseNumber_ProjectNumber_SectionNumber_LastName_FirstName*.a2w (where *LastName* and *FirstName* are your names), or use this filename as instructed by your professor:

____ File extension a2w stands for **A**lice version **2 W**orld, or use extension a3w if you're using Alice version 3.1. Save your file every 15 minutes to flash memory or somewhere that will survive a crash. Files on your USB flash memory should survive a crash.

Drag a comment tile into the editing area and edit it to include your filename. Based on one of the themes in the file Alice Themes.docx, create a scene that includes these objects: a **land or water vehicle** (from Vehicles**)**, some **aerial vehicle** (Vehicles), a **building** (Buildings, Farm, or Medieval), five **people** (People, but not HeBuilder or SheBuilder), three nonflying **animals** (Animals), two flying **birds or pterodactyls** (Animals), **table** and four **chairs** (Furniture or Beach), four **things on the table** (Kitchen), and a **baseball** or other ball also sitting on the table (Sports) that later you can get a person to pick up and throw. In the background (floating in the sky) include **3D text** with your first and last names. To add 3D text, click *Create 3D Text* in the local Gallery, type your names, choose some font and font size, and click *Okay*.

Use method instructions, the mouse, and quad view to position objects such as the stuff on the table so they're not floating in the air or buried in the table. Position the other objects on the ground or wherever they belong. Clicking the ground object and looking for its reference system in quad view will help you position objects that belong on the ground. Use your imagination, but don't be too ambitious. You can add a few more objects in later projects. These positions are initial point of views (POVs) for the objects (their POVs at the beginning of the program).

Extra credit worth 10/100: In the same Alice world and file as you used for this project, stand one person on his or her head on the ground, with arms out in front for support, as shown on the next page. The person's head and two hands touch the ground. This is an **initial pose** at the beginning of the program. You don't cause the body or arms to rotate while running the program (after clicking *Play)*. Chapter 2 describes how to use methods with object subparts to specify an initial pose. Expand a person into his or her body parts, then right-click on a part in the Objects window, choose *methods*, and experiment using some methods. Click *Undo* if you guessed wrong. You also can use mouse controls to orient body parts, but try using both ways (mouse and methods) to control the initial pose. Selecting the camera and right-clicking on the method *Camera get a good look at XX* (where *XX* is the person you're standing on his or her head) may help you see what's going on.

After completing the project and saving your latest version on your USB flash drive or desktop, check to see that the file size is not 0 KB and you can find where you stored it. Then close Alice. Open Alice and navigate through *File: Open* to open your file and see if all is OK. Then close your file and follow your professor's directions to submit your file. **Do not submit the autogenerated backup files.**

If you code a program off campus, remember to test it at your customer's site because tiny differences in software or hardware can cause a program to run OK on one computer but fail on another.

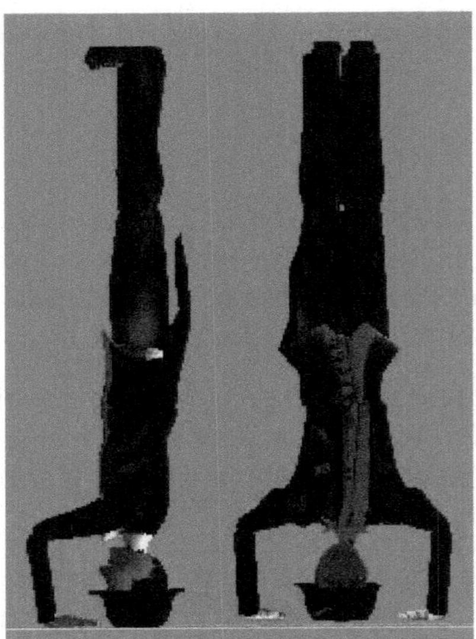

Side view and front view of a headstand. Two hands and head are on the ground to form a triangle. Hands are flat on the ground and turned toward the head. You also could have the upper arms rotated so they're straight out in the front.

CHAPTER 2 PROJECT: GRADING SHEET FOR CREATING THE INITIAL SETUP OF AN ALICE WORLD

Last name ____________________ First name ____________________ Section ____________________

☐ Project submitted after the deadline or not submitted (**No credit**).

☐ (–2). Filename should have the form *CourseNumber_ProjectNumber_SectionNumber_LastName_FirstName*.a2w with a _B or _C just after *FirstName* if you submitted several versions.

☐ (–2) **Omitted comment with your filename** in the editing window.

_____ **objects were omitted** (–4 each)

☐ **Land or water vehicle** (from Vehicles)

☐ **Aerial vehicle** (from Vehicles)

☐ **Building** (from Buildings, Farm, or Medieval)

☐ Five **people** (from People but not HeBuilder or SheBuilder)

☐ Three nonflying **animals** (Animals)

☐ Two flying **birds or pterodactyls** (Animals)

☐ **Table** and four **chairs** (Furniture; a beach chair is available in Beach)

☐ Four **things on the table** (Kitchen)

☐ **Baseball** or other ball also sitting on the table (Sports)

☐ **3D text** with your first and last names

_____ **objects were positioned slightly too high or low** (–2 each). Use quad view and the zoom tool more carefully.

_____ **objects were wildly mispositioned** (floating way up in the air or underground or inside other objects) (–3 each). Learn to use quad view, the zoom tool, and the hand to see objects from top, front, and side as well as the world view as seen by the camera.

Extra credit

☐ (+10) **Person standing on his or her head. Include in the same file as the basic project.**

☐ (–5) Person standing on his or her hands rather than on his or her head (head and both hands on ground with hands in front and sides so the person won't fall over).

☐ (–5) Hands/arms have good elevation but are off to the side of the head rather than in front to form a triangle for support.

☐ (   ) Person is on his or her head but hands and arms are not well positioned, or head is off the ground.

Other comments:

Score _______ **out of 100.** Keep this sheet as evidence of the score you received.

Chapter 3 DESIGNING OR PLANNING YOUR PROGRAM USING COMMENTS AND OTHER DOCUMENTATION

Contents

INTRODUCTION

A **computer program** is a set of instructions and data that tells the computer what to do. The main controller of a computer where the instructions are carried out or executed is called the central processing unit (the CPU). Programs also include comments that tell people what the program is supposed to do.

A **computer programmer** is a person who analyzes, designs, codes, tests, and documents programs. Sometimes programs are so large that they may have analysts, designers, coders, testers, and documenters who specialize in one part of the overall task of programming, or one person may serve all these roles. In school, programming usually focuses on designing, coding (implementing), and testing. Documentation in school would certainly include comments and descriptive names for the things that can be named, such as the names of the dummy objects described in Chapter 2.

A program should be no more complex than necessary. Of all the possible ways for a computer to accomplish a task, some ways have fewer instructions, are easier for programmers to understand or implement, or execute faster. These programs would be considered more **elegant** than the others. Accomplishing the task is certainly essential, but how the computer program does that is also important.

COMMENTS

A **comment** is non-executable. That means that when the program runs, a comment doesn't cause the CPU to execute any instructions.

Comments are intended to be read by the programmer and other programmers (or other people analyzing, designing, testing, or documenting the program). Comments describe or document the program and its logic, which can be difficult or impossible to determine from the code (the statements and settings, especially in programs with graphical interfaces).

In Alice, comment tiles are colored green and have the form // No comment when you drag them into the coding area.You can drag comment tiles into the editing area from the group of statements listed below the editing area. Once a comment tile is in the editing area, you can click on the *No comment* and edit it.

Learning to program with Alice, Pearson/Prentice Hall 2006.

TOP-DOWN AND BOTTOM-UP[1] DESIGNS OF A COMPUTER PROGRAM

Top-down design, stepwise refinement, problem decomposition, or **reductionism** (as referred to by Plato and Aristotle over 2,000 years ago) is the process of breaking a task into smaller, more manageable subtasks. If all of the small tasks really are equivalent to the original one, then completing all the small ones would accomplish the full task.

Having fewer requirements to think about at one time means you can focus your attention on manageable tasks. If a subtask is still too complex, then break it into still smaller ones.

Some of the possible ways to break a task into smaller parts include merely slicing the task into pieces (what happens first, next, and last) or by pieces that can be reused, such as a person walking or waving his or her hands, a bird flying, a frog jumping, a person picking up an object such as a ball, and a person throwing the ball. These approaches and others can be combined.

Bottom-up design uses elemental pieces combined into more complex ones. In computer programming, you might create reusable programs with elemental programs that could be combined many ways into bigger systems. Exactly how they'd be used, in contrast to a top-down design, may not be known. The person who designs and codes a program would combine the elemental pieces into an animation. Alice has many built-in methods and functions that can be combined into more complex behaviors, and you can program your own methods and functions that can be reused.

The word **emergent** is sometimes associated with bottom-up design. An example is designing a robotic vacuum cleaner by combining some elemental behaviors into a program where the resultant emergent behavior is that the vacuum cleans a room.

In contrast, a top-down design for a robotic vacuum would first have the vacuum create a map of the room and its furniture. Then it would plan how to move back and forth and navigate around the room to completely vacuum it with little wasted motion. Finally, it would follow the plan and vacuum the room. A computer program based on this approach would require a more powerful computer to do all the computations, better sensors so the room's geometry and furniture can be detected, or a longer time to create a plan that's good enough that the family cat isn't sucked into the vacuum.

Both top-down and bottom-up approaches are used in some program designs, especially in object-oriented languages like Alice, Java, C#, C++, and others.

ABSTRACTION

Abstraction is the concept that the programmer need not be faced with or distracted by every last detail required by a task, but the programmer can think and work at a higher level. Rather than seeing the code for every last movement of arms and legs when a person walks, the details are moved into separate programs (methods and functions), and referred to and executed by referring to the name of that program. The details are available by looking at that module and perhaps changing the module if you wanted to correct some fault or improve it, but otherwise you can take a more standoffish view and refer to the module, perhaps repeatedly.

---

[1] *Top-down* and *bottom-up* adjectives are used far more broadly than only in computer programming. The reduction in population growth in mainland China has resulted from a top-down effort by China's federal government to enforce a policy that couples have only one child. In developed countries, the number of children has fallen by a bottom-up approach: with higher education and awareness of the costs to raise and educate children and better heath care reducing the likelihood that a child will die from disease, couples have fewer children. Sometimes both are actively used. For example, city governments have a top-down effort to fight crime through laws and police to enforce laws and jails and fines to punish offenders. But neighborhood organizations fight crime by bottom-up efforts to watch for suspicious activities and report them. (http://en.wikipedia.org/wiki/Bottom-up_design).

This process can be extended many levels, with each level using lower levels. An object person can be programmed to pick up a volleyball, separately hit the ball with a hand, and those two actions can be combined with walking or running in an ever-more-complex game of volleyball. The module for the volleyball game could be combined with others into ever-richer behaviors.

As an example, you are abstracting when you decide to go to the grocery store and buy a loaf of bread. In the many skills necessary to get that bread and get back home, you may consciously move a leg, but you cannot consciously control the individual signals to separate muscle cells. Nevertheless, the nervous system controls details that you can neither detect nor control, while leaving you to take a more abstract view.

ERRORS IN A COMPUTER PROGRAM

Syntax errors are errors in following the rules of a language. A natural language such as English has words spelled in a certain manner, uses words in phrases and sentences with a certain order of the words, and uses punctuation and capitalization. Computer languages also have syntax rules for spelling key words, their order, and punctuation. **If you violate these rules of a computer language, the errors are syntax errors**. Alice is designed so syntax errors are nearly impossible.

Logic errors. If you meant to add two numbers, say 3 + 2, but you subtracted them rather than added them, 3 – 2, that would be a logic error. The program would follow the instructions you programmed but would calculate the "wrong" (unintended) result because of the logic error. Another example of a logic error: You intended some object to move direction FORWARD but you inadvertently chose BACKWARD, and the object doesn't move as you intended. Failing to position or orient an object properly is a logic error. No rules of the computer language have been violated with logic errors (no syntax errors have occurred). The program runs but executes incorrect or illogical instructions, so it does the wrong thing.

While programming, you'd be committing a logic error if you intended to save your file on your USB device but saved it to your desktop instead.

Runtime errors. When a program runs, data to be used by a program may not be available, or the data have values that can't be used. Suppose you code a program that asks the user to enter two numbers, and the program takes the first number and divides it by the second. If the user of the program entered a *one* for the first number and *zero* for the second, the computer cannot carry out the division because one divided by zero (1/0) is infinite. This is an example of a runtime error.

Another common runtime error is that a program needs some data and expects to find it at a certain place, such as in a file stored in some hierarchy of folders on your C: drive or your USB flash memory. But when the program goes there, the file cannot be found because it was moved, renamed, or deleted. This would be a runtime error.

QUESTIONS

3.1 Top-down and bottom-up designs have what similarities and differences?
3.2 Do logic errors in a program violate the rules of a computer language?
3.3 Should computer languages be created to automatically correct logic errors?

KEY WORDS FOR THE CHAPTER

- abstraction
- comments in a method or function are not executable
- computer program and computer programmer
- design of a program
  - top-down design, stepwise refinement, problem decomposition, or reductionism
  - bottom-up design
- documentation of a program
  - internal documentation
    - good names for objects, programs, and storage places called variables and parameters
    - comments that describe the program (the pseudocode or outline of a program)
  - external documentation such as operating manuals and videos that describe what a program does or how to run it
- errors in a computer program
  - syntax errors
  - logic errors
  - runtime errors
- pseudocode (described in the Chapter 3 Project)
- scenario (described in the Chapter 3 Project)
  - background (e.g., grass)
  - list of objects in the world
  - significant positions or orientations of those objects
  - user story or plot of the animation in narrative form (i.e., sentences in a paragraph)
- scene (a collection of objects and its background)
- shot (one camera position)

CHAPTER 3 PROJECT: PLANNING YOUR ANIMATION WITH A USER STORY AND OUTLINE AS COMMENTS

Due ______________________________

The purpose of this project is to create a plan for your animated program that uses the objects from your Chapter 2 project. Planning and documenting a program are essential for large programs. Ignoring them in small programs is a bad habit. First plan, then code and test your programs. This breaks a big task into smaller ones that you can focus on and manage. This is an example of *dividing and conquering* or *top-down design*. The user story and other comments in this project will remain in later projects to document your program. They'll help you when you code the program and help you and others who study your program to understand the logic of your program. Planning should be a separate step from coding.

The plan consists of (1) your writing a **user story** (also called a scenario), which is a narrative or paragraph that tells your story in ordinary English. The plan also includes (2) an **outline** (also called **pseudocode**), which breaks your story into a step-by-step set of instructions in outline form. An **algorithm** is a finite series of instructions that accomplishes a task.

(1) With Alice running, open the file you created earlier based on the project at the end of Chapter 2. Then use *Save as . . .* with the new name *CourseNumber_ProjectNumber_SectionNumber_LastName_FirstName*.a2w where *LastName* and *FirstName* are your names, or follow the directions of your professor to name your file. Include a comment in the editing pane with this filename. As **one long comment** using the *// comment* tile from the lower right of the editing area, type a **user story**. Because Alice doesn't take a long comment and display it on several lines, you also could type the story in several comment tiles. Using sentences, **a user story describes your plot or the main ideas of your story, much like you'd describe your story if a friend asks you "What is your story?"** The scenario tells your story as a narrative. An example follows, but **don't use this** for your scenario:

    User story: With a grass background, at the beginning appear a frog and cheshireCat, both facing the camera. They turn to face one another and then the frog introduces himself/herself followed by the cat. Then at the same time, both turn, move apart, and turn to face each other. The frog says "I love you, Kitty!," then the cat says "I love you too, Froggie!"

(2) As **a series of comments in outline form**, type **pseudocode** that breaks down the user story into step-by-step actions that you can later code. For this project, only include the user story and pseudo-code. No coding is necessary in this project. This will be your step-by-step plan that you'll code in a later project.

    Include at least **three shots** (three different camera positions) in your story, and at least 30 separate actions (that later will be coded as moves, turns, says, thinks, settings of properties, etc.) in your story. The control structures (Do in Order and Do Together) are not counted as part of the 30 actions. Example of pseudocode (but **don't use this pseudocode** as your project):

```
Do in Order
    Do Together
        Frog turns to face the cat
        Cat turns to face the frog
    Frog says "I'm Froggie"
    Cat says "I'm Kitty"
    Do Together
        Frog turns a half-revolution away from cat
        Cat turns a half-revolution the other direction
```

```
Do Together
    Frog moves 1 meter
    Cat moves 1 meter
Do Together
    Frog turns to face the cat
    Cat turns to face the frog
Move camera close to frog's face
Frog says "I love you, Kitty!"
Move camera close to cat's face
Cat says "I love you too, Froggie!"
```

(3) Follow your professor's directions to submit your project.

This outline has one scene and three shots (three camera positions; one at the beginning of the story and two others close to the frog's and cat's face).

Pseudocode uses English phrases and sentences in an outline form. Use indentation (spaces) to show steps that are grouped together. Break your scenario into enough detail so that one line of your pseudocode will guide you when you write (or create) one line of actual code in later projects.

CHAPTER 3 PROJECT: GRADING SHEET FOR PLANNING YOUR ANIMATION WITH A USER STORY AND OUTLINE AS COMMENTS

Last name ____________________ First name ____________________ Section ____________________

☐ Project submitted after the deadline or not submitted (**No credit**)

☐ (–3) Filename wrong . It should have the form *CourseNumber_ProjectNumber_SectionNumber_LastName_FirstName*.a2w with a _B or _C or _D just after *FirstName* if you submitted several versions.

☐ (–2) Omitted comment with your filename in the editing window.

_____ Project 2 did not meet all specifications for the previous project: a **car**, an **aerial vehicle** (helicopter, plane, blimp, etc.), a **building**, five **people**, three **nonflying animals**, two flying **birds or pterodactyls**, a **table** and four **chairs**, five **kitchen things on the table**, a **baseball** or other ball on the table, and **3D text** with your first and last names.

_____ Objects have positioning or angular errors .

New tasks

User story or scenario is a paragraph in plain English that tells your story:

☐ (–40) User story completely missing.

_____ words misspelled (–1 each)

_____ punctuation errors (–1 each)

_____ capitalization errors (–1 each)

Pseudocode (your plan in outline form that you'll later code and use to document your logic):

☐ (–40) **Pseudocode completely missing**. You have used actual code rather than comments. That means you coded without a plan.

☐ (–1 each for fewer than 30 actions). Story is short. You need a **minimum of 30 actions** (not counting the control structures such as *doInOrder* or *doTogether*).

☐ (–5) Not satisfying the requirement that you have **three or more camera positions** (you only have one: the camera position at the beginning of your story).

☐ **Pseudocode needs to be broken into finer steps** with the objective of finally having a line of pseudocode that can be coded with one statement. Then when you code, you'll focus on implementing or coding one thing at a time, and not mix designing your program and coding.

☐ **Logic in the pseudocode can be simplified.**

Other comments:

Score _______ **out of 100.** Keep this sheet as evidence of the score you received.

Chapter 4 METHODS AND FUNCTIONS

Contents

INTRODUCTION TO METHODS AND FUNCTIONS

Methods and functions have similarities and differences.

Similarities: Both are computer programs (**instructions** that tell the computer what to do and **comments** that tell people what the computer is being told). Both have instructions and comments grouped together into a lump and given a unique name. Once they've been created, they can be referred to by their names and used repeatedly. Both methods and functions are widely used throughout object-oriented programming (OOP) in the OOP languages such as Alice, Java, C#, C++, VB.Net, and many others. Functions are commonly used throughout both object-oriented languages and procedural languages such as C. Both are programs tightly bound to a specific object or the world in an OOP. Through the use of parameters, data can be passed or transferred into the programs to influence how the method or function runs, but these programs don't require that data be passed to them. They may receive no data, one piece of data, or several pieces of data. Both methods and functions can use topics described later in Chapter 5 (Control Structures) and Chapter 6 (Variables, Expressions, Assignment Statements, and Parameters).

Differences: As you know, objects have properties. Most objects we've used in Alice are 3D virtual objects that you can see in the world view or quad view, although they may be made invisible. But you may have seen some 2D signs or displays with text perhaps used to describe how to run a program. Some objects in Alice and other OOP programs may not be virtual models of physical objects. Whatever the type, the object has properties, and we've said that **a method is a program used to change one or more properties of an object,** and **a function is a program used to find and tell you the value of a property such as its width or point of view** (which actually has six values).

In computer programming, a function is a program that returns (that is, gives back to you) one value. That value may be the value of some property of an object (as we've described before), or the value may be one returned by a function such as square root that receives, for example, the number 4 and returns a 2 (the square root of 4).

For these two uses, methods and functions are used differently. How you code them as you're creating them differs, and how you code them when you're using them or referencing them, as computer programmers commonly refer to with their jargon, differs. Methods cause something to happen to affect a property of the object, and a function returns a value. That's all: a function gives you a value. The jargon is that a function returns a value in the name of the function. You must use that value immediately, perhaps by giving it to another program. If not that, then store the value in a storage place in memory called a variable. In that case, the function has done its job to return a value, and a separate action causes that value to be stored and be accessible for later use. That separate action to store the value in a variable is called an **assignment statement**.

Functions always give back or return a value. Methods may return one or more values, but in a different way than a function. Although a method will cause something to happen, it might not give back or return any values.

In programming, if data are transferred either into or out of a program, you normally must be careful that the data type (text, number, a Boolean value for *True* or *False*, and others) can represent the value you want to transfer.

METHODS

World-level methods and object-level methods

Alice has many built-in or primitive methods for its objects, and a programmer can create new ones. Use a **world-level method** if the program affects or refers to more than one object. Use an **object-level method** if the method affects only one object such as frog. Conversely, don't use an object-level method if more than one object is used in the method.

To create a world-level method, select the world in the object tree, then under the world's details, select the methods tab, then click *create new method.* Name the method descriptively with a verb so the name suggests what the method will do. Good names for methods are part of the internal documentation of the program.

To create an object-level method, select the object that you want to create the method for, then select the methods tab, and finally click *create new method*. Name the method descriptively so the name suggests what the method will do.

In the editing pane for the new method is where you code and document the method by dragging tiles into the pane.

Once created, you can *call* or execute that method by dragging the tile for that user-created method into the coding window, just as you've done with the built-in methods.

Example of a user-created (also called a user-generated or user-coded) object-level method

- In a pristine world, add a frog and a cheshireCat.
- Create an object-level method named *flip* that causes a frog to flip (jump up and down while turning forward) and use it in a world-level *main* method. Direction is up or down relative to the ground rather than relative to the frog.

To make the *flip* method execute, drag the frog.somersault tile from the frog's methods into the *world.main* method. Now clicking the *Play* button triggers the event *When the world starts,* which, as shown in the Events window, causes *world.main* to run, which causes *frog.flip* to run.

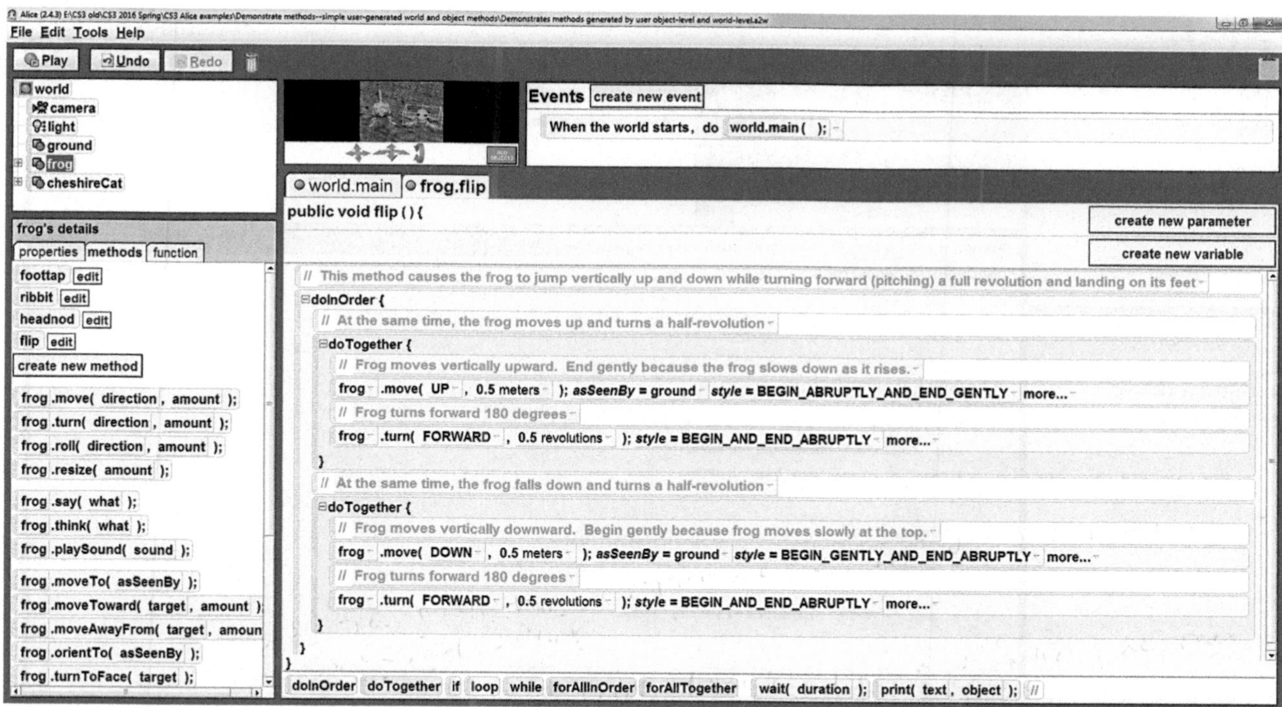

This object-level method causes the frog to flip (at the same time, jump up and turn forward a half-revolution, then, at the same time, move down and turn forward). The *move* and *turn* methods are separate programs, and the doTogether tile instructs the computer to run both programs at the same time. Method *main* calls method *flip*. Method *main* is shown later.

Example of a user-created world-level method

Now we'll create a new method that uses two objects. Because it uses two or more objects, the method will be world level. In the previous example world, add a cheshireCat (from Animals). Select the **world** (not the cat or frog) from the object tree, and in the world's details, click on the *create new method* button. Because the cat and frog will introduce themselves in this method, name the method *introduceCatAndFrog*, which begins with a verb and uses **camel case** to separate words by beginning new words with a capital letter (except for the first word, which begins with a lowercase letter).

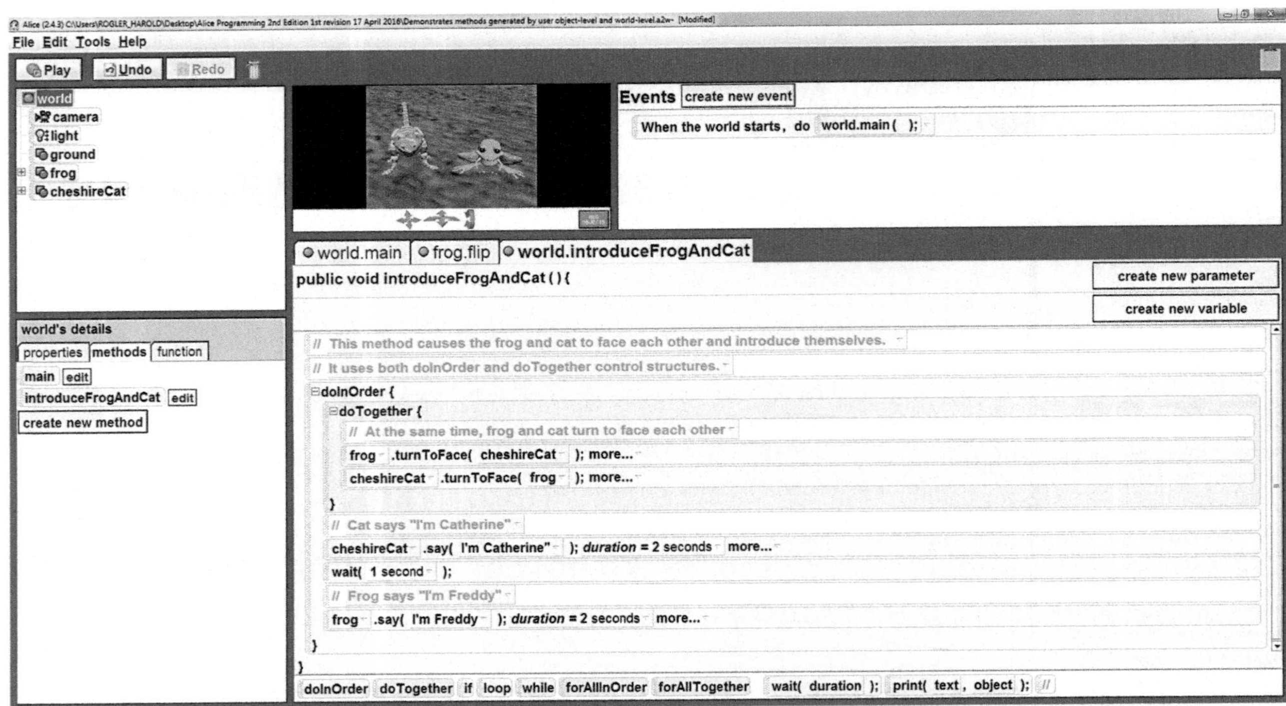

Here's the method *introduceFrogAndCat*. To make this method run, drag the tile *world.introduceFrogAndCat* into the *main* method, *world.main,* shown in the next image.

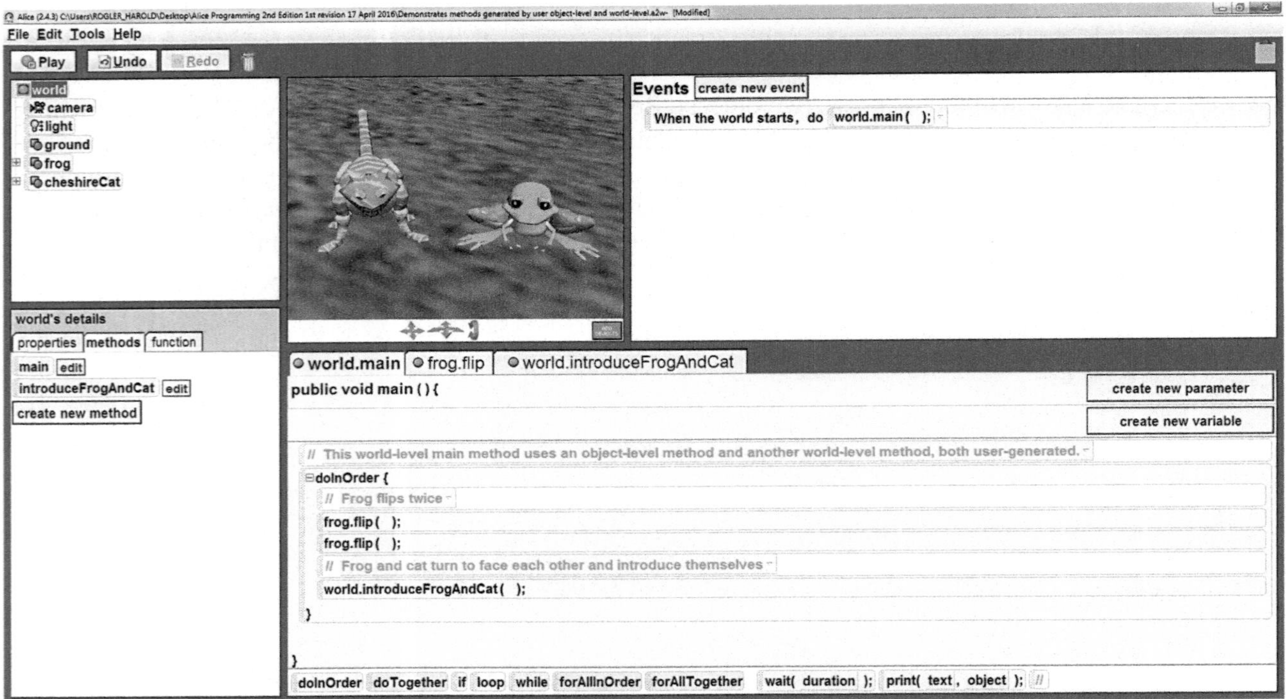

Now after the user clicks the *Play* button (which triggers the event *When the world starts*), the method *world.main* executes, and in that method appears the statements for two frog *flips* and *world.introduceFrogAndCat*.

USER-GENERATED FUNCTIONS

Alice has many built-in or intrinsic functions for the world, which are listed under the *functions* tab of the world's details. Objects have their intrinsic functions listed under each object's details. Functions, like methods, can be world level (if they use two or more objects) or object level (if they use only one object).

Programmers can create their own functions. An example of a **user-generated function** follows. As you know,surrounding any object is a rectangular prism (a brick shape) that shows when the object has been selected. As a simple example, the function will calculate the volume of that brick. The volume is the product of height * width * depth. These three values can be found from the built-in functions *getHeight, getWidth,* and *getDepth* for the object, which will be a frog.

In the Alice examples folder, this program has name Demonstrates user-generated function for frog volume.a2w.

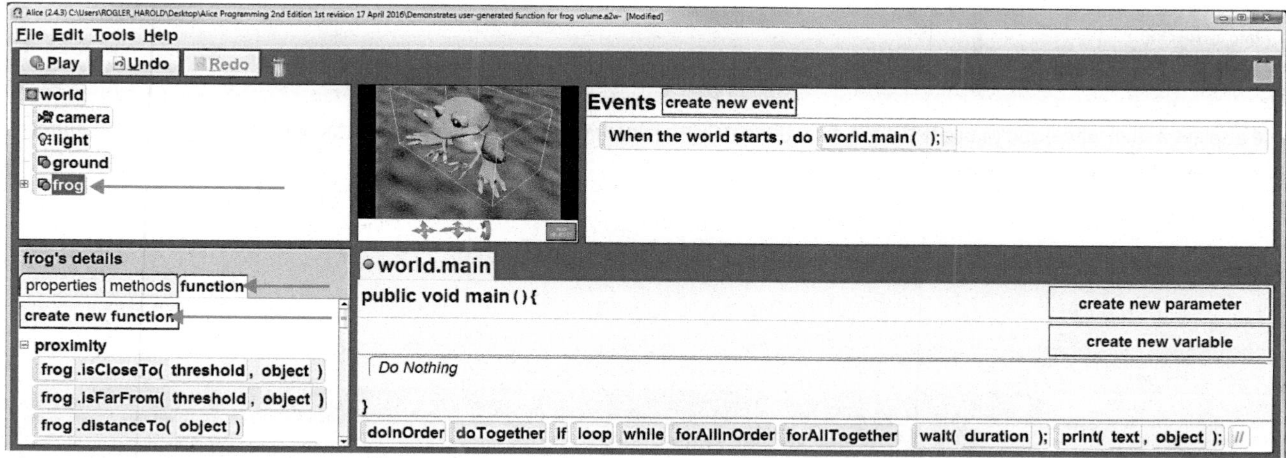

Here I've added a frog, selected it in the object browser near the top left, and clicked on the functions tab. Listed there are some of the many built-in functions for the frog. To create a new function for the frog, click on the *create new function* button.

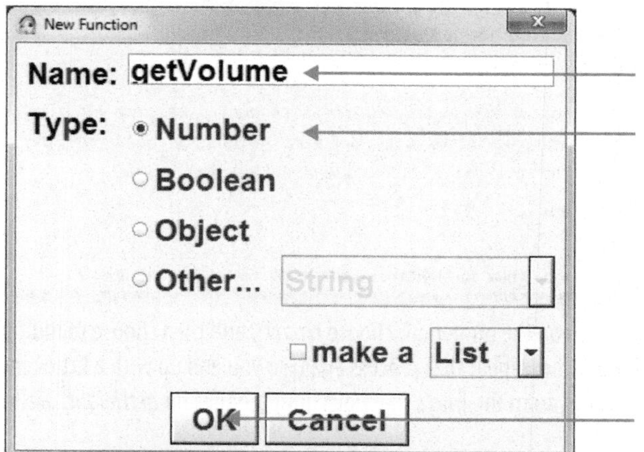

This dialog window appears, and you must give a unique name to your function. The name should be descriptive; the name should suggest what data or value will be returned or given back by the function. I've named it *getVolume*, using camel case to help separate words. You also must specify the type of data that will be returned, such as a number, a Boolean value, object, or text (one of the choices under *Other*). I chose a number data type because the function will return the volume of the rectangular prism that surrounds the frog. Click *OK*.

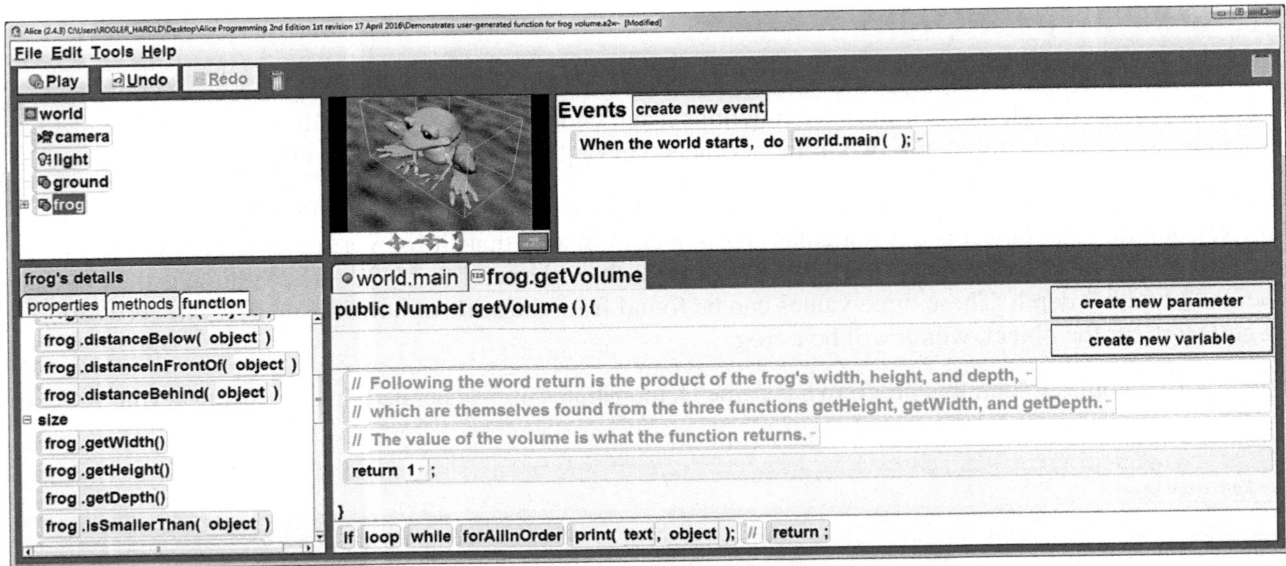

Alice displays a shell where you can code the function. Ultimately, the number for the volume of the rectangular prism that's to be returned appears where the *1 in return 1* appears above.

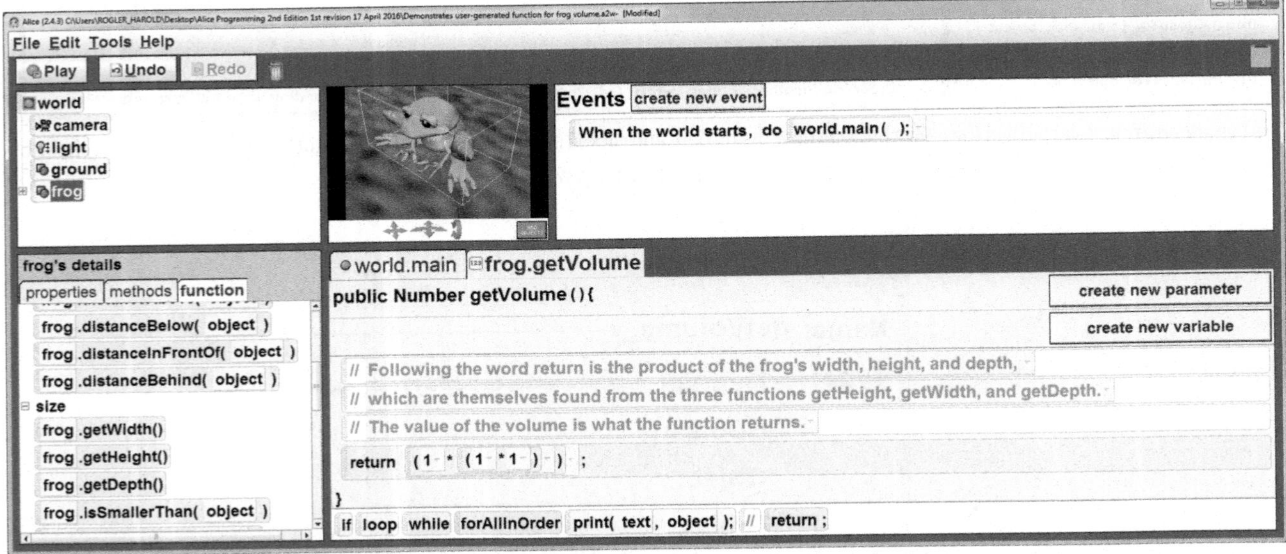

To calculate the frog's volume, right-click on the numeric 1, choose *math,* and then choose to multiply two numbers. Because we need to multiply three numbers to calculate the volume, repeat that process again so you end up with a little template to multiply three numbers as shown above. Into these three slots for numbers, from the frog's functions drag the tiles for *getHeight, getWidth*, and *getDepth*.

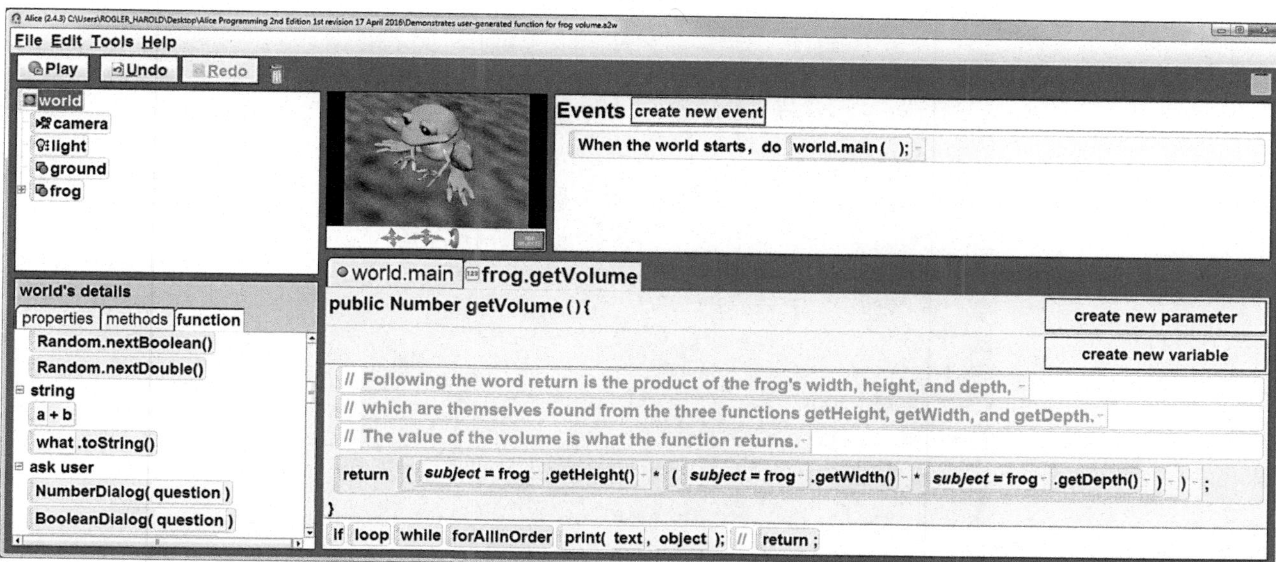

This completes the new function that will return the value for the volume of the prism that surrounds the frog. Now click on the tab for *my first method*, and from the frog's methods, drag in a *say* method. Because the *say* method can only say a string, and the volume is a number, from the world's functions, drag in a tile for *what.toString*, which will replace the *what* with the new *getVolume* method for the frog.

Now we're ready to run the program that will use our new function to return the volume. Click *Play*. After converting the volume into a string, the frog says its volume in the next figure.

When you click *Play*, the frog now uses the new function to say its volume. Some improvements to this program would be to concatenate two strings so the frog says "My volume is 0.0311 cubic meters" and to format the number so it has fewer significant places.

KEY WORDS FOR THE CHAPTER

- Alice's integrated development environment (IDE)
  - details of the world or an object
    - properties pane
    - functions pane
    - methods pane
  - editing or coding area
- camel case
- functions
  - descriptive name for the function
  - object-level and world-level functions
  - built-in and user-created functions
    - pane in details area of Alice's IDE
- methods
  - descriptive name for the method
  - object-level and world-level methods
  - built-in (or intrinsic) and user-created methods
  - pane in the details area of Alice's IDE
  - use to set up initial poses for objects

CHAPTER 4 PROJECT: CODE AND TEST YOUR STORY

Due ______________________________

☐ The purpose of this project is to **code and test your plan** from the previous project for Chapter 3. Your plan is your user story and outline of that story (your pseudocode). The pseudocode is the **algorithm** (the series of statements or instructions to carry out the task). **Implement** means **to code or program** and **test** your program. Keep your scenario and pseudocode from the previous project in this project. They serve as your plan while coding, and they document your logic after coding.

☐ Open your previous project from Chapter 3 and immediately save it as a new file named *CourseNumber_ProjectNumber_SectionNumber_LastName_FirstName.a2w,* or use a filename that your professor asks you to use. Edit the comment with your filename so it has the correct project number. Correct any problems from the previous project. Save your file every 15 minutes or so while you're working on it.

☐ **After** each line of your pseudocode and after selecting in the objects window what object you'll animate, drag and drop from the list of methods in the details window a method that accomplishes that step of pseudocode. You also can drag tiles from the properties tab and set new values for properties when that statement executes. Most methods require that you supply additional values for the method's **arguments** such as the direction and distance that an object moves and its duration.

Your pseudocode and actual code will be intermingled:

A line of pseudocode
Actual executable statement for the line of pseudocode just above
Another line of pseudocode
Actual executable statement for the line of pseudocode just above
Another line of pseudocode
Actual executable statement for the line pseudocode just above
etc.

After completing a step or two, test your program by playing the world you've coded thus far. After playing or replaying, close that window and make any changes necessary and retest. When all is fine, go on to code the next line of pseudocode.

Drag into your program *doInOrder*, *doTogether*, *If/else*, and *Loop* **control statement** or **control structure** tiles where necessary to control how other statements execute.

☐ If you code your program using your home computer or laptop, test the program at your school (your customer's site). Differences in hardware, operating system version, and configurations can cause a program to run on one computer but fail on another.

☐ After completing the project and saving your latest version, find where you stored the file, then check to see that the file size is not 0 KB and the file date and time are reasonable. Then submit the final version of your project as directed by your professor. Check the file size, filename, date, and time again to make sure you submitted the right version of your project. Don't submit an autosaved backup file.

CHAPTER 4 PROJECT: GRADING SHEET FOR CODE AND TEST YOUR STORY

Last name ____________________ First name ____________________ Section ____________________

☐ Project not submitted or submitted after the deadline. (**No credit**)

☐ (–3) Filename should have the form CourseNumber_ProjectNumber_SectionNumber_LastName_FirstName.a2w with a _B or _C just after *FirstName* if you submitted several versions.

☐ (-2) Omitted **comment with your filename** for this project in the editing window.

☐ **Project did not meet all specifications for the project of Chapter 2**:

A car or other ground vehicle, an airplane or other aerial vehicle, a building, five people, three nonflying animals, two flying birds or pterodactyls, table and four chairs, five kitchen things on the table, a ball on the table, and 3D text with your first and last names. Objects have positioning or orientation errors.

☐ **Project did not meet all specifications for the project of Chapter 3:**

_____A **scenario** or user story as a paragraph in English that tells your story. This remains in the project as documentation.

_____**Pseudocode** needs to be broken into finer steps with the objective of finally having a line of pseudocode that can be coded with one statement. Missing three or more camera positions (you have one or two). Story is short. You need a minimum of 30 actions (not including the control structures).

New tasks

☐ Executable code appears just after the pseudocode that describes the code. Program has groups of pseudocode comments followed by groups of actual code. Intermingle the comments so someone reading the program will have plain-English sentences describing the action, followed on the next line by the actual code.

☐ Logic in the doInOrder, doTogether, or other control structures can be simplified.

☐ You have a doTogether with one statement.

☐ When you were already in a doInOrder, you began another unnecessary doInOrder.

☐ Sometimes you used a doInOrder tile, then shifted to not using it (or the opposite).

Other comments

☐ Very good intermingling of pseudocode with executable code.

Score _______ out of 100. Keep this sheet as evidence of the score you received.

Chapter 5 CONTROL STRUCTURES

Contents

INTRODUCTION

Control structures or **control statements** are statements that control how other statements execute. This chapter revisits two control structures that you've seen before: *doInOrder* and *doTogether*. They're described here as graphical displays called **flow charts** that use rectangles, pathlines (arrows), diamonds, and other shapes. Later, we'll add a diamond graphic when we describe two new control structures in this chapter: the **If control structure** that controls which of two possible statements will execute, and two kinds of **loop control structures** that cause other statements to execute repeatedly. We'll also show how control structures can be placed inside (**nested in**) other control structures.

STATEMENTS

A **statement** is an instruction to the computer. It may make an object move, resize, change color, speak, and so on. Some statements in Alice and other object-oriented languages have the form **object.method** (*arguments*) or **world.method** (*arguments*). **Arguments** are values for parameters used by a method or function. These values affect what the method or function does. For example, the *move* method requires that the direction of the move be specified (for example, *up*) and the distance or amount to move (e.g., 3 meters). The parameters are *direction* and *amount*, and the arguments are the values *up* and *3 meters*.

Methods are programs (instructions) that can be either built in or programmer created:

- **Built-in methods** (also referred to as **primitive** or **predefined methods**), which are included with Alice and are listed in the details area under the methods tab), or

User-created methods (also referred to as **user-defined** or **user-generated methods**, but better named **programmer-created methods** because the programmer can create the method, but a user while running a program cannot create a method).

A **method** is a program that groups together a series of statements and gives that series a name, the method's name. In Alice, methods cause the properties of objects to change.

A function is also a program with a series of statements, and that series has a name, the name of the function. But a function is not a statement. It may be part of a statement, it may return a value that controls a statement, or it may return a value that is stored for later use. Functions associated with an object return the values of the object's properties, but don't change them. Other functions in Alice and most computer languages evaluate mathematical functions (and others) and return one value.

Another kind of statement is one that stores a value in a variable, or one that stores a value for a property. This is called an **assignment statement** (or **set statement**). Here's a place a function might be used: the value that the function returns could be stored in a variable or property.

The **control statements** (or **control structures**) described next affect the order in which other statements execute. They include ***doInOrder*** (executes statements sequentially), ***doTogether*** (executes statements simultaneously or at the same time), ***If*** statements (execute different statements as controlled by a condition), and two ***loops*** (with different ways to execute one or more statements repeatedly).

In summary, a statement can be a method, an assignment or set statement to either store a value or set a property value, or a control structure that controls the order in which other statements execute.

This chapter describes control statements and shows how they're used in programs.

HOW TO CONTROL THE ORDER IN WHICH STATEMENTS ARE EXECUTED

Introduction to the control structures

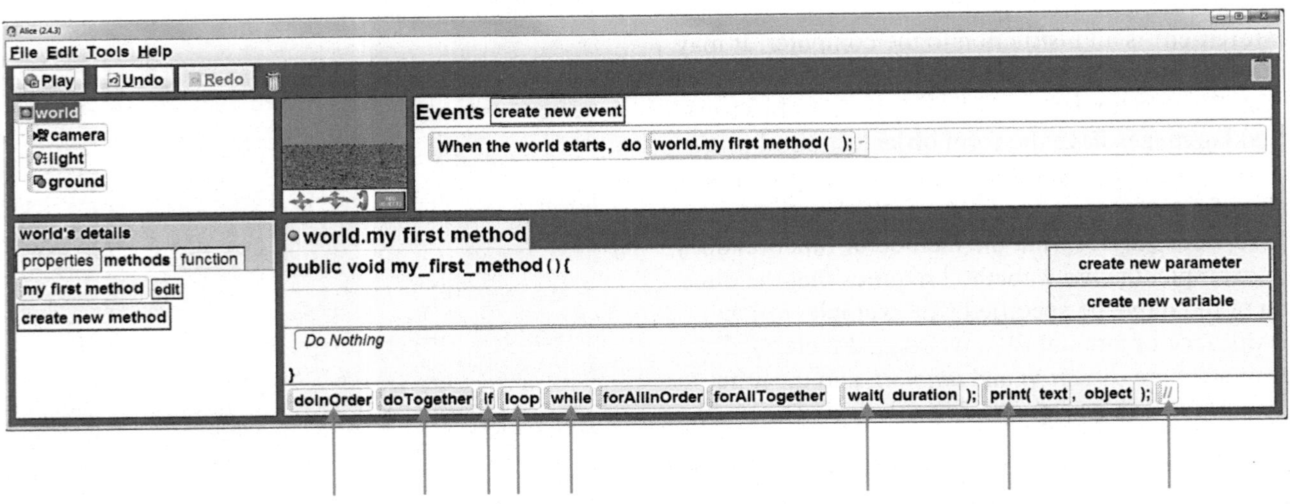

Shown here in **Java style** along the bottom of the editing area are the tiles for the control structures. Also shown are the wait, print, and comment tiles.

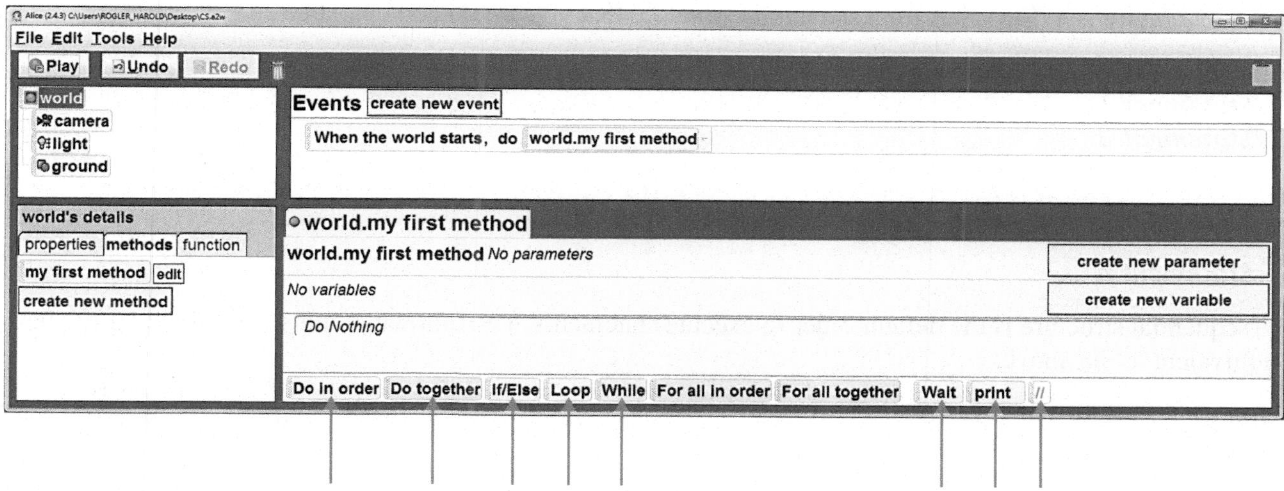

Shown here in **Alice style** along the bottom of the editing area are the tiles for the control structures.

Sequential. Execute statements in the order they're listed from top to bottom. Complete one statement before beginning the next statement. In Alice, this is **doInOrder.** Like the other statements described in this section, this is a statement that controls the order in which other statements are executed.

doTogether. Execute statements at the same time.

Conditional. Controls which of two groups of statements is executed and which is ignored. In Alice, this is the **If** (or **If/else**) control statement).

Repeatedly execute one or more statements (**loops**)

Repeat them a definite number of times. In Alice, this is the **For loop**.

Repeat one or more statements while (as long as) some condition is *True*. When the condition becomes *False*, exit from the loop. In Alice, this is the **While loop**.

Sequential structure (doInOrder)

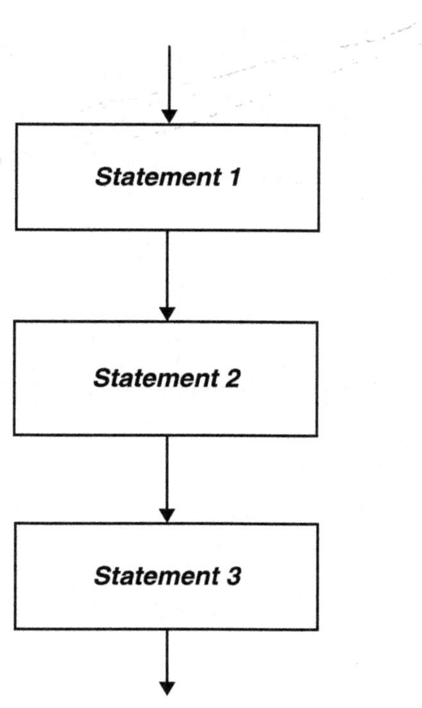

The above figure is a flow chart for a sequential structure that you would code in Alice as

```
doInOrder
    Statement 1
    Statement 2
    .
    .
    .
    Statement n
```

The sequential structure is the default order to execute statements. The following omits the doInOrder tile but is equivalent to the above:

```
Statement 1
Statement 2
.
.
.
Statement n
```

Although equivalent, using the *doInOrder* structure tile is better because (1) it explicitly states the order and therefore makes the order more obvious, and (2) it allows you to copy the entire doInOrder tile to the clipboard in one step, and later, in another program, copy that entire tile from the clipboard into the editing area when you're moving or rearranging code. Hence, rather than separately copying the individual statements, all statements within the doInOrder tile can be moved at once.

doTogether control structure

Several statements are executed "at the same time" or concurrently either by executing the statements on separate processors or by sharing one processor between several tasks. Each path is called a **thread**, and a program that uses this *doTogether* structure is a **multi-threaded program**.

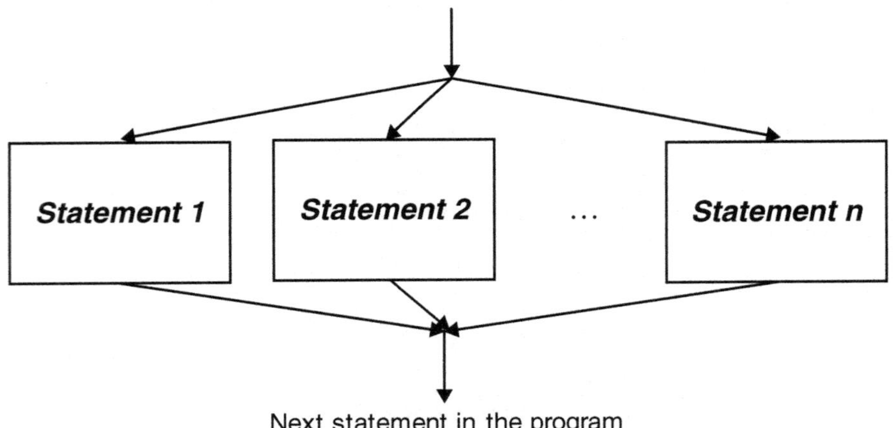

The doTogether tile appears in your editing window as

doTogether
    Statement 1
    Statement 2
    .
    .
    .
    Statement n

Statements begin executing at the same time; for example, an object moves 2 meters in 4 seconds while raising arms 90 degrees in 4 seconds.

However, different statements could take different times to complete, and some may continue executing after others have finished. The entire doTogether would take as long to execute as the individual statement that takes the longest time.

If you have only one statement in a doTogether, then you have no need for the doTogether statement:

doTogether
    Statement 1

is equivalent to

Statement 1

Programs should be no more complex than necessary.

When you want a bird or airplane to circle around forever while your story, as a sequence of actions, takes place, one way to program this is

doTogether

    Statement for bird circling around forever or for a long time

    doInOrder
        First statement in your sequence
        Second statement in your sequence
        ...
        Nth statement in your sequence

If (or If/else) selection structure

This control structure controls which statement of two statements is executed. When it executes, it makes a logical decision on which statement to execute.

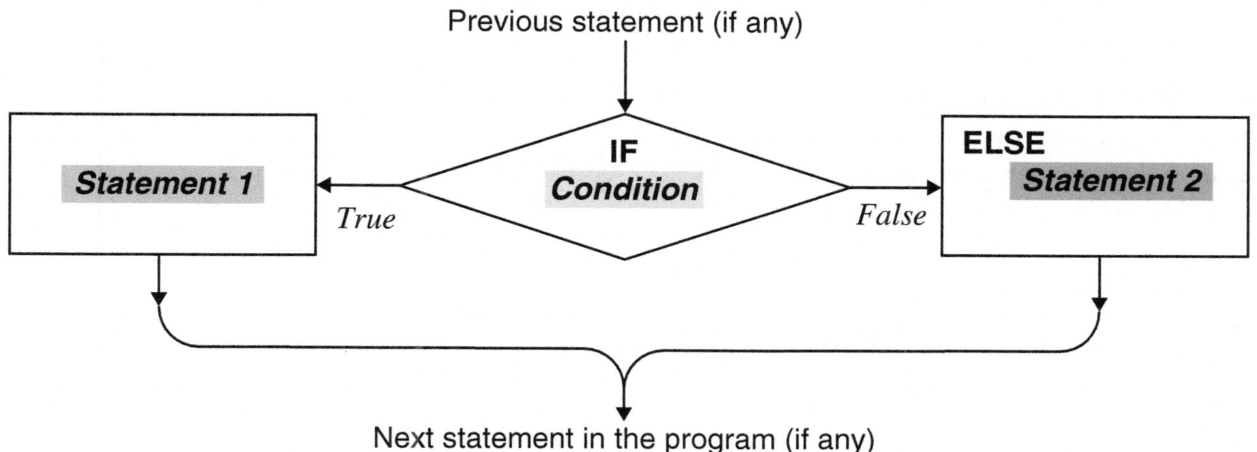

IF *Condition*

Statement 1 (or a block of several statements) executes if the ***Condition*** is *True*

Then skips over the statements that follow ELSE and exits from the If/else.

ELSE

Skips over Statement 1

Statement 2 (or a block of several statements) executes if the ***Condition*** is *False.*[1]

Statement 1 and ***Statement 2*** can each be a series of statements, including other control statements that are **nested** within the If statement. For example, what appears as *Statement 1* in the above flow chart could be one statement or several statements in a *doInOrder* tile, several statements in a *doTogether* tile, a loop, or even another *If* statement. If a control statement is coded within another control statement, the inner control statement is said to be **nested** within the outer one, or the two are nested. Alice allows more than two levels of nesting.

You also can leave the *Do Nothing* in one of the two slots for statements if you want nothing to execute for one of the values of the condition.

When you drag an If statement into your coding window, you (as a programmer) face the task of coding the slots where statements are required and coding the condition that controls which of the two statements will execute. Before showing some examples of If statements coded, let's survey the five forms for conditions.

Conditions can be Boolean constants (literals), Boolean expressions, Boolean functions, Boolean variables, or Boolean parameters

Introduction to conditions

All of these forms for conditions have values either ***True*** or ***False***. Conditions are used in If structures (as noted earlier) and in While loops described later, which continue looping as long as the condition is *True.*

How can you set the value of a condition? Alice allows the use of

- The **literal values** or constants, *True* or *False.* These are useful while learning how the If structure works and testing the Statements 1 and 2. You may find these literal values to be good placeholders temporarily chosen but later replaced while coding. Although *True* and *False* are words in ordinary usage, when they're used as conditions, they are key words and their values are stored in a special way in the computer and different from how text is stored.
- **Boolean expressions** that compare two values. You could ask if the two values are equal, or if the first one is greater than (larger than) the second value, or other comparisons. The relational operators used in Alice are == (equals), != (not equals), < (less than), > (greater than), <= (less than or equal to), and >= (greater than or equal to). The equivalent operators used in mathematics have symbols =, ≠, <, >, ≤, and ≥. The result of the comparison is again one of the values *True* or *False.* These also could be logical Boolean expressions that combine simple ones by using AND, OR, or NOT.
- **Boolean functions** (questions) that return (give back or are answered as) *True* or *False*.
- **Boolean variables** that store either *True* or *False.* These are storage places in random access memory (RAM) chips of the computer. Variables and the assignment or set statement that stores a value in a variable are described in Chapter 6.

[1] If you're displaying your code as *Java style in Color,* a new tile that you drag into your coding window appears as Java would be typed with parentheses and curly brackets much like this:

```
If ( true ) {
   Do Nothing
} else {
   Do Nothing
}
```

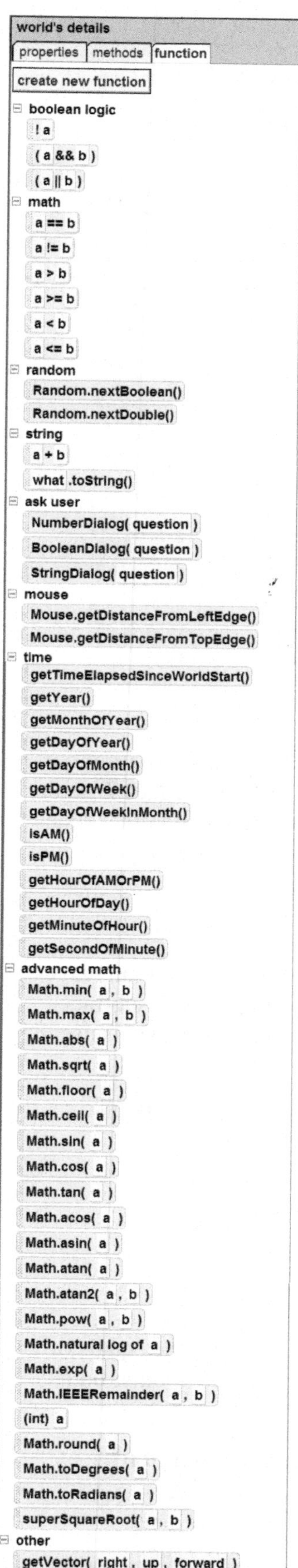

World's functions in Java Style

Templates for the **logical or compound Boolean expressions** are listed under the world's functions. These use Java and Alice versions of the NOT, AND, and OR operators. a and b here are slots for Boolean literals, expressions, functions, variables, or parameters.

Templates for the **relational Boolean expressions** are also listed under the world's functions.

a and b here are slots for two numbers (literals, , expressions, functions, variables, or parameters), so these are used to compare numeric values. In computer languages with datatypes for dates, they're used to compare dates, with > meaning *later than.* You can adapt a==b and a!= b to compare strings, objects, colors, and values in other datatypes.

world's details
properties
methods
function
create new function
boolean logic
not a
both a and b
either a or b , or both
math
a == b
a != b
a > b
a >= b
a < b
a <= b
random
choose true probabilityOfTrue of the time
random number
string
a joined with b
what as a string
ask user
ask user for a number
ask user for yes or no
ask user for a string
mouse
mouse distance from left edge
mouse distance from top edge
time
time elapsed
year
month of year
day of year
day of month
day of week
day of week in month
is AM
is PM
hour of AM or PM
hour of day
minute of hour
second of minute
advanced math
minimum of a and b
maximum of a and b
absolute value of a
square root of a
floor a
ceiling a
sin a
cos a
tan a
arccos a
arcsin a
arctan a
arctan a
arctan2 a b
a raised to the b power
natural log of a
e raised to the a power
IEEERemainder of a / b
int a
round a
a converted from radians to degrees
a converted from degrees to radians
the b th root of a
other
right , up , forward

World's functions in Alice Style

- **Boolean parameters** that each store either *True* or *False* are used to pass (transfer) that value to a method or function from another method or function. Parameters are described in Chapter 6.

Boolean literals

The following is executable if the program includes the two statements:

IF *True*
  Statement 1
ELSE
  Statement 2

It executes ***Statement 1*** and skips ***Statement 2***.

Similarly, the following is executable if the program includes the two statements:

IF *False*
  Statement 1
ELSE
  Statement 2

It skips past ***Statement 1*** and executes ***Statement 2***.

Except for using a literal *True* or *False* in an If/else as

- a temporary placeholder so you can finally see the If statement on the screen, or
- a value you can set for teaching or experimentation to see how an If statement works

a programmer wouldn't leave the condition as a literal *True* or *False* because neither the Alice program nor a user could change the condition. Under different situations (identified through the different values *True* or *False*), the programmer uses an If/else so the program can sometimes execute one statement and other times a different statement. Never do both statements execute. Thus, If/else allows the program to control which of two statements to execute.

Boolean expressions

Alice also lets you build up **Boolean expressions** in the forms commonly used in many computer languages. Just as the symbols + – * / are arithmetic operators that specify which arithmetic operation (add, subtract, multiply, divide) is used with two numbers (e.g., 2 + 3, or 5 – 3, or 2*3, or 2/3), Boolean expressions use the following six **relational operators** to specify how two values are to be compared:

OPERATOR	MEANING
==	is equal to
!=	is not equal to
<	is less than
<=	is less than or equal to
>	is greater than
>=	is greater than or equal to

a and b here are slots for two numbers, so these are used to compare numbers. You can adapt the equals (a == b) and the not equals (a != b) to compare strings, compare objects, and compare values in other data types.

a == b Does **a equal b**? Answer is *True* or *False*.
(No space appears between the two equal signs.)
  5 == 5 is *True*
  5 == 6 is *False*

a != b Is **a not equal to b**?

  3 != 3 is *False*
  3 != 4 is *True*

−1 == −1 is *True*
0 == 1 is *False*
−1 == 1 is False

The numbers being compared don't have to be whole numbers:

1.5 == 1.5 is *True*
1.5 == 1.6 is *False*
1.5 == 1.55 is also *False*, so be careful about the number of decimal places in the two numbers being compared.
1/3 == 0.33 is *False* because Alice carries out the division 1/3 to a large number of decimal places, many more decimal places than the two-place value on the right side.

−1 != 1 is *True*

a < b Is **a less than b**?
3 < 4 is *True*
3 < 3 is *False*
−4 < −3 is *True*
−3 < −4 is *False*

a > b Is **a greater than b**?
3 > 4 is *False*
4 > 3 is *True*
0 > −1 is *True*
−1 > 0 is *False*

a <= b Is **a less than <u>or</u> equal to b**? The **or** means that

a <= b will be *True* if either a = = b is *True* or a < b is *True*. Never will both be *True*.
If both are *False* (a < b is *False* and a = = b is *False*), then a <= b is *False*.
3 <= 4 is *True*
3 <= 3 is *True*
3 <= 2 is *False (both* 3 < 2 and 3 = 2 are *False)*
−1 <= −1 is *True*

a >= b Is **a greater than <u>or</u> equal to b**?
4 >= 3 is *True*
4 >= 4 is *True*
3 >= 4 is *False*

In most coding, a Boolean expression would be used with things other than literal numbers on both sides, although a literal on one side is common. Usually what appears is a function that returns a number on one side (or both sides). Chapter 6 describes variables and parameters that are also frequently used for the values a and b.

The previous examples use literal numbers for a and b in the tiles you drag from the world's functions. Much like choosing the value *True* or *False* for the condition when dragging an If tile into a coding window, comparing literal values are good choices to practice these expressions. They also serve as placeholders or a template in your coding window so you can separately code one side at a time (either the "a side" or the "b side" of the values being compared).

The previous examples used numbers for the values a and b. The next section describes how to adapt the a == b and a != b tiles to compare strings of characters and compare objects, colors, and many other types of data in Alice.

Comparing two strings, two objects, or two colors (optional)

When you drag a tile for a Boolean expression from the world's functions, (e.g., a == b) the values being compared (a and b) are numbers. However, if you have a variable or parameter with another data type (such as a string of characters), you can drop that variable or parameter on the expression and Alice will transform the expression into a comparison of strings. Because it doesn't make sense to ask if the string *James* (the letters) is less than the string *Jim* (again the letters), because we're not looking at the number of characters in the string, then Alice will rightfully restrict the expression to either a == b or a != b (your choice being to determine if the strings are the same or different).

The values Jim, Jane, and Hello used below are literal strings.

a == b Does **a equal b**? Answer is *True* or *False*.
Jim == Jim is *True*
Jim == Jane is *False*
Hello == Hello! is *False* because the right-hand string has an exclamation mark.

a != b Is **a not equal to b**? Answer is *True* or *False*.
Jim != Jane is *True*
Jim != Jim is *False*

The values compared could also be objects, colors, or other types of data in Alice:

Number
Boolean
Object
Other
- String
- Color
- TextureMap
- Sound
- Pose
- Position
- Orientation
- PointOfView
- ReferenceFrame
- Transformable
- Light
- Direction
- Orientation
- PointOfView
- ReferenceFrame

Hence you could compare two objects or two colors to see if they're the same or different by using the a == b or a != b expressions[2].

Boolean functions

For conditions in If statements or While loops (described later), the programmer can use **Boolean functions** (questions that have *True* or *False* answers, or programs that return or give back *True* or *False* values). These functions are found under the functions tab in the details area for most objects and the world, but not all functions are Boolean ones that return *True* or *False* (some return numbers, some return strings of characters, and others return other types of data).

---

[2] Optional note: Alice 2.4.3 doesn't include a type of data for dates (or times or both). In Java and many other languages with that data type, it makes logical sense to ask if one date is less than another date because "less than" means "earlier than" when comparing dates. Hence, comparing dates allows the use of any of the six relational operators: ==, !=, <, <=, >, >=.

Most objects include these Boolean functions, where ***Object*** is the name of the object whose function you're using, and you supply the name of the ***object*** as you drop the tile into your coding window:

Object is within the ***threshold*** of another ***object***
Object is at least ***threshold*** away from ***object***
Object is smaller than another ***object***
Object is larger than another ***object***
Object is narrower than another ***object***
Object is wider than another ***object***
Object is shorter than another ***object***
Object is taller than another ***object***

The following functions are comparing the positions of the centers of two objects.

Object is to the left of another ***object***
Object is to the right of another ***object***
Object is above another ***object***
Object is below another ***object***
Object is in front of another ***object***
Object is behind another ***object***

The following world-level function also returns a *True* or *False*:

In Alice style: Ask user for a yes or no (clicking *Yes* returns *True*; clicking *No* returns *False*)
In Java style: BooleanDialog (*question*)

An example of using this interactive function is shown on the next page, where the user clicks *Yes* or *No* to a question, and the function returns a *True* or *False* as the condition for an If statement.

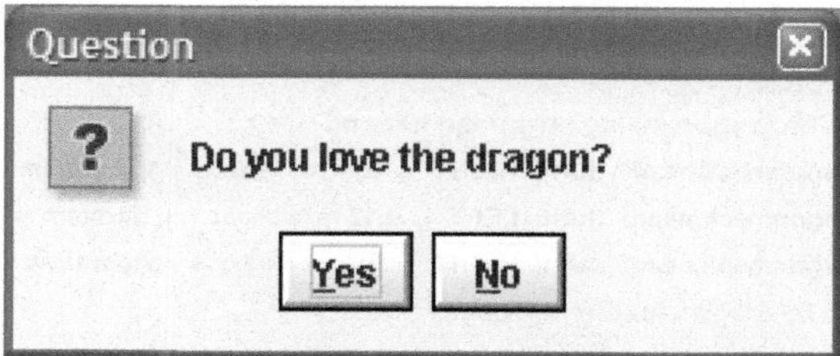

User-created functions also could return a Boolean value, so those functions can be used as conditions. That means that if Alice doesn't have a built-in function that serves your purpose, then you can code one and use it in your condition. If the coding for a condition becomes too lengthy or complex to include it all in the If statement or While loop, you may want to combine that condition in a function you program that finally returns a *True* or *False* when it executes.

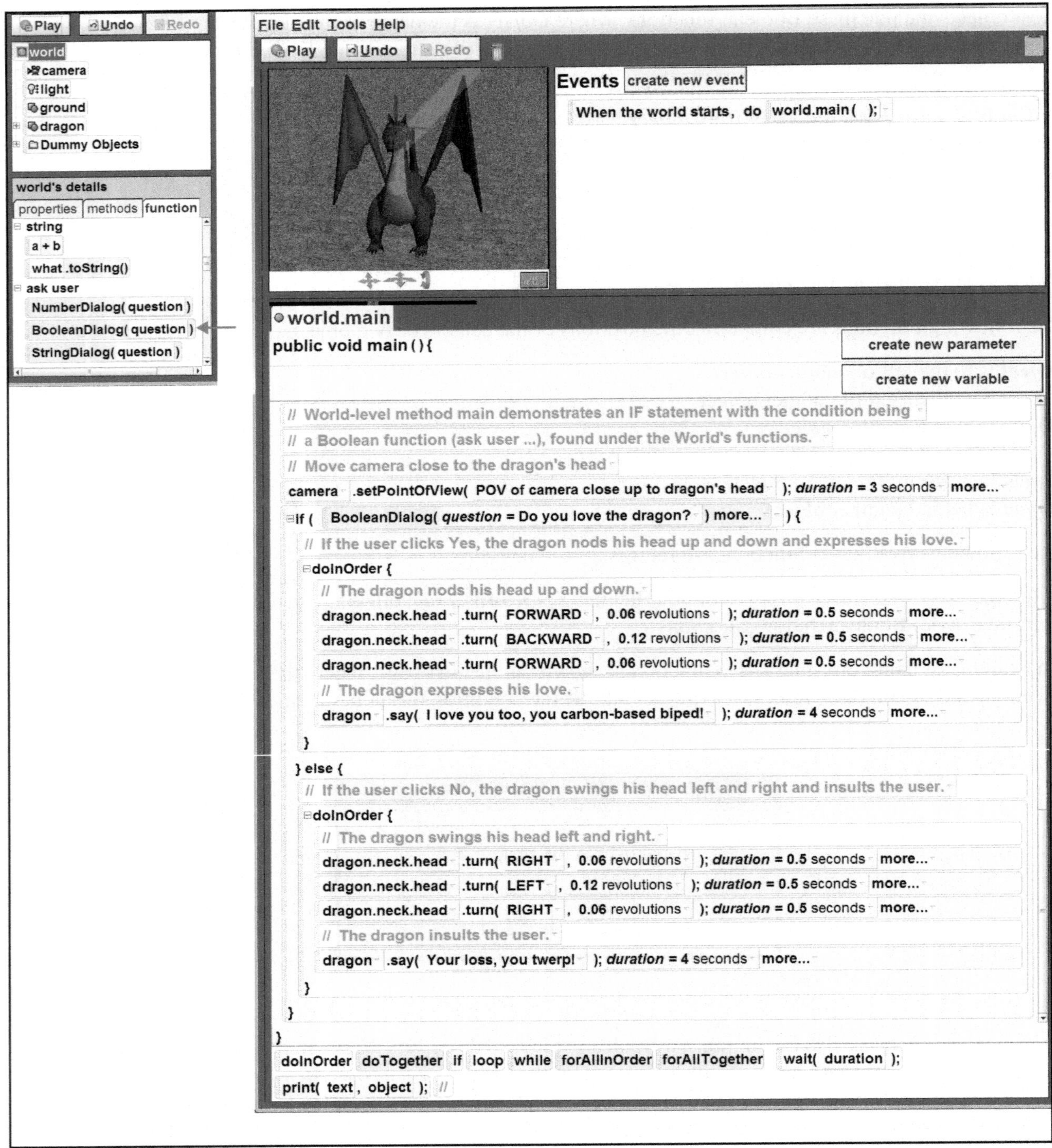

This program uses an If control structure and, as a condition, the world-level function *Ask user for yes or no* to interactively control whether the dragon shakes his head up and down or left and right. The user clicks *Yes* or *No*, and the function returns (gives back) a *True* or *False*.

Boolean variables

A variable is a storage place in the primary memory of the computer to store a value in some data type. That data type can be a Boolean type that can store *True* or *False*. If a Boolean variable has been assigned an initial value appropriate to control the If/else, or that variable has been later assigned a value for some Boolean expression, another variable, parameter, or literal, the variable's name can be used as a condition. The value it stores will control the If/else. Variables are described in Chapter 6.

Boolean parameters

A parameter is a value stored in primary memory and used to transfer a value from one program to another. The value transferred can influence how the receiving program runs. The Boolean value passed (transferred) to a method or function with a Boolean parameter could be used directly in an *If/else* by using that parameter's name as the condition. The value it stores will control the If/else. Parameters are described in Chapter 6.

In summary, we've seen that the condition used in an *If* statement can be a Boolean:

literal
expression
function
variable
parameter

Although we've emphasized Boolean forms of these, the same five forms arise for numbers, strings, and other types of data. For example, numbers can also be literals (e.g., 5), arithmetic expressions (3 + 4), functions that return numbers, variables that store numbers, and parameters that store and pass numbers from one program to another.

Using the logical operators (&& or AND, ! or NOT, and || or OR) in Boolean expressions (optional)

The Boolean expressions described earlier compared two values and found the comparison to be *True* or *False.* How the two values were compared was specified by using one of the six relational or comparison operators: ==, !=, <, <=, >, or >=.

In Alice and many other computer languages, Boolean expressions can be more general than these relational ones. These more general ones use the **logical or compound operators** shown below in both Java style and Alice style:

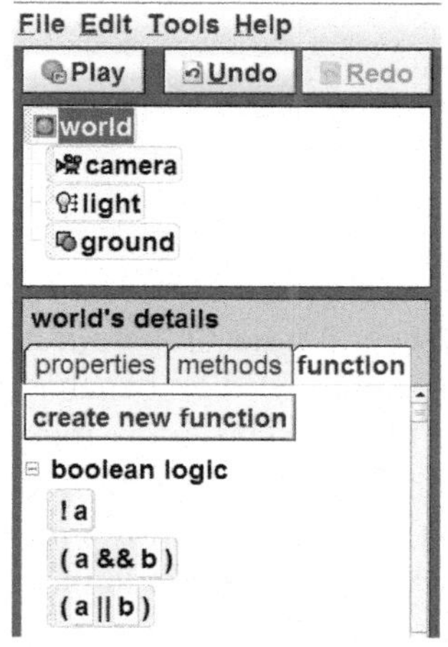

Boolean logic expressions
In Java style

Boolean logic expressions
In Alice style

Tiles with the logical operators (and slots where the Boolean values go that are used with the operators) can be found near the top of the world's functions, shown here in Java style. The values a and b, however, are always Boolean (not numbers and not strings and not any of the other types of data except Boolean, i.e., finally having values *True* or *False*).

While learning how these expressions work, it's useful to begin with the literal values *True* or *False*. Here's the values of expressions using the logical operators:

! a (read as **NOT a**) reverses the value for a:

!*True*	is *False*
!*False*	is *True*

The value **a** could be any of these five forms of Booleans: Boolean literals, Boolean expressions, Boolean functions, Boolean variables, or Boolean parameters.

a && b (read as **a AND b**) is *True* only if both a and b are *True*; otherwise *False*.

It has four forms because a and b can separately be *True* or *False*:

True && True	*is True*
True && False	*is False*
False && True	*is False*
False && False	*is False*

a || b (read as **a OR b**) is *True if one or both are True; otherwise False if both* a *and* b *are False:*

True || *True*	*is True*
True || *False*	*is True*
False || *True*	*is True*
False || *False*	*is False*

Using the literal values *True* or *False* is good for practice and learning (just as using literal numbers is useful while learning about the relational expressions), and you should be aware that there's five forms for Boolean values (the same five we're in the middle of describing in this chapter), and any of these forms can be used for a and b in the logical expressions (!a, a && b, a || b):

1. literal values *True* or *False* that were used in the examples above
2. Boolean functions
3. Boolean expressions (both the relational ones and logical ones)
4. Boolean variables (described in chapter 6)
5. Boolean parameters (described in chapter 6)

Repetition structures

A loop that executes a specified number of times

If you want to execute a method several times, you could list it several times in a doInOrder statement. This approach is OK if you want to execute the method a couple times, but you'd go bananas if you had to list it a 100 times or change the list from 100 to 50. Such long lists take longer to program, make your programs bigger, and may take longer to execute. Fortunately, high-level computer languages have loop control statements so you can easily execute some statements as many times as you want. (Alice allows *infinity*.) A loop is a control statement that allows you to repeatedly run a statement or several statements in the loop. Without a loop, if you wanted to run a method 100 times, you'd have to drag the method tile into your program 100 times, which would be no fun. You can specify the number of times that the statement(s) repeat, which is a whole number (no fractional passes). Alice allows the number to be "infinity," which means the loop continues until the program is stopped by the user or runtime errors occur because numbers used in the loops become too large. The flow chart for this simple loop is shown below.

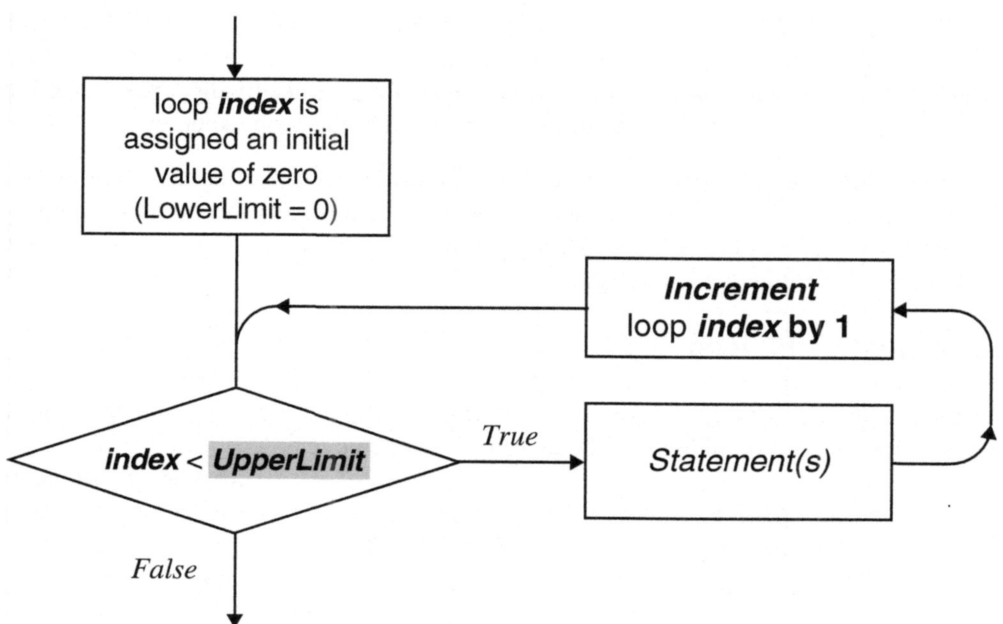

In the **simple FOR Loop**, you specify the ***UpperLimit*** to control how many cycles you want the loop to execute and include what statements you want to execute repeatedly. The loop first zeros the loop **index**, then tests to see if its value is less than the ***UpperLimit***. If not (i.e, ***index < UpperLimit*** is False when the **index** is equal to or greater than the ***UpperLimit***), you exit the loop. If the **index** is less than the ***UpperLimit***, the loop executes the statements and increments the ***index*** by one (increases its value by one). The cycle repeats to test the loop index to see if it's still less than the ***UpperLimit***. If any of the tests fail (i.e., index < ***UpperLimit*** is False) then you exit the loop. Until that time, you execute your statements over and over.

Java style

```
for (int index = 0; index < 10 times; index++) {
  Statement(s)
}
```

++ means to increment the loop index by one

Alice style

```
Loop 10 times
  Statement(s)
```

If you know the number of repetitions you want the *Statement(s)* in the loop to execute, this loop is perfect. It also may be the best choice if you can code Alice to calculate from a formula the number of repetitions.

Where the literal number *10* appears above can be these forms of the same list you've seen before, except now the values are **numbers**:

1. a **literal** number (e.g., 2 or 5 or 10)
2. an **arithmetic expression** that does arithmetic using one of the arithmetic operators (+ – * /)
3. a **function** that returns a number; this could be the *NumberDialog* or *Ask user for a number* or many other functions
4. a **variable** that has a number type
5. a **parameter** that has a number type

The number should be a positive whole number because loops execute completely a whole number of times. However, if the number has a fractional part such as 2.6, Alice **truncates** the number (drops the fractional part). Thus 2.6 truncates to the integer 2. The value 1.9999999 truncates to 1. The number 0.9 truncates to zero, so if you code **Loop 0.9 times**, then the statements inside the loop will never execute because you've exited from the loop before executing the statements.

In most computer languages, using a number with a fractional part to specify how many times a loop is to execute would be a syntax error. Alice is permissive here, which allows you to use functions that probably return a non-integer in the loop. An example is Loop **getHeight(frog)** times to allow the frog's height (after automatically truncating the number) to be the number of cycles that the loop executes.

Truncating a number isn't generally the same as **rounding** a number. Truncating a number means to drop any fractional part, so 2.3 and 2.5, and 2.7 all truncate to 2 (a whole number). A common rounding rule is to round down if the fractional number is 0.0 to 0.4, but round up if the fractional part is 0.5 to 0.9. Thus 2.3 rounds down to 2 and both 2.5 and 2.7 round up to 3.

"Complicated version" of this loop

You can toggle between the "simple" and more complicated versions of the loop by clicking the *more complicated version* button. This version gives you more control over the index by allowing you to specify the LowerLimit and how much the loop index is to be incremented each cycle.

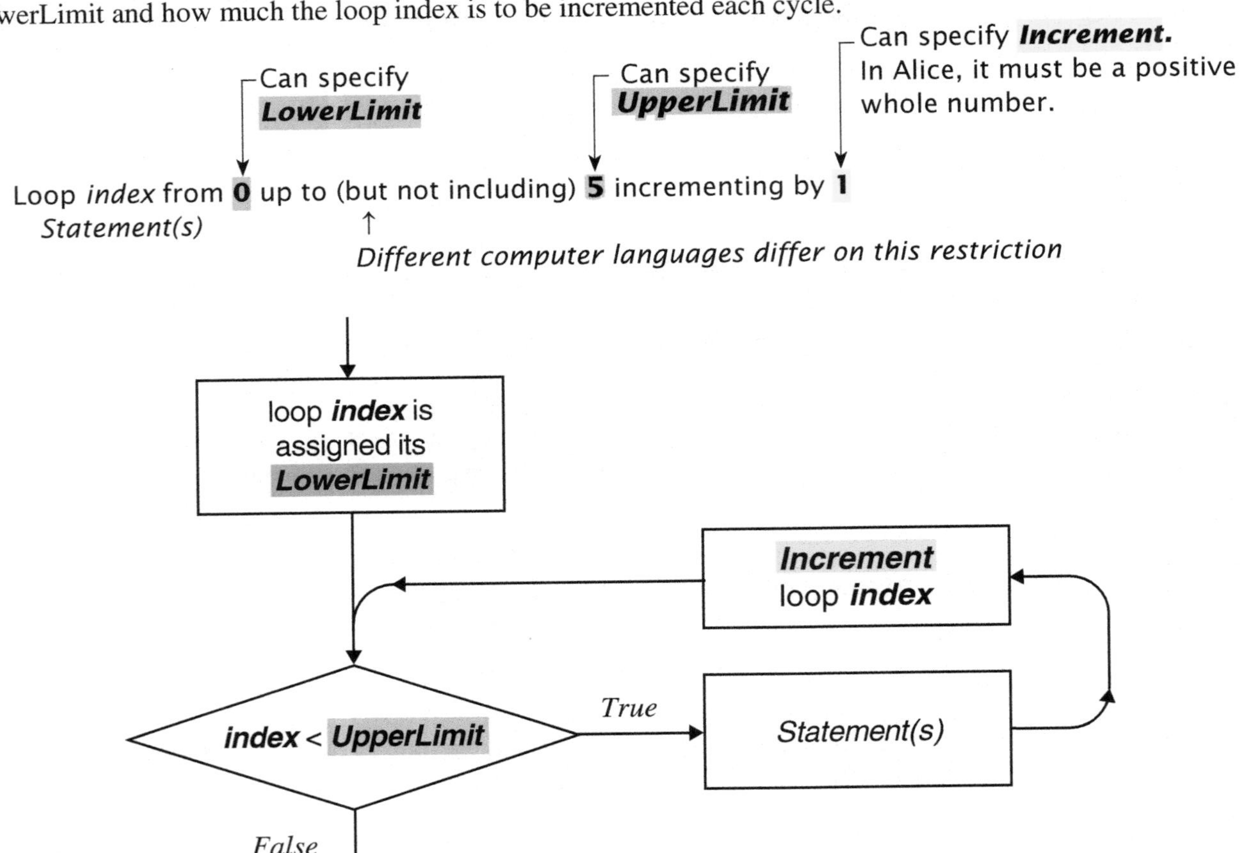

Flow chart for the more complicated version of the loop. The simpler version fixes the *LowerLimit* to be 0 and the increment to be 1, but the more complicated version allows you to control the *LowerLimit*, ***UpperLimit***, ***Increment*** and the statements that execute repeatedly.

Notes:

1. Incrementing the loop index (the counter) takes place after the statement(s) in the body of the loop have executed. The incrementation is automatically carried out by the loop structure and acts as if the following assignment statement executes:

   index set value to **index** + ***Increment***

2. Exiting from the loop occurs when the index is greater than **or equal to** the number ***UpperLimit***.

3. We shall show later (and you can see from the test for Index < **UpperLimit**) that **LowerLimit** must be less than **UpperLimit**. If they are the same, then the first test, **UpperLimit** < **UpperLimit**, is *False* and the *Statement(s)* in the loop never execute.

In the following example, the loop index begins with value **0** and increments by **1** each cycle through the loop, but when the upper limit of 5 is reached, the looping stops because it says up to **(but not including)** 5:

```
Loop index from 0 up to (but not including) 5 incrementing by 1
  Statement(s)
```

What are the values and actions that take place as the loop executes?

Cycle number through the test on loop index	Loop index	Test: Loop index < UpperLimit	Action
1 (first cycle)	0 (***LowerLimit***)	0 < 5 is True	*Statement(s)* execute
2	1	1 < 5 is True	*Statement(s)* execute
3	2	2 < 5 is True	*Statement(s)* execute
4	3	3 < 5 is True	*Statement(s)* execute
5	4	4 < 5 is True	*Statement(s)* execute
6	5 (***UpperLimit***)	5 < 5 is False	*Statement(s)* don't execute because **5** < **5** is *False*

Suppose you changed the increment from **1** to **2**:

```
Loop index from 0 up to (but not including) 5 incrementing by 2
  Statement(s)
```

Cycle number through the test on loop index	Loop index	Test: Loop index < UpperLimit	Action
1 (first cycle)	0 ***(LowerLimit)***	0 < 5 is True	*Statement(s)* execute
2	2	2 < 5 is True	*Statement(s)* execute
3	4	4 < 5 is True	*Statement(s)* execute
4	6	6 < 5 is False	*Statement(s)* don't execute because **6** < **5** is *False*

Suppose you changed the loop as follows:

```
Loop index from 1 up to (but not including) 1 incrementing by 1
  Statement(s)
```

Cycle number through the test on loop index	Loop index	Test: Loop index < *UpperLimit*	Action
1 (first cycle)	1 ***(LowerLimit)***	1 < 1 is False	*Statement(s)* don't execute because **1** < **1** is *False*

Whenever the **LowerLimit** = **UpperLimit**, the *Statement(s)* in the loop don't execute.

Why use the "complicated version" rather than the simpler one (Loop n times)?

- **The programmer wants to use the index** for some purpose, maybe saying or printing its value, using it in some calculation, or passing it to another method or function for use.
- Rather than starting with a LowerLimit of 0 or an increment of 1, the programmer wants to "count" from another LowerLimit such as 5 and increment differently (say, increment by 2).

An **infinite loop** has a practical use in Alice if you want something like windmills to rotate, birds to fly back and forth or circle, and other cyclic activities to continue throughout your animation. This means that your program never ends. However, in the computer world, "infinity" is surprisingly small. The program runs until the user stops the execution, the computer breaks (intentionally breaking the computer is not a good way to stop a program!), the program fails because the loop causes a number to be calculated that's too large (or too small) for the computer to store, or your electrical supply fails (or you starve to death watching your infinite loop and no one pays your utility bill).

Having an infinite process in the middle of a sequence of statements:

```
doInOrder
    Statement 1
    Infinite loop (program will never get past this loop)
    Statement 2 (this statement never executes)
```

never allows the program to execute *Statement 2* because the loop never ends or maybe the program crashes because the computer can't store some huge number. A similar problem can occur if Statement 1 and Statement 2 are separated by some excessively long process, even if it's not infinite.

Using any computer language, your responsibility as a programmer includes programming that uses the computer resources wisely. The resources include the use of the CPU, which has a tremendous task to calculate where all the polygons are that make up the 3D objects as they change position and orientation and finally send out data to all the pixels on the screen where you're viewing the program. Calculations continue even if the camera doesn't show an object because it's off the screen or occluded (hidden) by another object. Ending a program in some infinite loop while some turtle crawls into the sunset without telling the user that this is the end isn't a good way to end an animation.

Example method that uses the "complicated version" of the loop

Suppose you want the ground to count by threes (0, 3, 6, . . ., 27) in *says.* The loop automatically increments the index each cycle by 3. The index of the loop is available for use in the loop, and the goal here is that the ground say the index. However, because the index is a number, and *says* require string data, the index must be converted into a string by using the world's string function what.toString(). After that conversion, the result is a string that the ground can say:

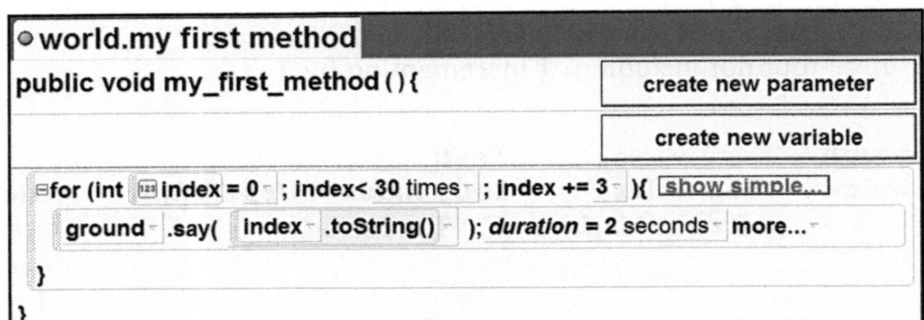

Use of the complicated version of the For loop.

In this loop appears the condition **index < 30 times**, but this loop does not execute 30 times because the increment is 3. Thus the index takes on the values 0, 3, 6, 9, 12, 15, 18, 21, 24, and 27. The value of the index must be less than 30, so this loop executes the method *ground.say* 10 times. When the index is 27, then 27 < 30 is *True* and the ground says *27*. The next time through the loop, the index is again incremented by 3, and now has value 30, but 30 < 30 is *False* and the loop exits without saying that value.

While loop (repetition statement) with its pretest condition

You may want to execute a statement several times, but you're unable to specify or calculate the number of loops. In the previous loops, the number of repetitions is supplied when the loops begins, then the loop is left alone to finish. Because a user can interactively change the program by clicking on an object with the mouse and moving it and many other things, a programmer may be unable to calculate the number of repetitions. Even worse is the case that whether to continue or exit the loop depends on what's happened as the loop executes.

The **While loop** can handle these situations as long as it can decide, just before it executes the body of the loop, whether to execute the statement or not execute it and exit the loop.

Before executing the statements in the body of the loop, the While loop evaluates a condition. If the condition is *False* the first time through the loop, the statements are not executed (control passes out of the loop). If the condition is *True*, then the statements execute. Again the condition is evaluated, and if *True*, the statements are executed again; if *False*, the loop is exited. This cycle of examining the condition and executing the statements if the condition is *True* and exiting the loop if the condition is *False* continues until you exit because he condition is *False*. If the condition never becomes *False*, then you're in an *infinite loop*.

If the Boolean expression never becomes *False*, you're in an **infinite loop**.

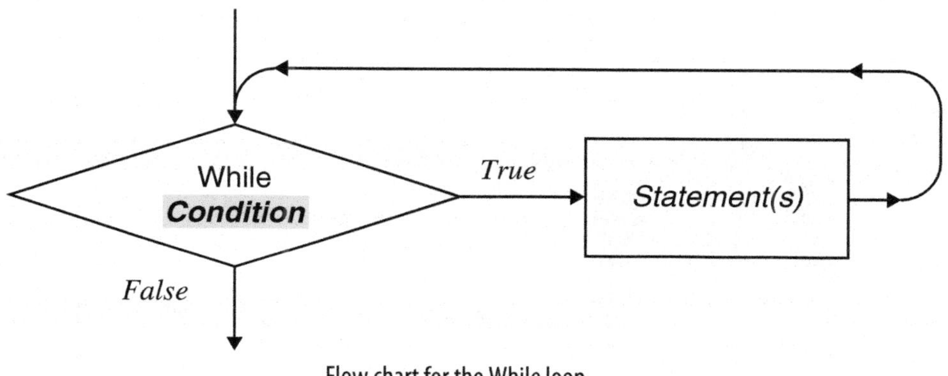

Flow chart for the While loop.

The tile for this loop appears as

WHILE *Condition*
    Statement(s)

The test occurs before the body of the loop is executed. The body of the loop could be a simple statement or a series of statements (including control statements). While the ***Condition*** is *True*, cycling through the loop continues. When the ***Condition*** becomes *False*, you exit the loop without further execution of the statement(s) which are part of the loop, shown in the above flow chart as the rectangle with *Statement(s)*.

Just as with the ***Condition*** in an If/else control statement, the ***Condition*** in this loop can be any one of the five forms:

1. **literal Boolean values**, but if a literal *True* is used, you have an infinite loop, and if a *False* is used, no statements that are part of that While loop will ever execute.
2. **Boolean expressions** such as a < b or others that use the relational operators (==, <, <=, >, >=, !=) with examples shown earlier in the chapter, or maybe forms that use logical operators.
3. **Boolean functions** that return *True* or *False* (i.e., questions such as *Is Object within the threshold of another object?)*
4. **Boolean variables**
5. **Boolean parameters**

} These are storage places that store Boolean values. They're described in the next chapter.

Example of a while loop, with kelly chasing randomGuy1[1]

In this method, kelly chases randomGuy1, but in this interactive program, the user can use the arrow keys so he can escape. Since the programmer doesn't know how skilled the user will be so randomGuy1 escapes from kelly, or whether the user vicariously wants kelly to catch him or not, the programmer can't know how many cycles kelly should turn and move toward him. Hence, a FOR loop with its definite number of cycles wouldn't work.

A while loop is quite suited for this task. The condition in the while loop is that the distance between kelly and randomGuy1 is greater than one meter:

```
kelly.distanceTo( randomGuy1 ) > 1
```

If this is True, then she continually moves toward him. She also turns toward him because the user, with the arrow keys, can be moving randomGuy1 and turning him at the same time. Once the condition evaluates False because the distance between them at that instant is one meter or less, the loop is exited and kelly rests.

As coded, you may notice that the condition is tested only once in a second, then for the next second, kelly moves and turns. In that one second, randomGuy1 might momentarily be closer than one meter to kelly as he blows quickly past her, and she won't have caught him if he's further than one meter from her when the condition is evaluated. How would you modify the while loop to eliminate this possibility or make it very difficult?

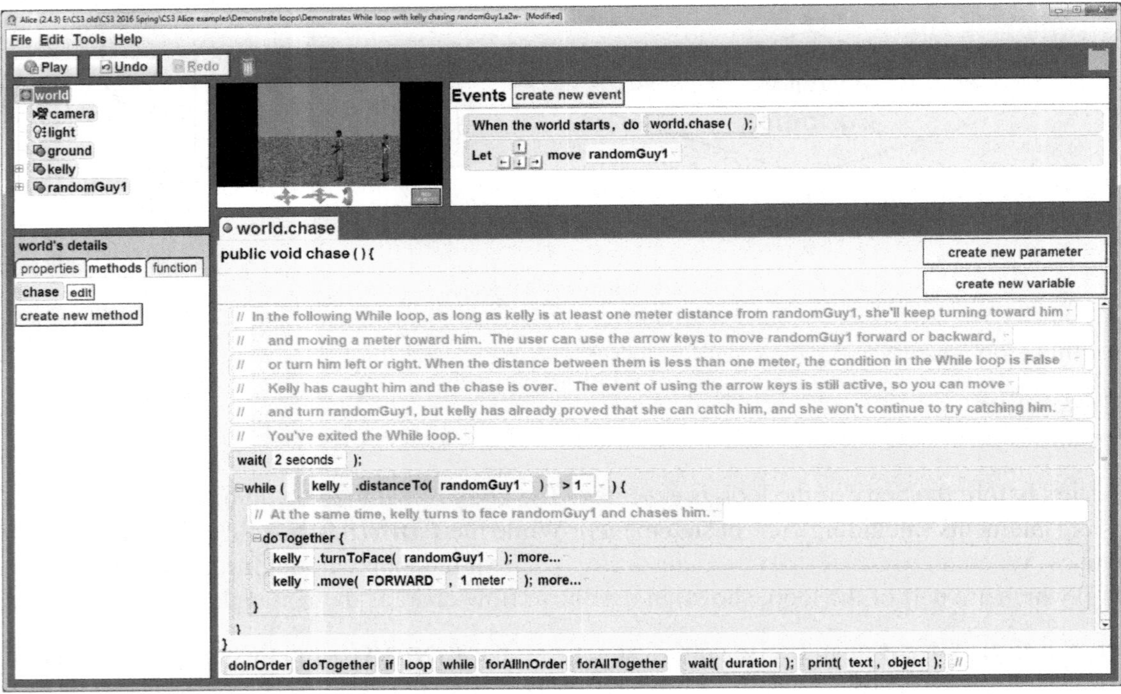

The user uses arrow keys to move randomGuy1 (so he can escape, or he can tease, or he gets captured), and the method uses a while loop to repeatedly turn and move kelly toward him until she's one meter or less from him. When that happens, ...!

[1] This world is stored as Alice Examples\demonstrates loops\Demonstrates While loop with kelly chasing randomGuy1.a2w.

SUMMARY OF THE CHAPTER

Programs can mix the control structures described in this chapter in any order:

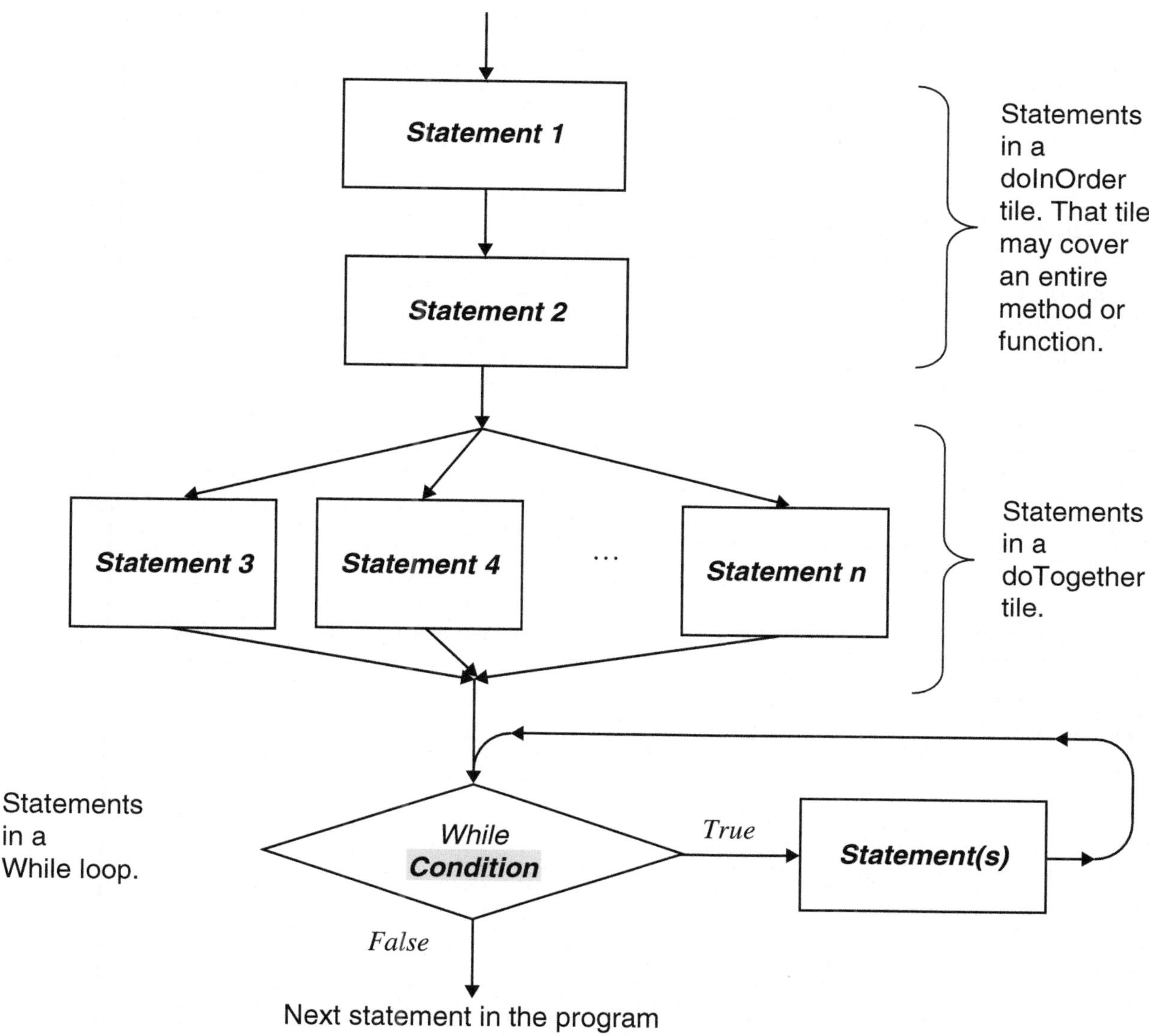

The control structures also can be **nested**. That means anywhere you see a statement in a control structure, it could be replaced by a control structure. Ultimately, however, within some control structure will appear a method or assignment statement that executes.

I've shown how control statements can control other statements by controlling the order in which they execute (either **sequentially in the doInOrder** or at **the same time in the doTogether**), controlling which of two statements will be executed (using the **If statement** with its condition as the controller to pick which statement will execute), or **executing a statement repeatedly in a loop**. The loop may execute a statement the number of times indicated (or perhaps controlled by an index that keeps getting incremented until it reaches a specified limit). Or the While loop repeatedly executes its statements until a condition becomes *False*, which is useful if you can't know in advance how many times to execute a statement.

Boolean values to control If/else and While statements were categorized as literals, expressions, functions, variables, and parameters. These five forms are also useful for numbers, strings of characters, and other types of data.

Flow charts for the control structures were drawn. These graphical ways to plan and document a program or a control statement use rectangles for statements, diamonds where a decision is being made, and pathlines with their arrowheads to show how the steps connect.

KEY WORDS FOR THE CHAPTER

- Boolean variables and the Boolean values *True* and *False*
- condition (controls If/else control structure and While loop)
  - literal Boolean (*True* or *False*)
  - Boolean expression
  - Boolean function
  - Boolean variable
  - Boolean parameter
- flow chart
  - symbols: rectangles, diamonds, pathlines
  - for control structures
- infinite loop
- logical or compound operators (optional)
  - Java style (!, &&, ||)
  - Alice style (NOT, AND, OR)
- relational operators (==, !=, <, <=, >, >=)
- statements
  - assignment or set statement (see Chapter 6)
  - control statement
    - doInOrder (the sequential structure)
    - doTogether
    - if with its condition (a selection structure)
    - loop (repetition structure)
      - For loop
        - simple (increments by +1)
        - "complicated version" (with control over the LowerLimit and increment)
      - While loop
    - statement of form *object.method*
    - statement of form *world.method*

EXERCISES

In the following, a line such as Statement A or Statement B is a statement like frog.move, aliceLiddell.say, or an assignment statement that stores a value in a variable or property. Each also could be a control statement (such as a doInOrder, doTogether, If, or one of the loops). The indentation denotes that the statement is within another control structure. The logic (the use of the control statements and their arrangement) should be no more complex than necessary.

5.1 Are the following functionally equivalent? In the choice on the left, the doInOrder structure has not been explicitly dragged into the coding area. In the choice on the right, the statements appear within a doInOrder tile.
Answer: a. Yes b. No

Statement A
Statement B
Statement C
Statement D

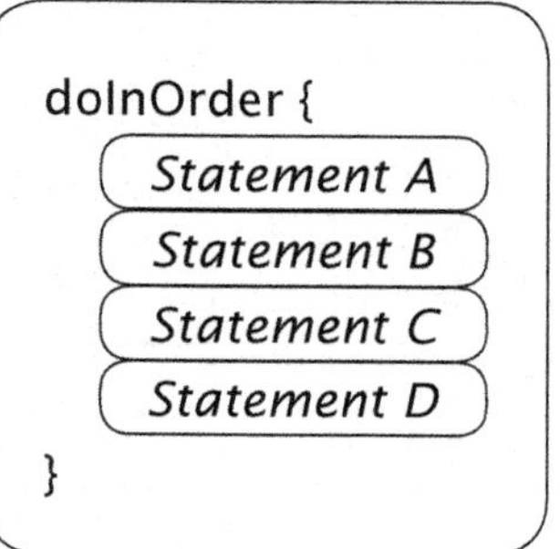

5.2 Simplify the following logic. In the grid on the right, neatly print the control statement(s) and use indentation to show that the statements are a part of a control statement. This overly complex logic is commonly seen in student projects.

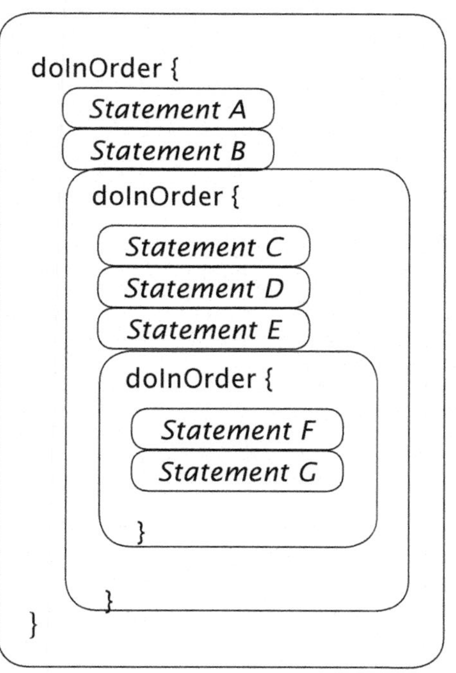

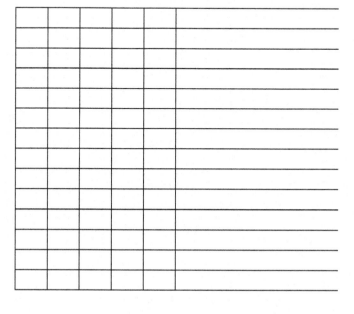

5.3 Simplify the following logic. In the grid on the right, neatly print the control statement(s) and use indentation to show that the statements are a part of a control statement. This overly complex logic is not being consistent in the use of a doInOrder, and unnecessarily uses some doInOrder statements.

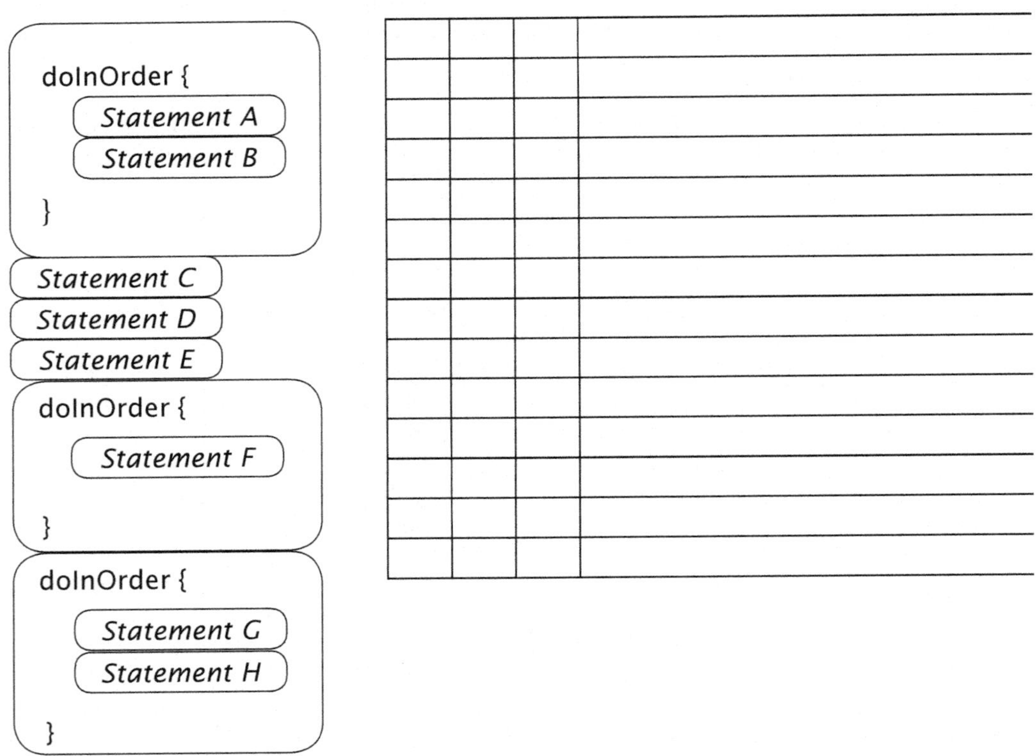

5.4 Are the following control statements functionally equivalent? Answer: a. Yes b. No

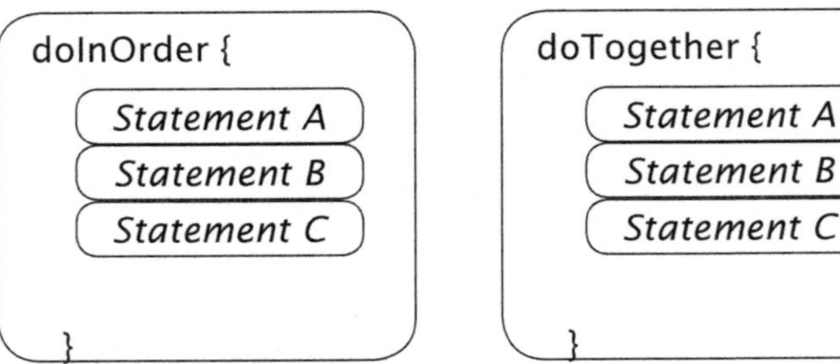

5.5 Simplify the following logic. In the grid on the right, neatly print the control statement(s) and use indentation to show that the statements are a part of a control statement. This overly complex logic unnecessarily uses some doTogether statements.

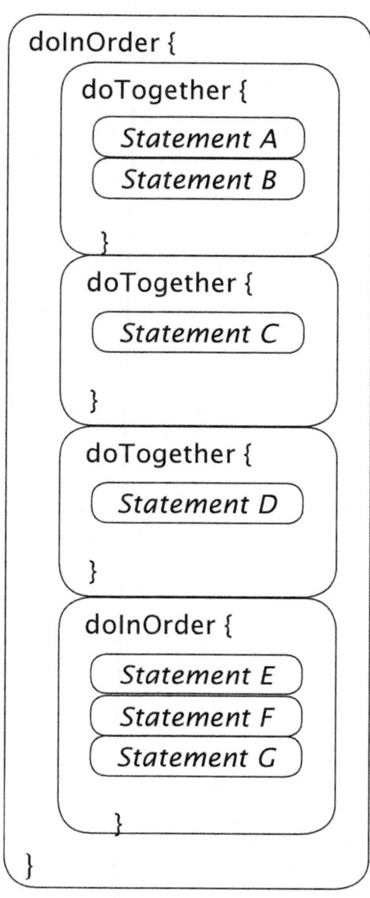

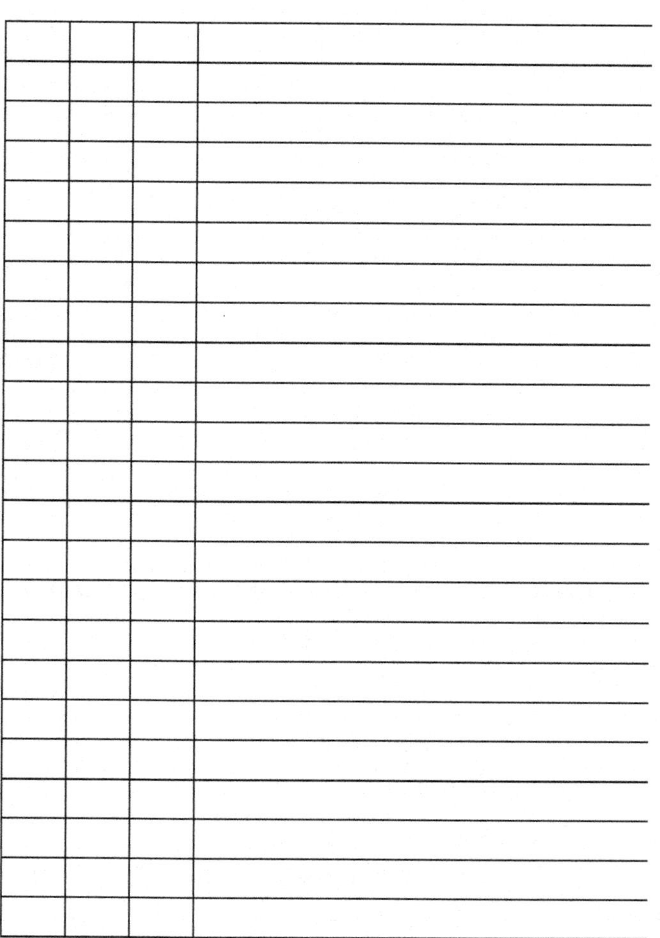

5.6 Are the following functionally equivalent? Answer: a. Yes b. No, each functions differently. c. No, _______ and _______ function the same (specify Left, Middle, Right).

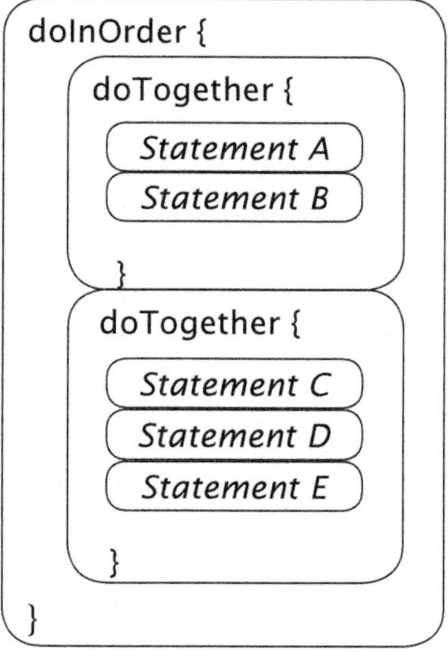

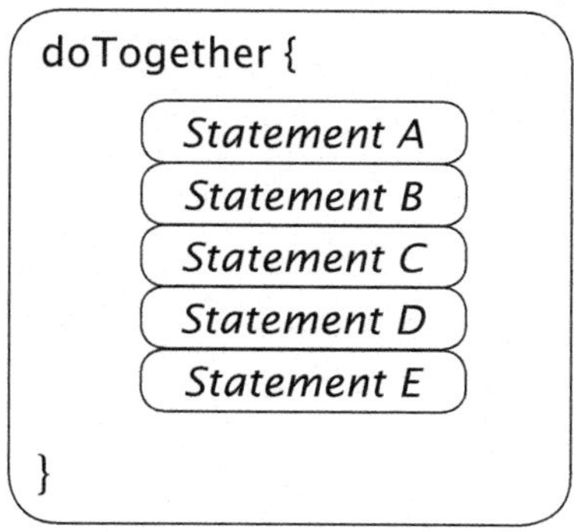

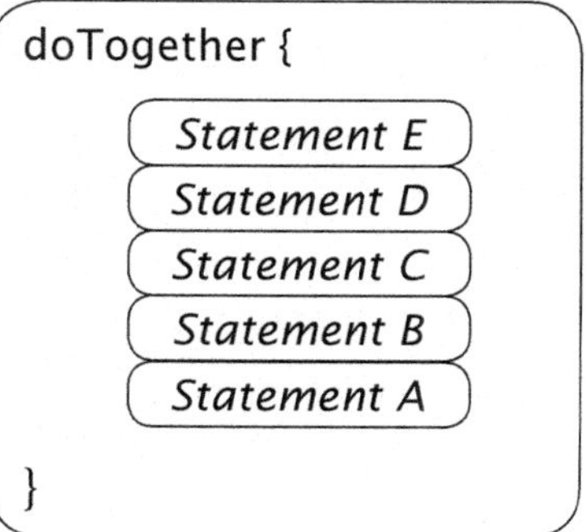

5.7 Using a loop, show the equivalent of the sequential structure on the left. When a statement is repeated many times, the sequential structure is unwieldy, and a loop to cause repetition is much better.

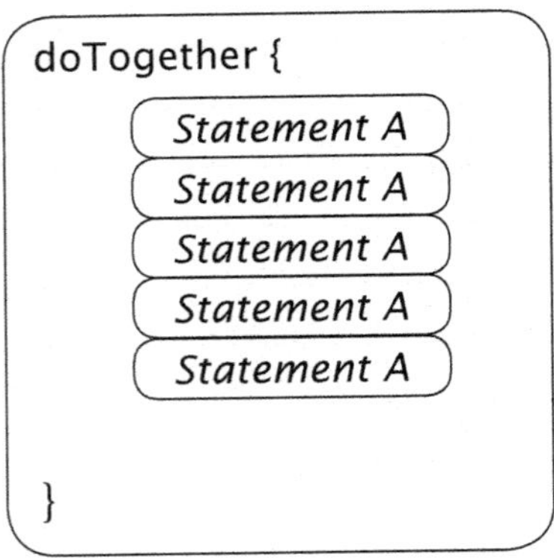

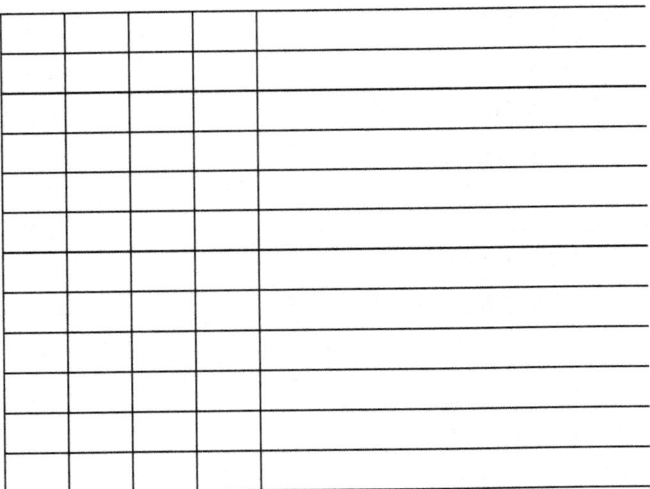

5.8 In the following, will Statement E (located after the loop) execute? Answer: a. Yes b. No

```
doInOrder {
    Statement A
    Statement B
    Statement C
    for (int index=0; index< Infinity ; index ++) { Show complicated version

        Statement D
    }
    Statement E
    Statement F
}
```

5.9 If you would like a cyclic behavior such as a hawk flying in a circle continuously (either in an infinite loop or for a very long time) while the rest of your animation proceeds sequentially, you can use a doTogether that has the infinite loop and the rest of your animation in a doInOrder that's inside your doTogether.

Suppose that Statement D in the infinite loop of Exercise 5.8 is the method **hawk.flyOneCircle,** and the other statements A, B, C, E, F are what you want to execute sequentially. In the following grid, show how you'd organize your program. Use indentation to show what statements are part of a control structure.

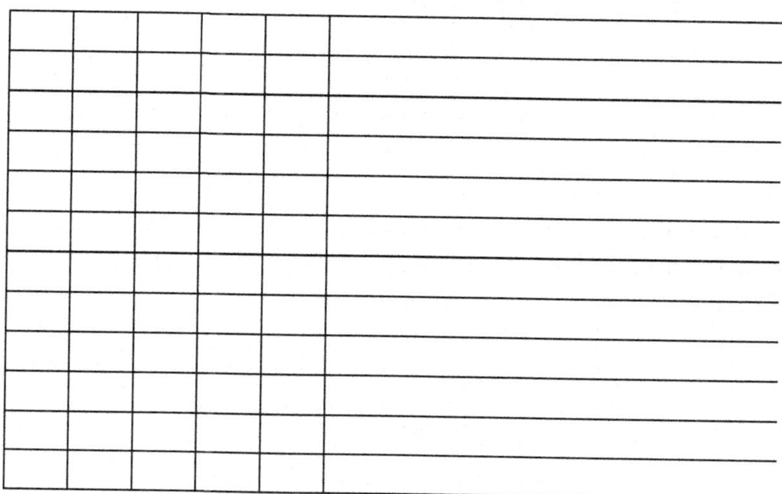

5.10 In Exercise 5.9, if each of the five statements A, B, C, E, F takes 10 seconds to execute, how many seconds should the loop execute so the loop ends at the same time as those five statements? Answer: ___________ seconds.

5.11 In the following, the durations of the statements are shown. How long does it take the loop to execute? Answer: ________ seconds.

```
for (int index=0; index< [5 times] ; index ++) { [Show complicated version]
    doInOrder {
        Statement A with duration 3 seconds
        Statement B with duration 4 seconds
    }
}
```

5.12 In the following, the doInOrder from the previous question was replaced by a doTogether and the durations of the statements are shown. How long does it take the loop to execute? Answer: ________ seconds.

```
for (int index=0; index< [5 times] ; index ++) { [Show complicated version]
  doTogether {
    Statement A with duration 3 seconds
    Statement B with duration 4 seconds
  }
}
```

5.13 The *condition* in an If control statement controls which of two statements executes. Here, literal values (true or false) are being used. Which statement executes? A. Statement A   B. Statement B

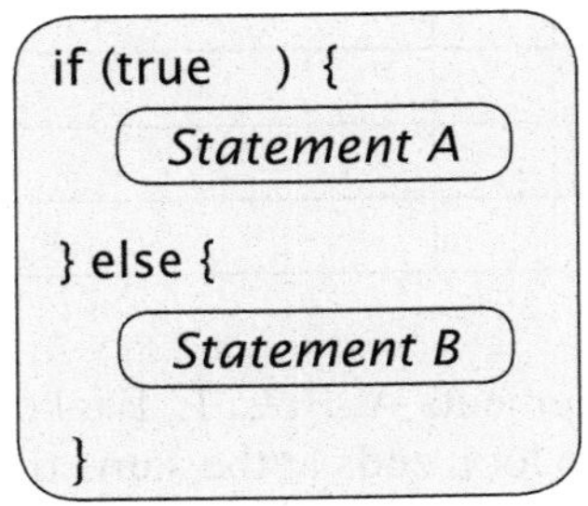

5.14 Which statement executes in this nested If? A. Statement A   B. Statement B   C. Statement C

```
if (false ) {
  Statement A
} else {
  if (true ) {
    Statement B
  } else {
    Statement C
  }
}
```

Chapter 6 VARIABLES, EXPRESSIONS, ASSIGNMENT STATEMENTS, AND PARAMETERS

Contents

INTRODUCTION

This chapter introduces a way for you to create variables, use them to store values, and later retrieve the values and use them. The chapter also summarizes expressions for arithmetic, string, and Boolean operations, so you can add, subtract, multiply, and divide numbers; combine strings of characters into longer strings; and compare values to see if one is larger or the same value as another value.

Finally, parameters are described, which allow you to pass or give a value to another program. You've been using parameters when you use the *move* method and give it a direction and distance. This chapter shows how you can use parameters in the methods and functions you code. The value of a parameter that's passed to a method or function is intended to influence how the program runs. For example, when you use the *move* method to move an object, you set values for the direction and amount (distance) to control the direction and distance that the object moves.

VARIABLES

Variables allow you to store values in the random access memory (RAM) of your computer, and later retrieve those values and use them. **Variables are well named because the values they store can *vary* or change while your program is running**.

A variable has

- a **name**,
- a **data type** (Alice refers to it as *type*, which can be a **number**, **Boolean**, **object**, Other: **string** (a string of characters), and other types, and

- an **initial value** (a value that it is given initially or in the beginning). Because the value stored in a variable can be changed by the programmer (or sometimes by a user in an interactive program), this initial value can be changed if needed. Sometimes the initial value is one that will be used; other times, the initial value is merely a placeholder that will be changed to another value later.

The process of creating a variable is referred to as **declaring a variable.** Variable names are nouns. The programmer should name each variable so the name describes what it stores so the code you write can be more easily read and its logic understood. The beginning programmer may choose a name that is short and cryptic, such as using x as the distance between two objects. A more descriptive name for the variable could be distanceBetweenHareAndJoey. Another style of naming is to begin the variable name with its data type so you'll readily see the variable type. Example: numberDistanceBetweenFrogAndHare.

Variables store values in the primary memory (the Random Access Memory or RAM) of the computer. The interpreter (the program that translates your Alice program, the a2w file, into machine code) converts the variable's name into an address. When you "assign" a value to a variable (using *set* in Alice), the program stores that value beginning at the address in RAM dictated by the interpreter and the operating system and often some memory management chips. This conversion from a name into an address is handled automatically. How many bits or bytes to be used to store that value depends on the variable's **data type**, which also includes the rules used to store the bits (the binary data: the1's and 0's) that represent that value. These rules are also used when a value is retrieved from RAM.

When do you use variables? Four **uses of variables** are:

- **Storing a value that you'll use repeatedly**. Find or calculate the value once, store that value in the variable, and use that stored value repeatedly rather than spending a lot of programmer time and computer resources to find or calculate the value again. For example, you could store Pi (3.14159...) in a variable and use the variable again and again rather than typing its value many times.
- **Store intermediate values in a complex operation** that helps you focus on each part of the operation. When the values for all parts are available, combine them into the whole. This can be better than doing too many things in one statement. This is another example of **reductionism**, where you solve a problem by breaking it into smaller parts and later combining those parts into a whole.
- **Store values that the user enters** from an *Ask user for a Yes or No*, or *Ask user for a number*, or *Ask user for a string* question. This is really an example of breaking a complex task into steps that include soliciting data from the user. Sometimes, the process of getting a value and using the value can be pretty complex, and separately getting the value and storing it for later use will help you. Trying to think about too many tasks at once will confuse you.
- **Store a value for a property or characteristic of an object**. For example, maybe a frog is given the name *Heavenly Frog* stored in a variable named nameOfFrog. Throughout your program, you can refer to the variable nameOfFrog and the program will know the name as *Heavenly Frog*.

In this textbook, the **main data types for variables and parameters** are

Number
Boolean
Object
Other: String (i.e., a **string of characters** used in words, phrases, sentences, and other strings).

More data types are listed under *Other* that you may need, but string is a commonly used type in many computer languages.

Your job as a programmer includes choosing the data type that "best" accomplishes the task. Some data types simply cannot store some values. For example, a Boolean data type can store a *True* or *False* but cannot store a number and cannot store a string (of course, the words True and False exist, but the Boolean values are not words). A variable or parameter with number data type can store numbers but not *True* or *False* and not objects. A string cannot store an object. If you have several choices of data types that could work, then you'd consider their sizes and how efficiently they could be used. Computer resources are neither infinite nor free, and a good programmer uses the resources wisely.

A program may have many methods that a programmer has coded and tested. Where can variables be used? A **local variable** or **method variable** is a variable created in a method. Such a variable can only be used in that method where the variable is declared (created). Programmers refer to such a limitation as the **scope of the variable** being restricted to the method or function where the variable is declared. Such a variable is a **local variable**.

Local variables also can be used in functions that you code.

In contrast, a **property variable** is created by a programmer in the details area of an object under the properties tab. There you can create, name, specify a data type, and set a value for a new property for the object. Throughout your program, that variable can be used. Such a variable would be said to have a **global scope** because it can be used globally or everywhere in the Alice world where it was declared.

Example program that uses number variables with values input interactively

This program asks the user to input two numbers, which are added and the answer then is output to the screen using a *say* method. The numbers that the user enters are stored in variables, and the sum of the two numbers is also stored in a variable. To use the *say* method, the program must convert the answer (stored as a number) into a string (the type of data that the *say* method expects to receive).

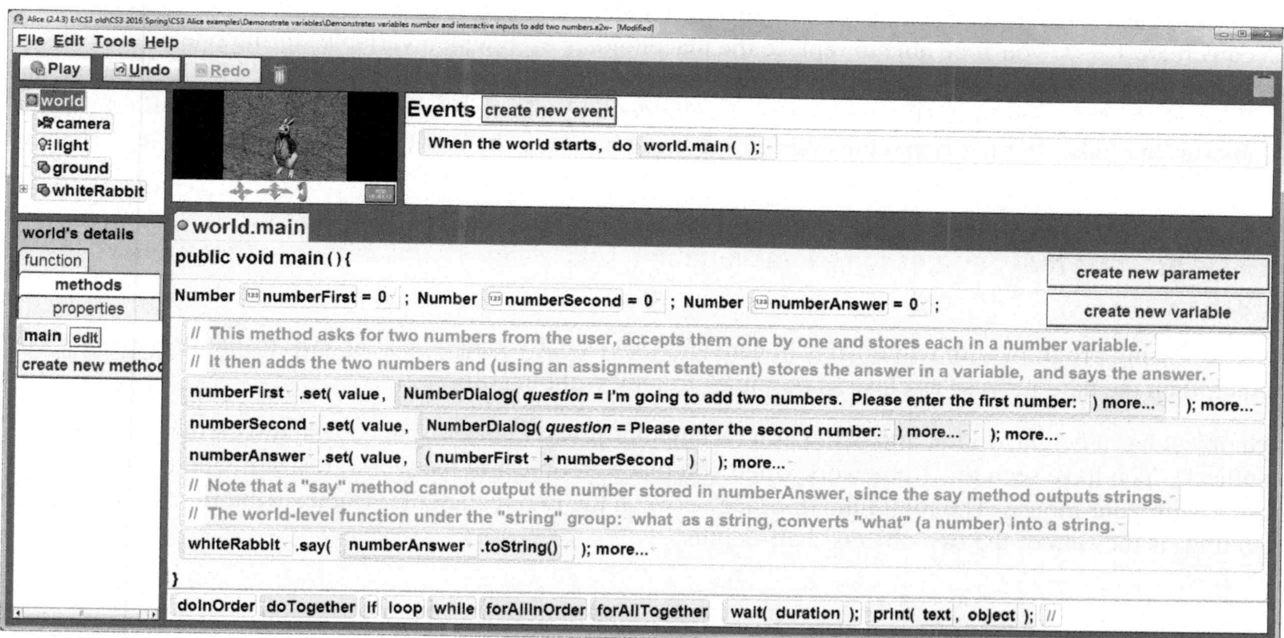

File: Demonstrates number variables and interactive inputs.a2w. This program also uses *assignment statements* to store values in variables.

The method declares three variables of type number (*numberFirst*, *numberSecond*, *numberAnswer*). In the method where you want to use these variables, click the *create new variable* button. A window will appear where you can type the variable's name, specify the type, and give an initial value:

This is the process of **declaring a variable**. Because a syntax rule requires that a variable must store a value, then you must type an initial value (a literal value). The value you type either could be a value you may use in your program, or a temporary value that you'll replace later in that program.[1]

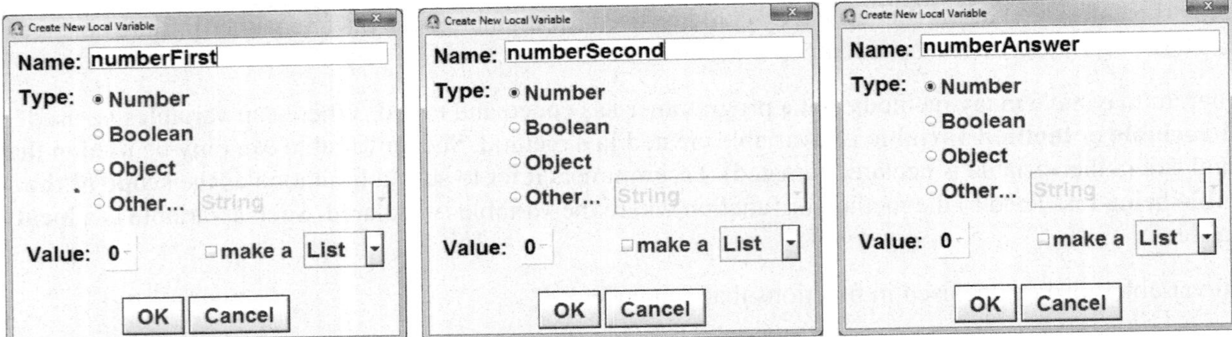

Three local variables were declared by naming them, setting their datatypes to be numbers, and initializing their values to be zero.

Drag the tile for *numberFirst* into the editing pane, and temporarily set its value to be 0 (or anything just to get the set statement into the editing area). Now drag the tile for the world-level function *ask user for a number* to replace the 0 you used as a placeholder, and type in the question that the world will ask the user.

Similarly, ask the user for the second number and store it in the variable *numberSecond*. Finally, drag down the tile for *numberAnswer*, and temporarily set its value to 0 (a placeholder). Add the two numbers stored in the two variables, which stores the answer in the variable named *numberAnswer*. This can be accomplished by dragging the variable *numberAnswer* into the editing area and temporily setting its value to 0 (or whatever as a placeholder). Then right-click the placeholder and under *math* you find the addition of two numbers. (If you can create 1 + 1, you'll be able to replace the placeholders each with a variable storing one of the two numbers supplied by the user. Again, addition and other arithmetic operations (subtraction, multiplication, and division) can be accessed by right-clicking the placeholder and selecting *math.* Finally, the WhiteRabbit says the answer, but only after it's been converted into a string by using the world-level function *what as a string*, listed under the "string" group of world functions.

Example program that declares some local variables, sets (assigns) new values to them, then uses the variables

In the following program with two objects (a hare and joey, a baby kangaroo), the task is that the two face one another, then the hare moves "as close as possible" to joey without colliding.

Each object has a height, width, and depth as a rectangular prism (a brick-shaped framework that surrounds the object). You have seen this framework when you place an object in the world, resize it, and move and rotate it with your mouse. The minimum distance between the two rectangular frames without overlapping (colliding) is the sum of the two objects' half-depths:

[1] If a temporary value, a good habit is to set the initial values for number variables to be 0, and the initial value for string variables to be an empty string (i.e., you don't type anything and delete every letter and space), but these initial values are not essential.

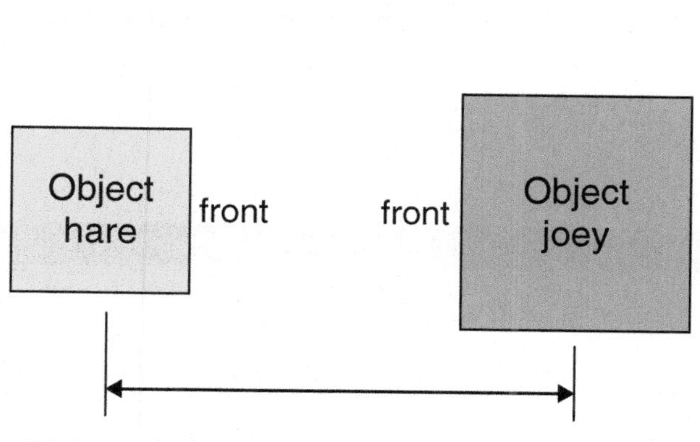
Object
hare
front
front
Object
joey
Distance between the centers of the two objects, which can be found from a function

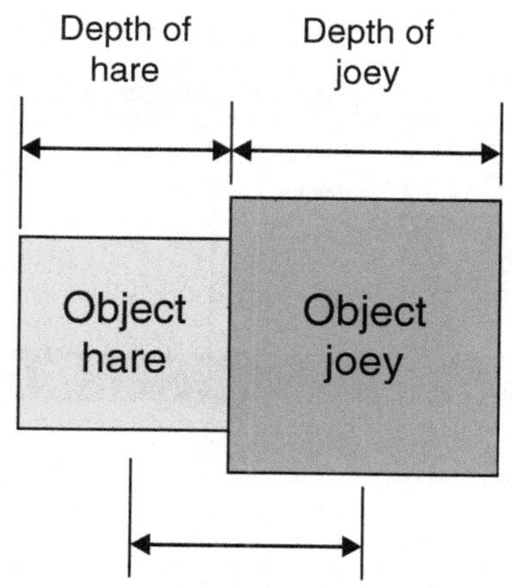
Depth of
hare
Depth of
joey
Object
hare
Object
joey
Minimum distance between the centers without colliding is the sum of half the hare's depth and half joey's depth. This is not exactly correct because the centers of the objects are not exactly halfway between their fronts and backs.

Top view of the rectangular frames for two objects, which are facing each other.

In the following code, three variables were **declared**, each by clicking on *create new variable*, naming the variable, and specifying its data type. These variables are

distanceToMove	Number	initially assigned to have a value of 0
hareHalfDepth	Number	"
joeyHalfDepth	Number	"

Think of these initial values as placeholders with values that will be replaced when we get around to it in the program. Then in three lines of code, the hareHalfDepth and joeyHalfDepth are calculated from functions for those objects' depth, then the distance for the hare to move toward joey without colliding is calculated. In each assignment statement where a value is assigned to a variable, the variable tile was dragged to that place in the code, then the initial values were replaced by expressions. Finally, the distance for the hare to move is the total distance between the centers minus the sum of the two half depths so the objects don't collide.

In each of the three cases, an arithmetic expression was set up to calculate some number, then this number was assigned to the variable (i.e., stored in RAM as a pattern of 0's and 1's that follow the rules of the data type). The form of the assignment statement is

variable set value to **value**

The effect of this statement is that the **value** (on the right) is stored in the **variable** on the left. Actually, the value is stored in RAM at the address that is assigned to that variable. This task of linking the variable name to an address in primary memory is carried out by the interpreter without programmer intervention. The interpreter is the translator of code written in the Alice language into the machine code language that the CPU "understands."

Now that you know the distance to move, move the hare that distance as the last line of code.

The final code is shown below. Before running the program, you can move and/or turn one or both of the hare and joey.

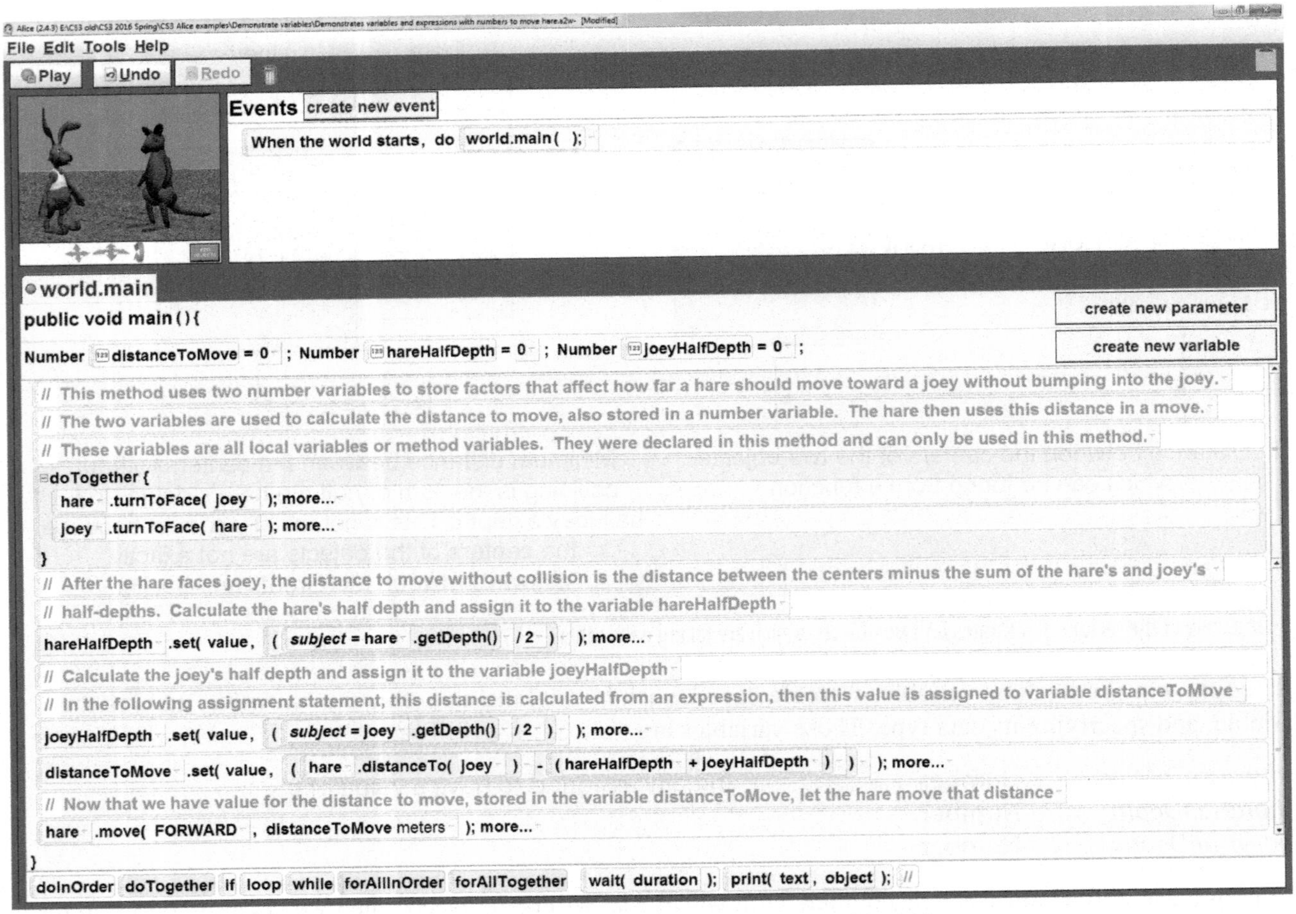

File Edit Tools Help
Play
Undo
Redo
Events
create new event
When the world starts, do world.main( );
world.main
public void main (){
create new parameter
create new variable
Number distanceToMove = 0 ; Number hareHalfDepth = 0 ; Number joeyHalfDepth = 0 ;
// This method uses two number variables to store factors that affect how far a hare should move toward a joey without bumping into the joey.
// The two variables are used to calculate the distance to move, also stored in a number variable. The hare then uses this distance in a move.
// These variables are all local variables or method variables. They were declared in this method and can only be used in this method.
doTogether {
hare .turnToFace(joey); more...
joey .turnToFace(hare); more...
}
// After the hare faces joey, the distance to move without collision is the distance between the centers minus the sum of the hare's and joey's
// half-depths. Calculate the hare's half depth and assign it to the variable hareHalfDepth
hareHalfDepth .set(value, (subject = hare .getDepth() / 2)); more...
// Calculate the joey's half depth and assign it to the variable joeyHalfDepth
// In the following assignment statement, this distance is calculated from an expression, then this value is assigned to variable distanceToMove
joeyHalfDepth .set(value, (subject = joey .getDepth() / 2)); more...
distanceToMove .set(value, (hare .distanceTo(joey) - (hareHalfDepth + joeyHalfDepth))); more...
// Now that we have value for the distance to move, stored in the variable distanceToMove, let the hare move that distance
hare .move(FORWARD , distanceToMove meters); more...
}
doInOrder doTogether if loop while forAllInOrder forAllTogether wait(duration); print(text , object); //

File: Demonstrates variables and expressions.a2w stored in Alice Examples/Demonstrate variables folder.

Pause
Play
Restart
Stop
Take Picture

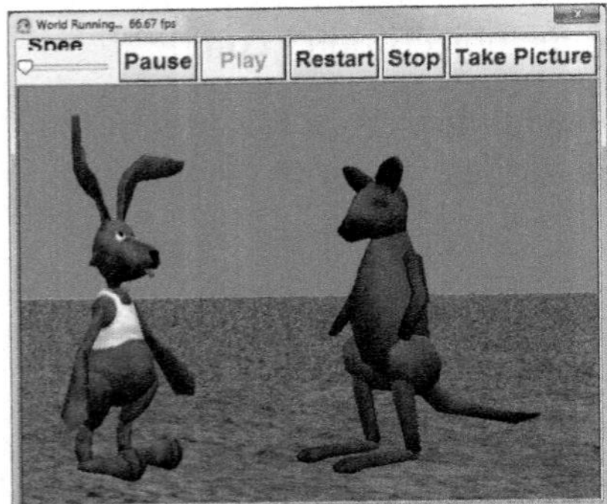

Initial positions and orientations.

Pause
Play
Restart
Stop
Take Picture

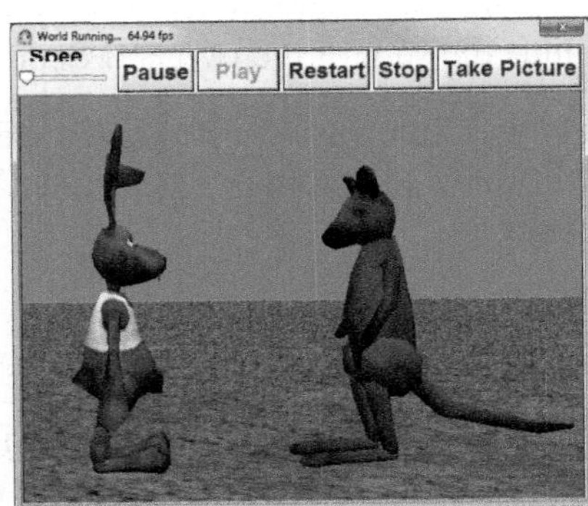

After both have turned to face each other.

Pause
Play
Restart
Stop
Take Picture

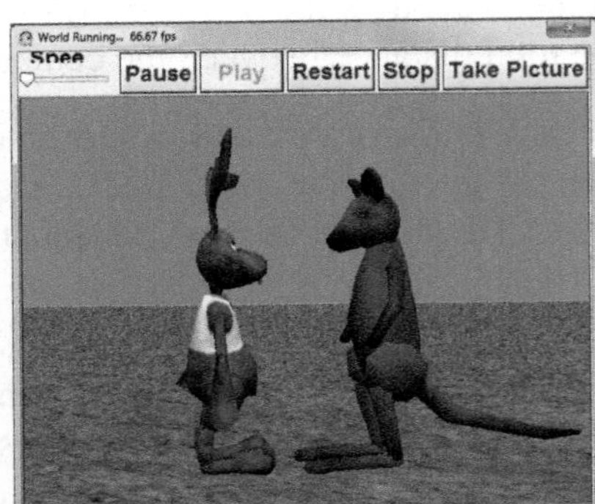

After the hare has moved.

Although you could have built up the *distanceToMove* and included that expression in the final line of code without using variables, the use of variables is convenient here because they allow you to design, code, and test subtasks that each require thought. You also could "print" these intermediate values (display them on the screen below your world when running your program). The expressions used in these subtasks are shorter, their logic is easier to follow, and they are easier to document with comments. The result is a variable that stores the distance to move without colliding, and this variable is used in the final move rather than some **literal constant** such as 3 meters.

EXPRESSIONS

Expressions in Alice include arithmetic expressions, concatenation of strings, and Boolean expressions.

Arithmetic expressions

Arithmetic expressions, where two or more numbers are added, subtracted, multiplied, or divided, as determined by the arithmetic operators + – * / (for add, subtract, multiply, and divide). Some computer languages have operators for exponentiation (raising a number to a power) and others.

The choices that you have after selecting *math* to set up an arithmetic expression.

From any numeric field (where the data types are numbers), you can find the templates for adding, subtracting, multiplying, and dividing by right or left-clicking and selecting *math*. The four choices appear from which you choose the operation you want to carry out (here I selected adding two numbers). Because Alice is designed to avoid almost all syntax errors, values must be selected for both a and b in $a + b$. You may want to carefully set the desired values, or maybe you prefer to create a template that you can later edit to set values.

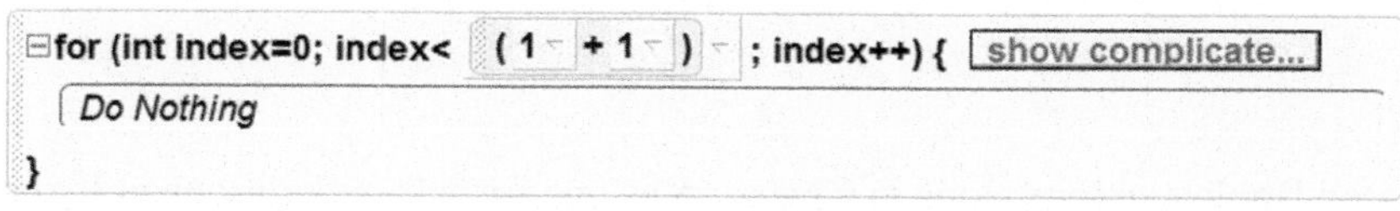

After selecting 1's for *a* and *b*, here's an arithmetic expression for adding

Because a and b are numbers, each can be a literal number, a function that returns a number, another arithmetic expression, a number variable, or a number parameter. Although literal values can be kept (and are useful while experimenting and learning), usually one or both are merely placeholders for numeric values you'll later code. Aside from those uses for literals, replacing 1 + 1 with 2 would simplify the coding. You can delete an expression by right-clicking on the expression and selecting *delete*.

If you chose the wrong arithmetic operation, you can right-click on the tile and choose *change to,* and Alice allows you to change from whatever you have to one of the other three arithmetic operations.

The "numbers" can be literal numbers (2, 10, –5, 12.356, –5.4, 0, etc.) or the arithmetic expressions could use variables or parameters. They also could use functions that return numeric values (i.e., a question that is answered with a number), a variable with type number, or a parameter with type number.

If an arithmetic expression has so many pieces that the tile gets too wide or so many things are happening at once that you're confused (or someone reading your code would be confused), consider the use of variables to store parts of the expression and combine the results. Use comments to describe what you're doing.

String expressions (concatenating strings to combine strings into longer strings)

String expressions combine two or more strings into one longer string. This operation is called **concatenation**. This allows letters, punctuation, and other characters to be built into words, phrases, sentences, and more. It allows two separate words to be combined into a bigger string. For example,

> "Harold" + " " + "Rogler" concatenates (combines) the three strings (the middle one-character string is a blank) into one string, "Harold Rogler"

The pieces of strings that can be concatenated include **literal** strings, **functions** that return strings, other string **expressions**, string **variables** (either method variables or property variables), and string **parameters**.

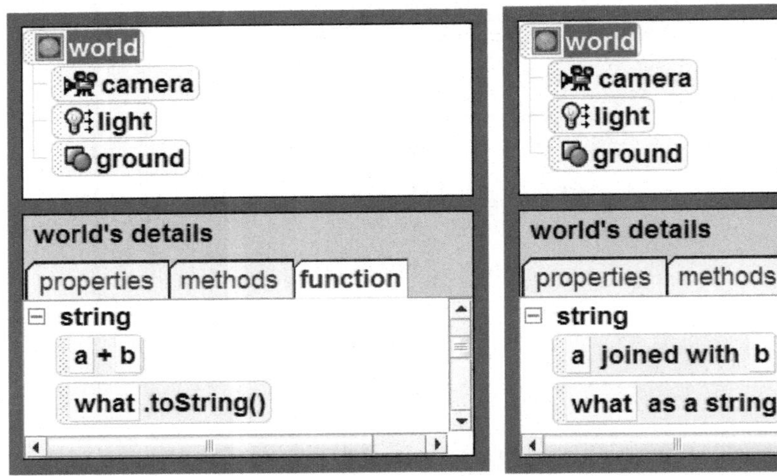

Java style. Alice style.

The template for concatenation, **a + b,** where a and b are strings, can be found under the world's details menu under the functions tab under the group for a string if you're displaying your code in Java style. In the Alice style of display, concatenation is **a** *joined with* **b**. As with other expressions in Alice, you may carefully set the values for the two strings, or you may accept the defaults to proceed ahead to display the concatenation template, and edit the strings later.

Boolean expressions

Because we've introduced Boolean expressions in Chapter 5 as one form for conditions in If statements and While loops, here we'll summarize them and show the pattern of all expressions: combine two or more values into one value. Unlike arithmetic expression that combine two numbers into one number, and string concatenations that combine two strings into one longer string, Boolean expressions compare two values and yield one True or False. **Boolean expressions** either

(1) Compare two values and evaluate as *True* or *False*. How the two are to be compared is determined by the relational operators == (equals), < (less than), > (greater than), <= (less than or equal to), >= (greater than or equal to), and != (not equal to). Any of these can be used to compare numbers. Strings and many other types can be compared with == (equals) and != (not equal to).

or

(2) Form expressions using the logical operators !, &&, and || (the Java versions for NOT, AND, and OR).

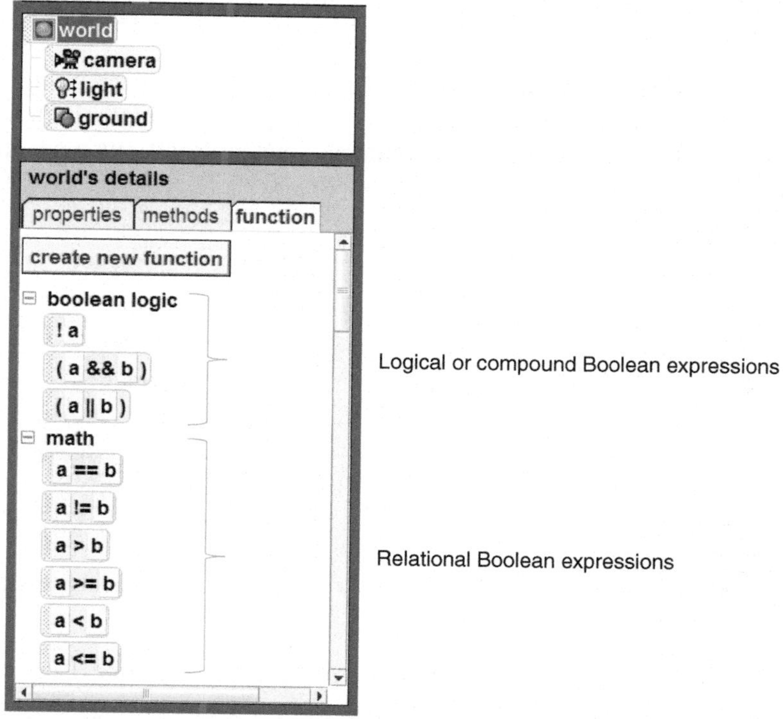

The templates for these Boolean expressions were described in Chapter 5 and can be found under the world's details menu under the functions tab. These are in Java style.

PARAMETERS

Introduction to parameters

Both variables and parameters have names, both store values in the computer's primary memory, and the program specifies a data type for each. But parameters have a specific use of transferring a value from one program (a method or function) to another program. The parameter transfers a value for the purpose of influencing how the receiving program runs.

Built-in methods such as *move* have parameters such as *direction* that store your choice of six values (FORWARD, BACKWARD, LEFT, RIGHT, UP, DOWN) and another parameter named *amount* that stores whatever distance the object is to move, such as 2.5 meters. Method *move* also has some parameters with **default values**, such as the parameter *duration* having the default value of 1 second. If you accept that default, then you don't have to do anything and the duration will be one second, but you can also change the value to another duration, such as 2 seconds or 2.345 seconds.

The value stored in a parameter is called an **argument**. What takes place hidden from the programmer and user is that the computer converts the parameter's name into an address in primary memory (RAM) where the value (the argument) is stored. This address is transferred from one program to another, and hence the value stored at that address is shared between the two programs. This is what we mean by transferring a value between programs.

Parameters are also useful to pass data to your user-created methods or functions that those programs require and use. They will affect their operation just as you have set values for the built-in parameters such as the direction or amount (distance) that an object moves. This information is an argument (the value that the parameter stores), and it will have one of the data types (number, Boolean, object, string, or other types).

While you're coding a method that uses a parameter, act as if the method or function knows the value of the parameter. Once a parameter has been declared in a method, Alice requires that you supply a value for the parameter when you call the method or function.

In a method where you want to receive a value for some number, Boolean, object, string, or other data type, the process to create the parameter begins with clicking the *Create new parameter* button near the top of the editing area for that method. Give a descriptive name to the parameter, specify its type, and click *OK*.

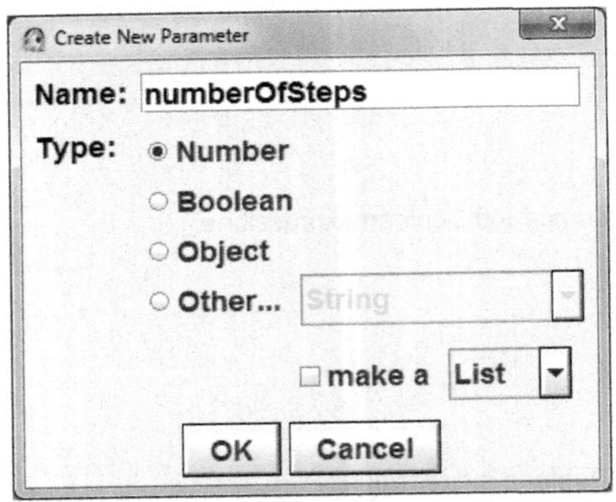

Declaring a parameter with datatype number.

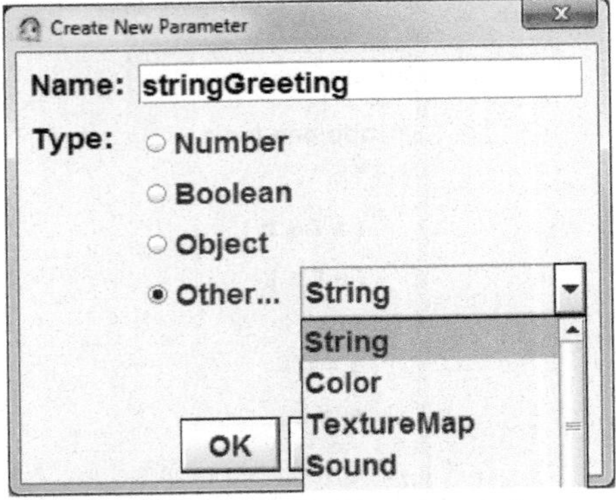

Declaring a parameter with datatype string.

Parameters are used to transfer or pass values from one program to another. Like variables, they have descriptive names and data types suitable for storing the data that will be transferred. In the method or function where the parameter is declared (defined), you need not specify an initial value because the value will be supplied when the programmer uses the method or function, just like you supply an amount (distance) when you use the built-in method *move*. The built-in methods like *move* have many parameters (direction, amount, duration, etc.) for which you set values when you use the method. In user-generated methods and functions, the parameters similarly are created. When you use the method, you specify the value you want to store in the parameter and transfer to another program.

Method1 that calls (executes) **Method2** below and where the value of a parameter is set. This method executes either because some event causes it to run or it appears in another program that's running.

transferred

Method2 that receives the parameter, which influences how the method runs. Here's where you declare (create) the parameter in programs you code. Name the parameter descriptively and specify its data type.

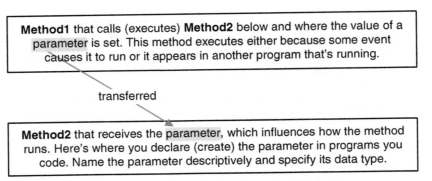

This figure shows where a parameter is declared and where its value is set.

Example program with parameters of type *number, object, string, and Boolean*

The following program has several objects and a world-level method that uses parameters to make

any object jump (even including the ground to simulate an earthquake),
any number of times,
to any height,
do either a straight jump without rotating or a flip with a 360° forward turn, and
make the object say something.

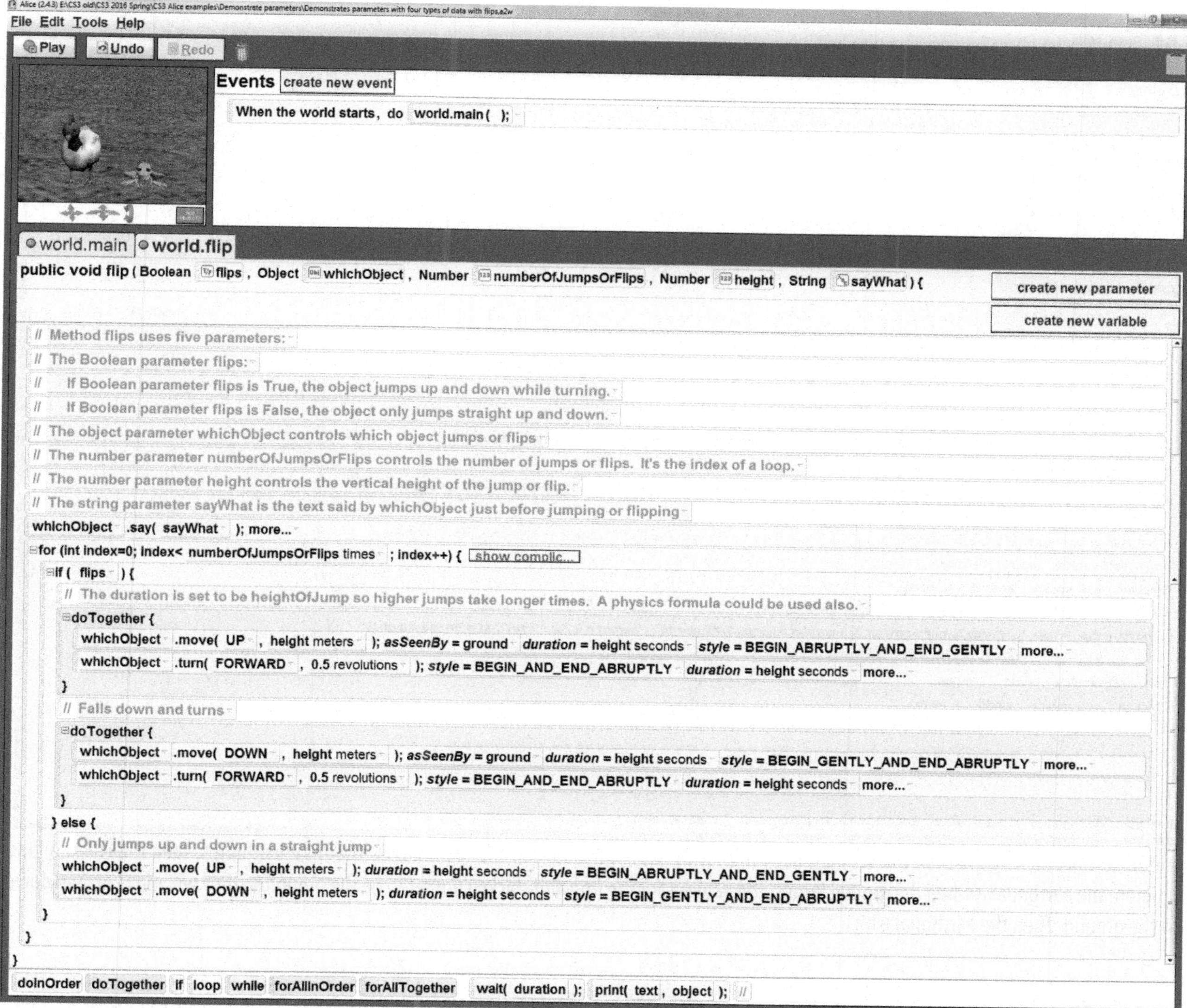

File: Demonstrates parameters with four types of data with flips.a2w.

First code a world-level method to make the frog jump to height 1, then move down the same distance. Use a world-level method for flip because later we'll generalize it to allow any object to jump. This was placed in the "False" part of the *If* statement, and expanded in the "True" part of the *If* by adding some forward turns. Finally, the *If* was placed within a simple loop, and a *say* method was added.

Now create five parameters:

One named *whichObject* that controls which object of the three objects jumps or flips, data type *object*
One named *height* that controls how high the object jumps, data type *number*
One named *numberOfJumps* that controls how many jumps the object takes, data type *number*
One named *flips* that controls (in an If/else statement) whether the object flips or does a straight up-and-down jump, data type *Boolean*
One named *sayWhat* that stores a string that the object says just before the object jumps or flips

Then drag the parameters into the *move, say,* or *turn* statements, or the loop and *If/else* control statements.

When you code a method with a parameter, act like the value of the parameter is known. When the method is used, the parameter will have a value. It acts like a variable; its name corresponds to an address that stores a value when the method is used.

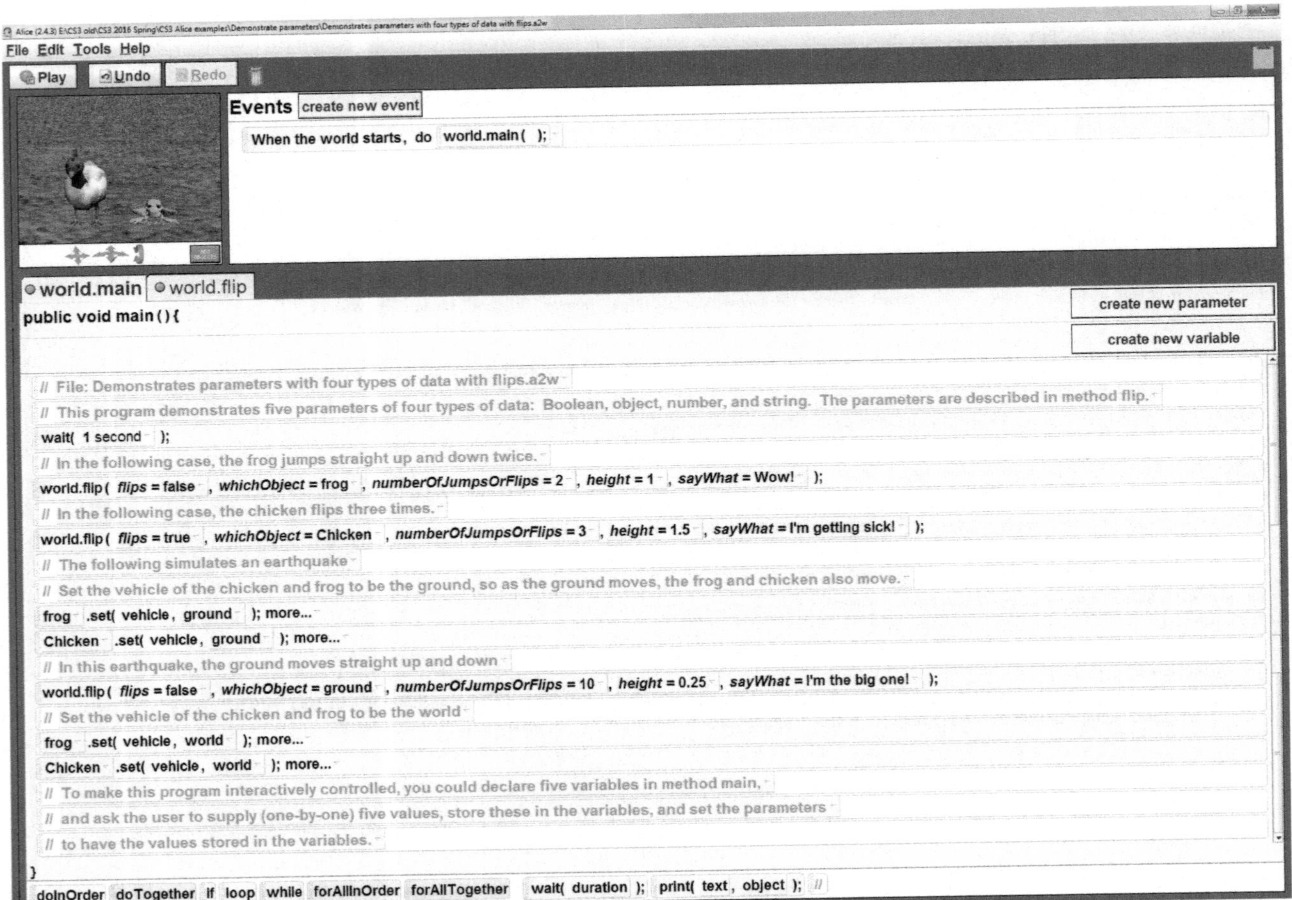

World.main calls the *flip* method three times, each time with different values for the parameters. The frog first jumps, then the chicken flips. Just before the earthquake when the ground jumps, the vehicles for the frog and chicken are set to be the ground so they will move up and down with the ground. Then the earthquake hits.

In the *main* method here **literal values** were used for the arguments (the values of the parameters) such as the *height* having value 2 and *numberOfJumpsOrSomersaults* being 2. You also can use variables, other parameters, arithmetic expressions, or functions for those values as long as the data types are correct.

The loop is a control structure that repetitively executes the statements in its tile. The loop just shown is a simple loop. It executes exactly the number of times shown and is controlled by the parameter *numberOfJumps*.

Taking one full step with straight legs and arms

An algorithm to take a full step is sketched below with a stick figure. The knees and elbows don't bend. When coded as a method named stepOne, it can be used in a loop so the person can take several steps as shown in the following pages. One cycle of this walking begins and ends with the person standing straight.

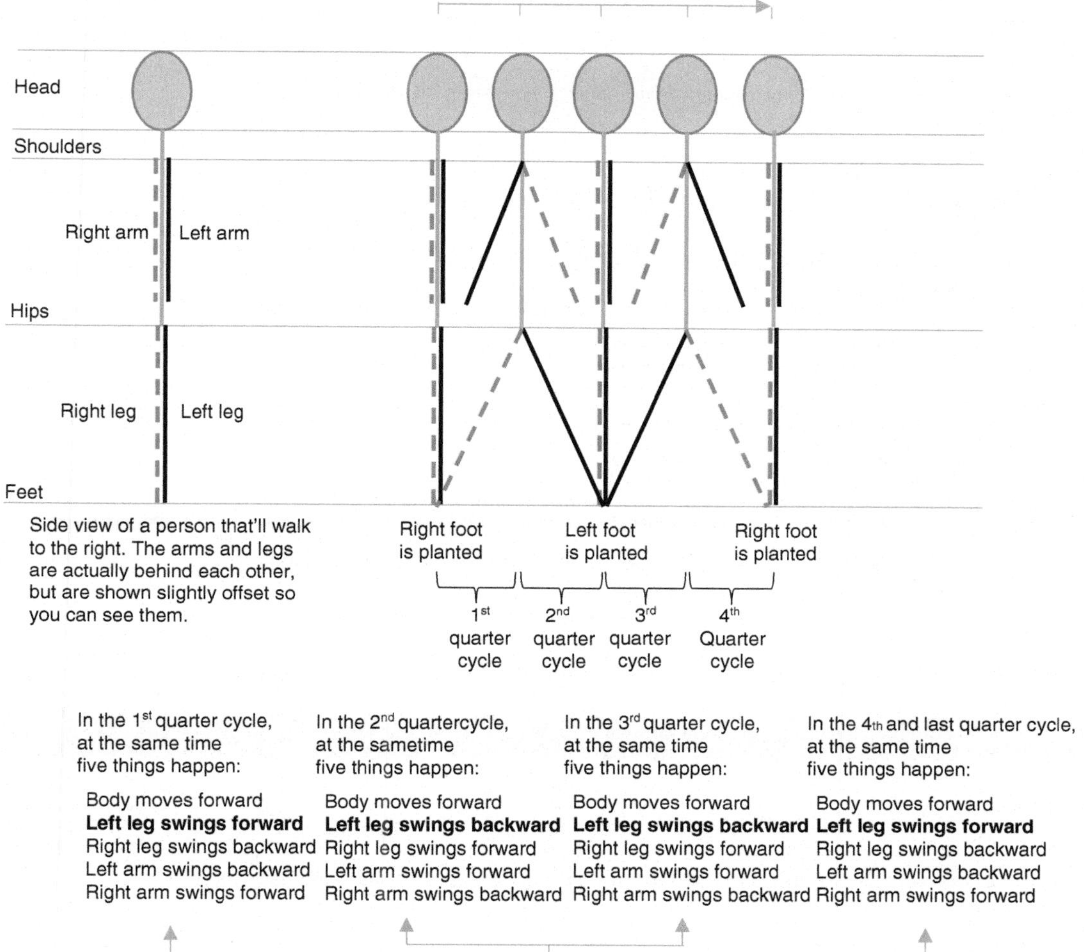

One full step (one cycle of walking)
Head
Shoulders
Right arm
Left arm
Hips
Right leg
Left leg
Feet
Side view of a person that'll walk to the right. The arms and legs are actually behind each other, but are shown slightly offset so you can see them.
Right foot is planted
Left foot is planted
Right foot is planted
1st quarter cycle
2nd quarter cycle
3rd quarter cycle
4th Quarter cycle
In the 1st quarter cycle, at the same time five things happen:
Body moves forward
Left leg swings forward
Right leg swings backward
Left arm swings backward
Right arm swings forward
In the 2nd quartercycle, at the sametime five things happen:
Body moves forward
Left leg swings backward
Right leg swings forward
Left arm swings forward
Right arm swings backward
In the 3rd quarter cycle, at the same time five things happen:
Body moves forward
Left leg swings backward
Right leg swings forward
Left arm swings forward
Right arm swings backward
In the 4th and last quarter cycle, at the same time five things happen:
Body moves forward
Left leg swings forward
Right leg swings backward
Left arm swings backward
Right arm swings forward

The changes in leg and arm angles are the same in these two quarter cycles.
For example, the **left leg swings backward** in both.
The same code can be used for both.

The changes in leg and arm angles are the same in these two quarter cycles.
For example, the **left leg swings forward** in both. The same code can be used for both.

One cycle of walking with straight legs and arms. After programming one cycle, you can repeatedly take one step in a loop, and thus walk several steps. In other methods, you could combine this walking with turning so the person walks in a circle.

The first two quarter cycles are coded in the two screens below.

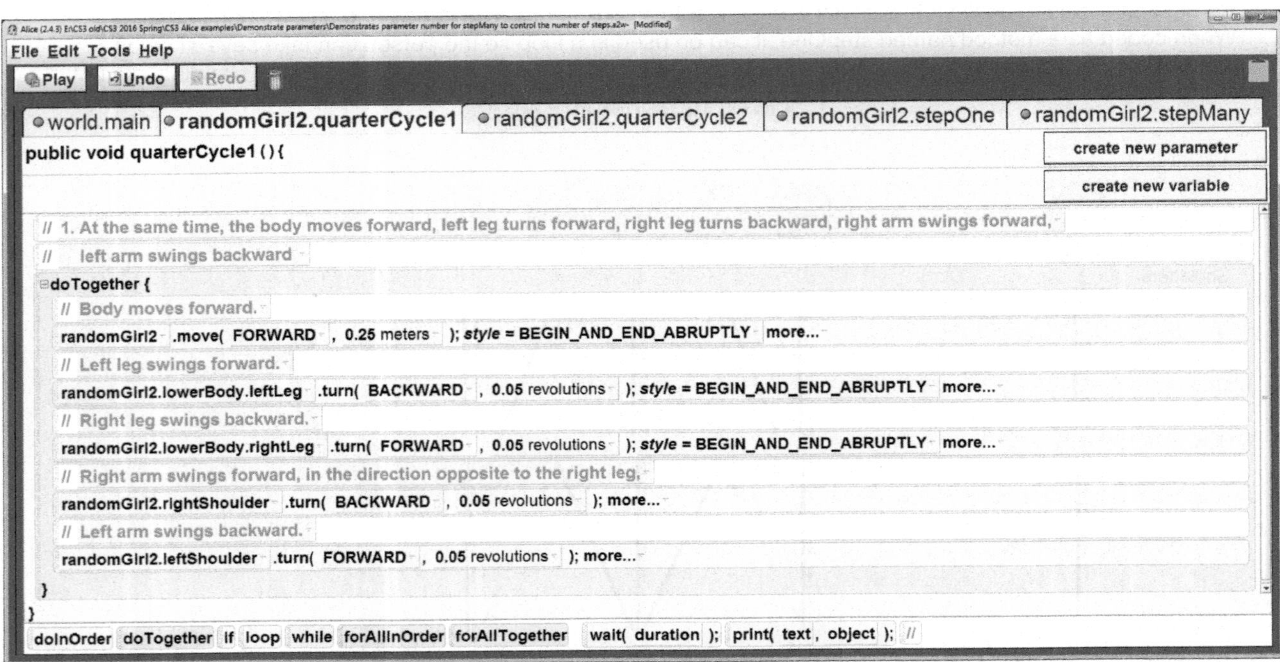

First quarter cycle with the left leg swinging forward (out in front) and right leg swinging backward (behind).

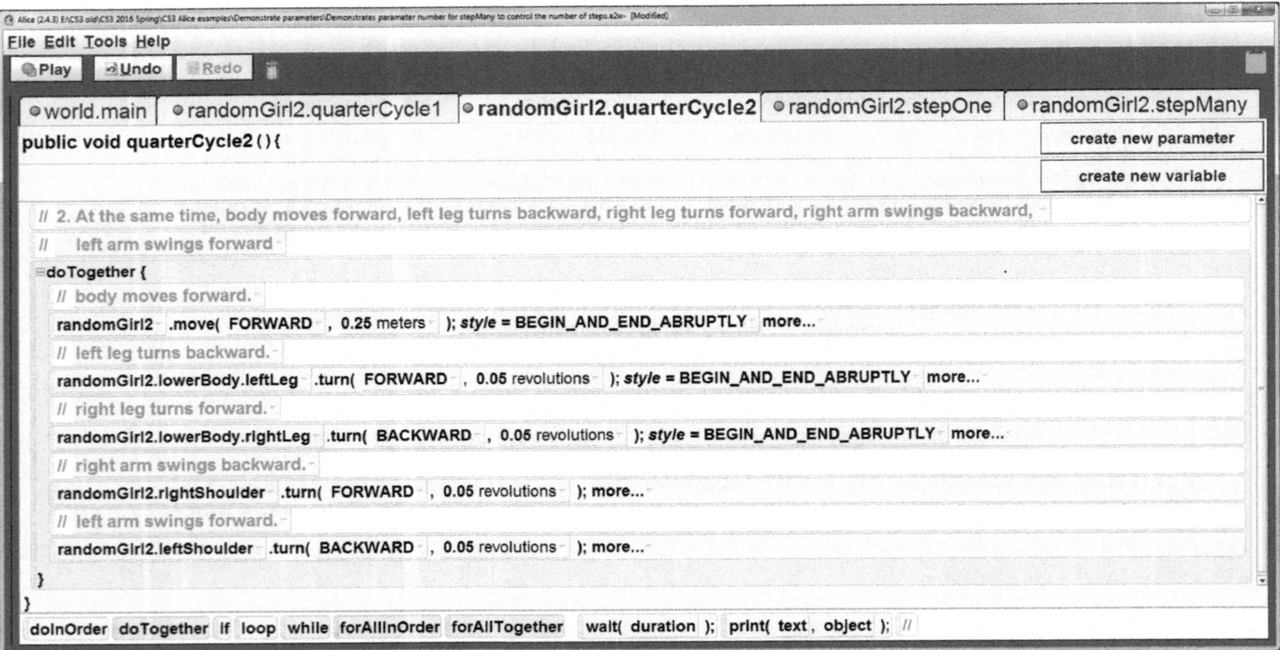

Second quarter cycle with the left leg swinging backward and right leg swinging forward.

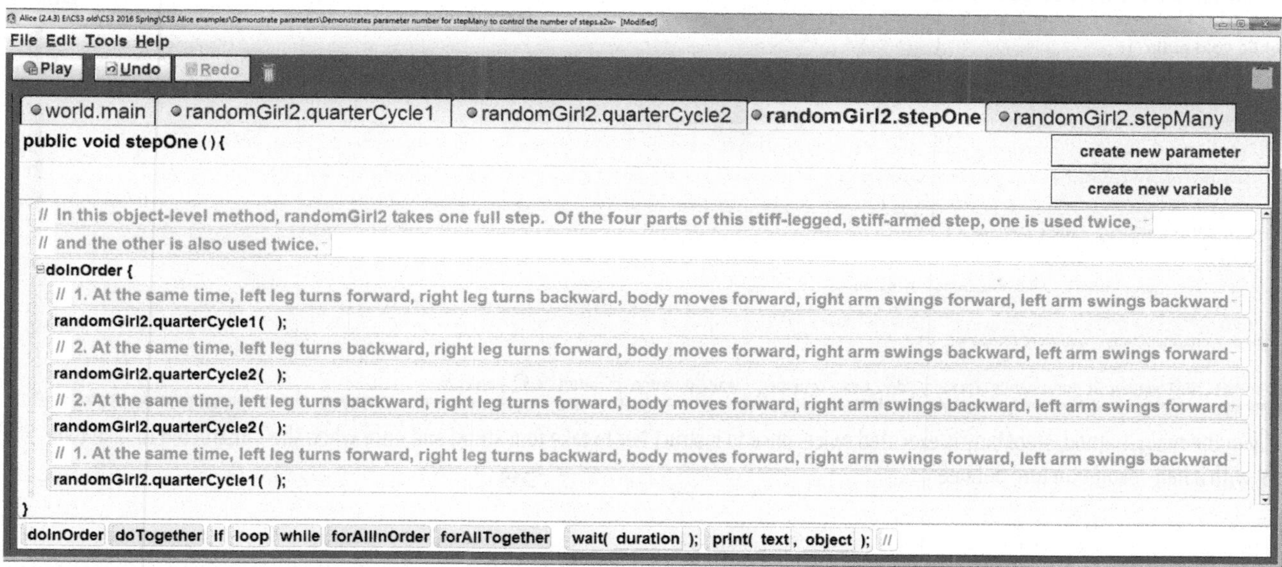

randomGirl2 takes one full step here. The third quarter cycle is the same as the second. The fourth quarter cycle is the same as the first. At the beginning, the person is standing straight, and after this step and each cycle, a person is again straight.

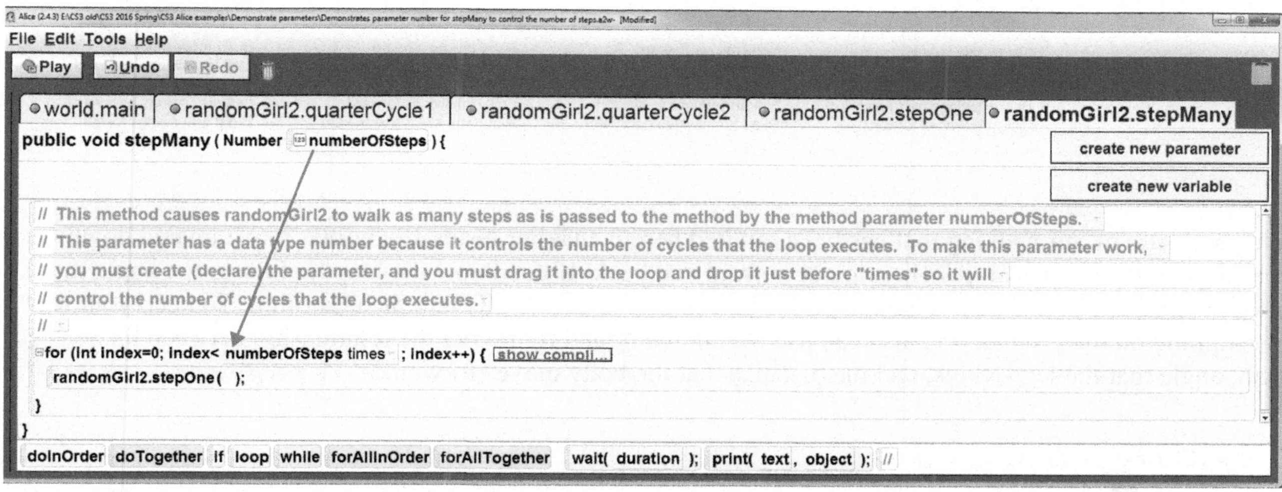

This stepMany method allows randomGirl2 to take any number of steps so she can walk straight continuously. A number parameter, numberOfSteps, controls the number of steps she takes. It has been dragged down into the For loop as the UpperLimit of the index. Each time through the loop, she takes one step.

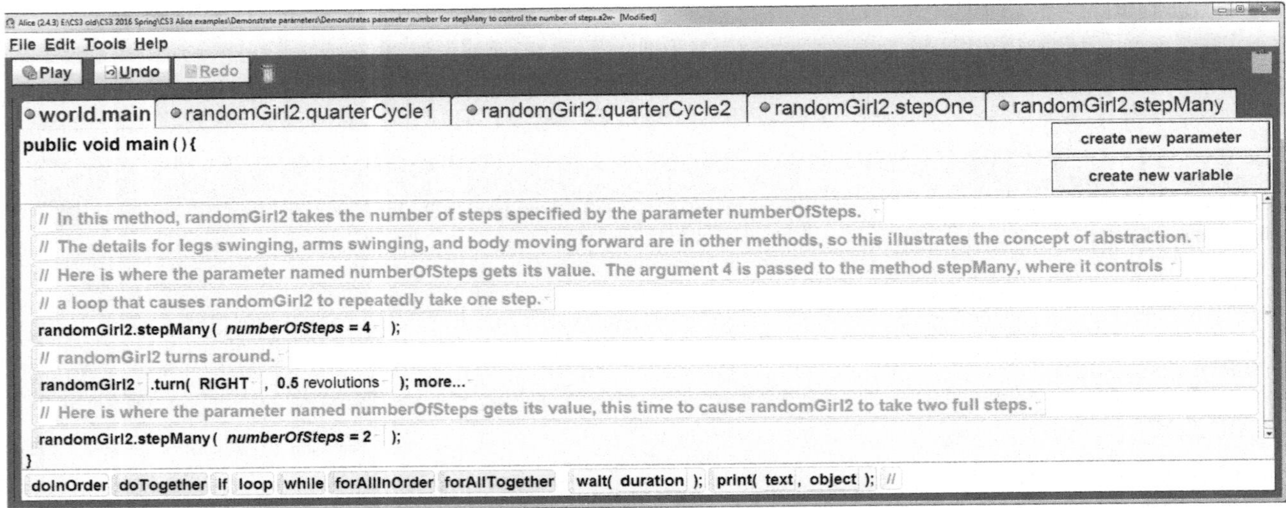

Finally in the main method, stepMany is executed twice: once to instruct her to take four steps, and once when she's instructed to take two steps, with a half-revolution turn between.

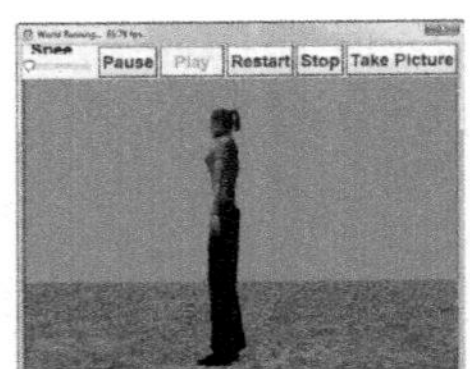

After the 4th quarter cycle, randomGirl2 has completed one full step and she can stop or begin another step.

After the 3rd quarter cycle, at the same time five things happen in the 4th quarter cycle:

Body moves forward
Left leg swings forward
Right leg swings backward
Left arm swings backward
Right arm swings forward

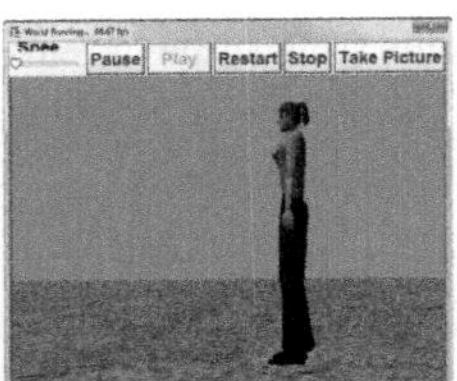

After the 2nd quarter cycle, at the same time five things happen in the 3rd quarter cycle:

Body moves forward
Left leg swings backward
Right leg swings forward
Left arm swings forward
Right arm swings backward

After the 1st quarter cycle, at the same time five things happen in the 2nd quarter cycle:

Body moves forward
Left leg swings backward
Right leg swings forward
Left arm swings forward
Right arm swings backward

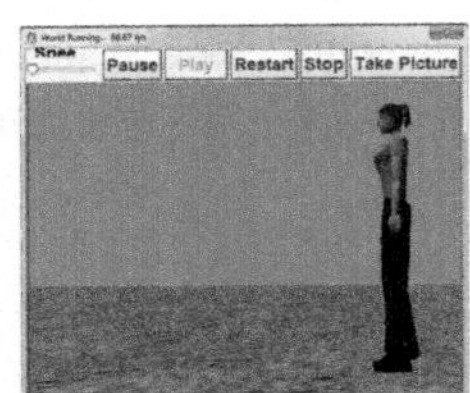

From this initial pose, at the same time five things happen in the 1st quarter cycle:

Body moves forward
Left leg swings forward
Right leg swings backward
Left arm swings backward
Right arm swings forward

A characteristic of our walking that has been omitted here is that our heads and bodies move up and down as our legs go from vertical to swinging out in front and back. If you know the length of a leg, the angle that the leg swings, and some basic trigonometry, you could incorporate this into the algorithm. To keep your feet from slipping on the ground, you also can use trigonometry and figure out the relationship between the leg length, angle that the leg swings, and the distance that the body moves forward.

Using parameters that are objects

Simple example: a jump method in which the object to jump is input into the method as a parameter. Two "animate" objects appear in the world. Which object jumps is controlled by the parameter passed to the jump method.

More advanced example: edit the *stepOne* method (the method where Alice takes one step) so it can be applied to other "people" objects by passing to the method the object as a parameter.

Parameters and variables with *Other* data types (optional)

Not just any string can be typed as a value for the color of an object. The acceptable values are limited to a set of colors such as red, blue, green, and so on or whose name you have typed and specified. Because Alice does much to avoid syntax errors, which includes correctly spelling such colors, Alice has many data types whose purpose is to eliminate such errors. For these reasons, Alice has more data types than just number, string, Boolean, and object. These appear under *Other* data types. This ensures that each variable has a proper initial value and later is assigned (set) proper values. Similarly, values passed into a method by parameters will have the correct values.

INTERACTIVE INPUT BY THE USER ANSWERING QUESTIONS

Interactive input by the user answering questions for *Yes* or *No*, numbers, and strings

You have interacted with an Alice program while it was running by triggering some event by using arrow keys, typing or continually pressing other keys, and using your mouse to move the camera, click on objects, and so forth.

Another way for the user to interact with the program is to select *Yes* or *No* to some question that the programmer types or for the user to enter a number, again to respond to some question. These are implemented as functions.

The Yes/No question (function) returns a *True* when the user selects *Yes* and returns *False* when the user selects *No*. Such a question can appear as the Boolean expression or condition in an If/else statement or in a While loop. The function also can be assigned to a Boolean variable, and then this variable can be used wherever Boolean expressions are used.

Similarly, a function for the world object can display a question, accept a number that the user types, and return that number. This number could be assigned to a variable that you have declared to have a number data type, and then this variable can be used in arithmetic expressions, in Boolean expressions, as the counter in simple loops (Loop n times), and in other places where numbers are used.

In the world below with aliceLiddell, I dragged an If/else tile into my first method, then dragged in the function *ask user for a yes or no* (which eventually returns a *True* or *False*) as the condition that appears after the

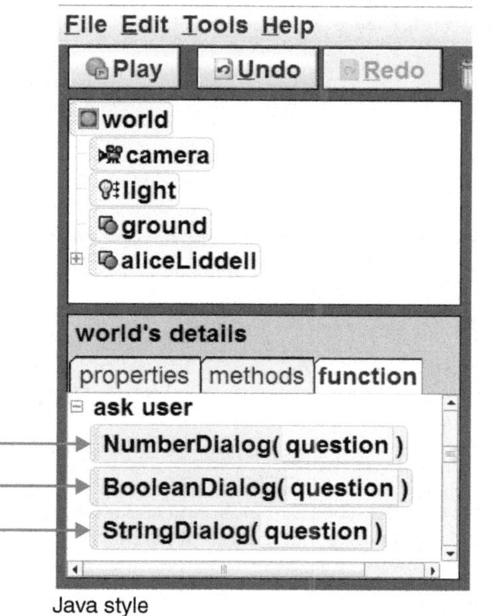

Java style

Alice style

These world functions are one way to make your programs interactive.

keyword If, and I typed a suitable question. The question was *Do you want Alice to jump?* If the user selects *Yes*, then the function returns a *True*. If the user selects *No*, the function returns *False*.

To demonstrate how a user can interact with a program by inputting a number, a variable named *NumberOfJumps* was created with a Number data type because it will store the number of jumps that Alice will make. We'll use this number in a simple loop to control how many jumps Alice will make. Click *create a new variable*, name it, and select data type *number*. Once created, drag its tile into the position shown, temporarily set its number to be 1 (or whatever you want because it will be replaced by the function that asks a question and returns a number).

Drag the tile for *ask user for a number* to replace the 1, then type a question such as *How many jumps for Alice?*

The effect of the statement is to display the question on the screen, accept the number that the user types, and assign it to the variable. We use the variable in the simple loop that causes Alice to jump up and down.

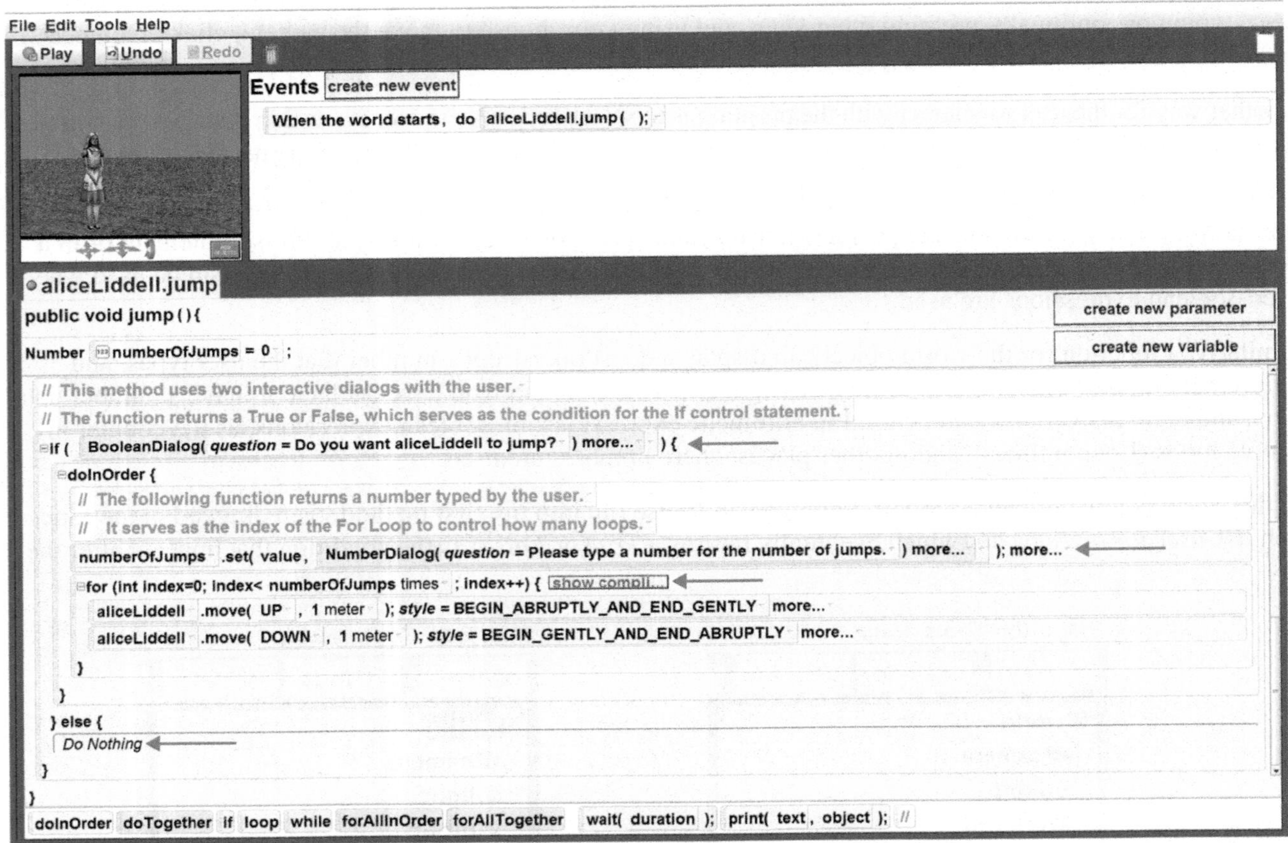

At runtime, the first question appears. If the user clicks *Yes*, then the second question (below) appears. If the user clicks *No*, nothing happens.

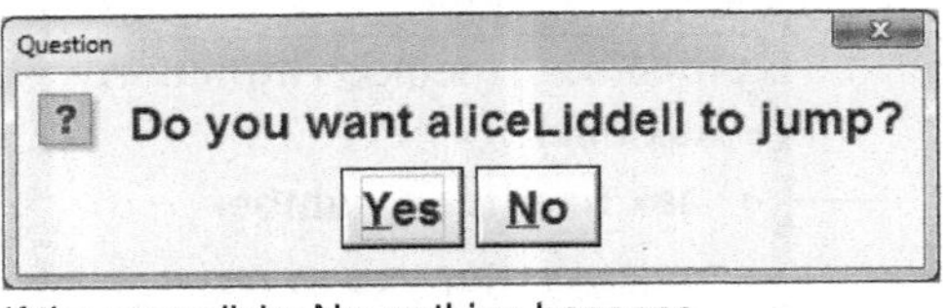

If the user clicks No, nothing happens.
If the user clicks *Yes*, then the instruction on the right appears.

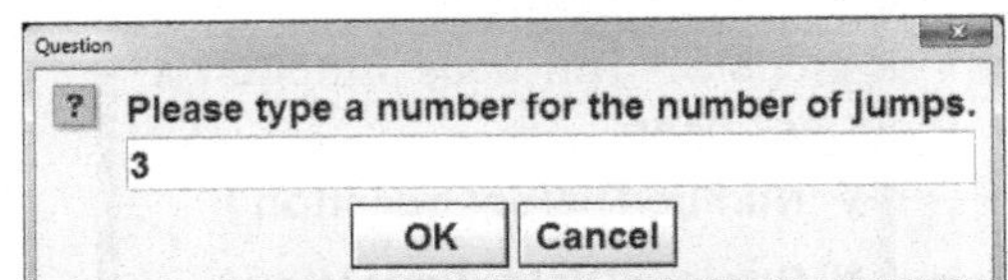

After the user types a number and clicks *OK*, aliceLiddell jumps that number of jumps.

Alice also allows the user to interactively enter a string, as shown in the next section.

Interactively entering a string and using it

The effect of the world function *ask user for a string* is to display a question on the screen and accept the string of characters that the user types. This string can be used wherever strings can be used. For simplicity, we'll then output the string using the *say* method on an object such as aliceLiddell.

Here a string variable named stringName has been created (declared). Then its value is set to be the string that the function StringDialog (in Java style) or ask user for a string (in Alice style) returns. Finally, Alice says the string that the user has input.

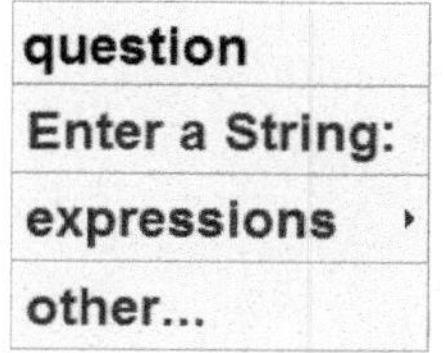

First step in setting up a string dialog.

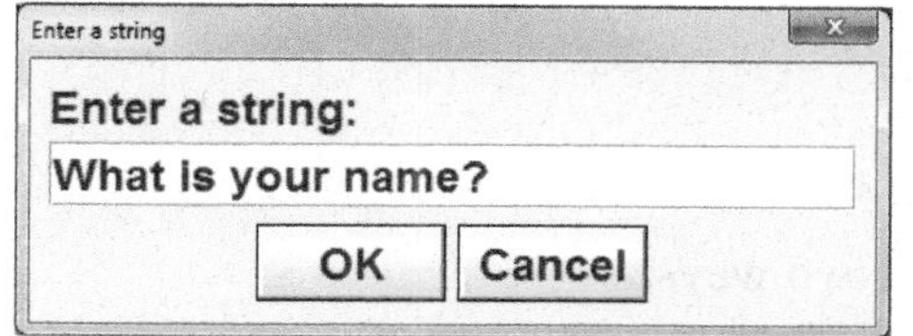

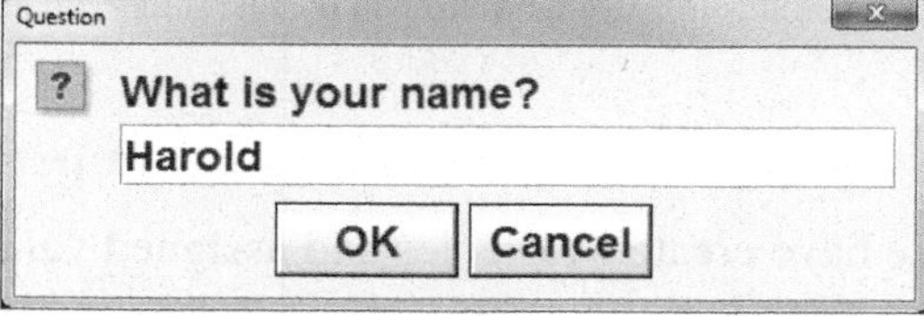

While setting up the function, you can specify what question or instruction appears on the screen.

The aliceLiddell method *say* then outputs the variable. This variable remains available throughout the method *My first method* (or wherever it has been created), so you can use it again. It also can be passed to another method as the value supplied to a parameter, then used in the other method. On the right is shown a say formed by concatenating three strings, as shown below.

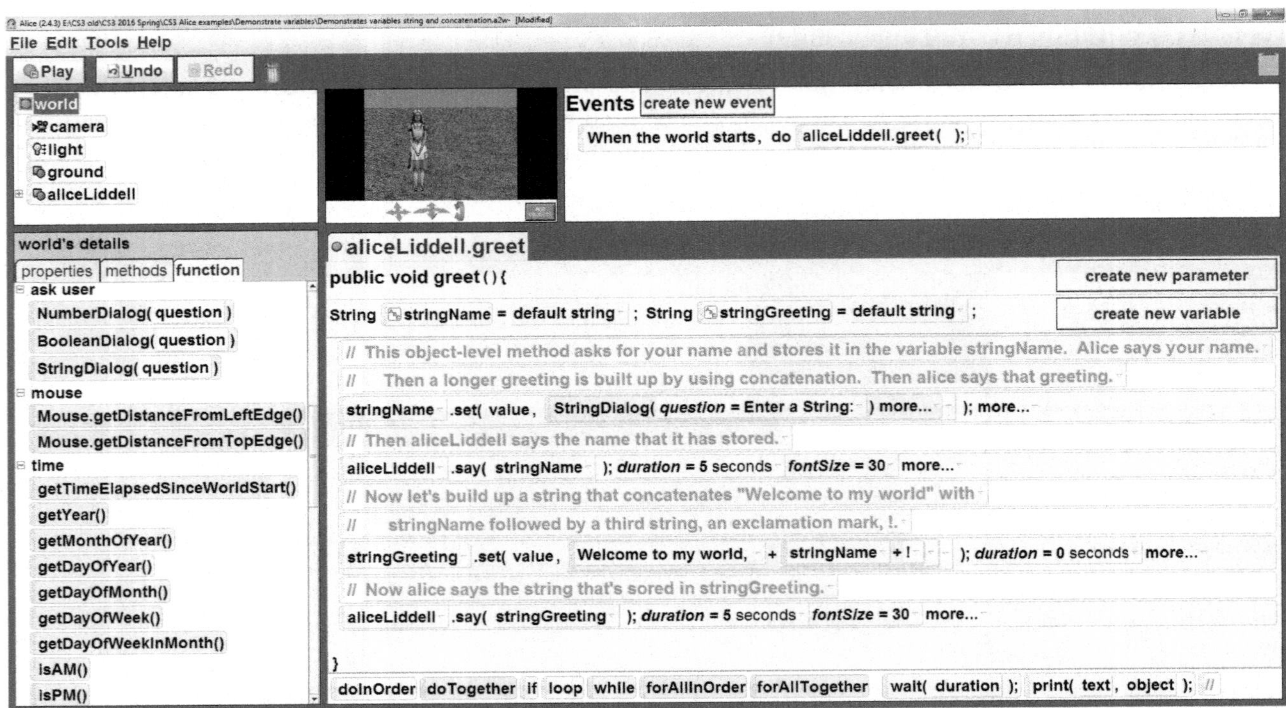

To improve the output and learn about joining several strings into one string (an operation called concatenation), here I've created another string variable named stringGreeting. It uses the world function a b (Java style) or a joined with b (Alice style) to concatenate the string Welcome to my world with the name stored in the variable stringName (such as Harold) and an exclamation mark to form one string(e.g., Welcome to my world Harold!) This string is output in the last statement above.

Assigning (setting) a value to the property of an object during runtime

We have created variables and assigned values in two ways:

(1) When the variable was first created, an initial value was set.

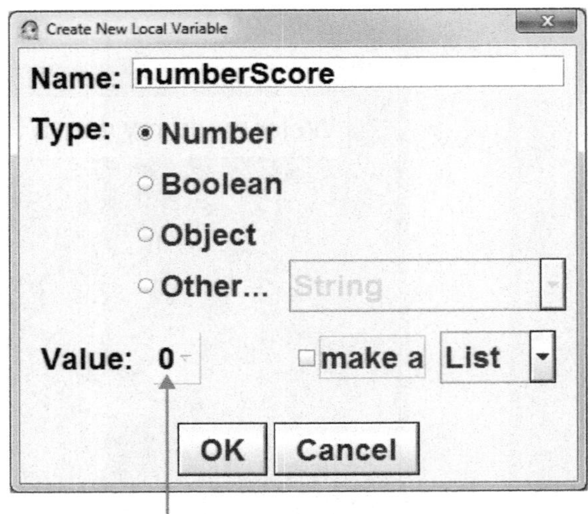

Initial value for the variable numberScore.

(2) In methods or user-generated functions, we drag the variable tile into the coding window and set a value.

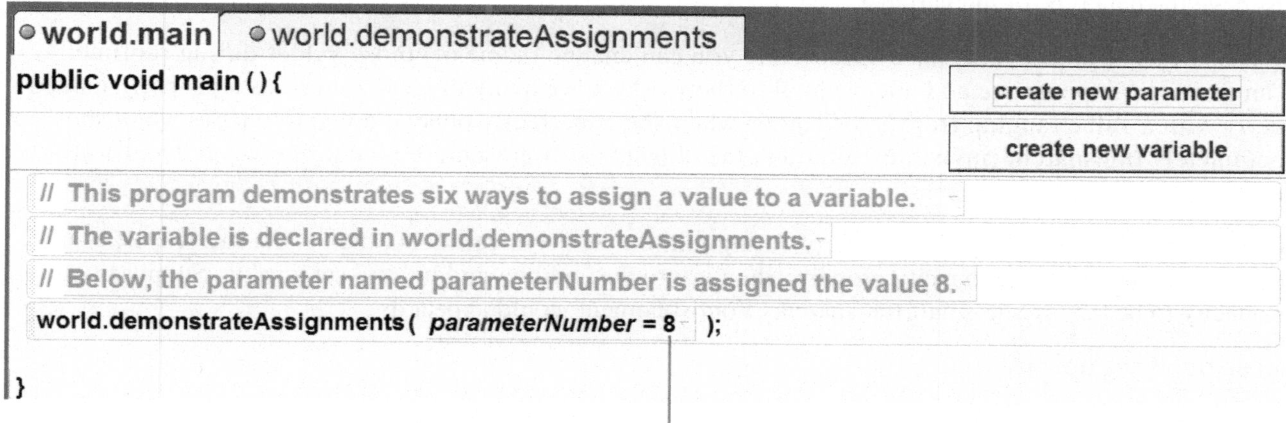


```
world.main | world.demonstrateAssignments
public void demonstrateAssignments ( Number parameterNumber ){      create new parameter
Number numberScore = 0 ; Number numberSecondScore = 5 ;              create new variable
  // Variable numberScore is assigned the literal value or constant 2.
  numberScore .set( value, 2 ); more...
  // Variable numberScore is assigned the value of an arithmetic expression..
  numberScore .set( value, (3 + 4 ) ); more...
  // Variable numberScore is assigned the value stored in another variable numberSecondScore.
  numberScore .set( value, numberSecondScore ); more...
  // Variable numberScore is assigned the value returned by a function.
  numberScore .set( value, camera .distanceTo( ground ) ); more...
  // Variable numberScore is assigned the value passed by a parameter.
  numberScore .set( value, parameterNumber ); more...
}
```

In addition to the initial value, 0, assigned to the local variable numberScore when it was declared, the lower method assigns a numeric value to the variable in five ways: a literal value, an arithmetic expression, another variable numberSecondScore, a function that returns a number, and the parameter that's been passed from method main at the top.

You could use the following to increment the value stored in the variable *numberScore*:

```
numberScore   set value to   numberScore + 1
```

The effect of this statement is to retrieve the value stored in *numberScore*, add 1 to it, and store the result back in numberScore.

In the previous examples, I dragged the variable named *numberScore* into the coding window and set its value to be 2, to be the result of an arithmetic expression (3 + 4), to be the value of another variable (here *numberSecondScore* that was previously given the value 5), and finally to be the value of a function (here, the function that returns the distance between the camera and the ground). If the method had a parameter, you also could assign the value of the parameter to the variable. In all cases, the value you set (assign) to the variable must have the data type of the variable.

The properties of objects also have values, and you can change (some of) those values during runtime. As an example, suppose we add aliceLiddell to the world. Like many objects, Alice has a property named *opacity* with a value ranging from 1 (or 100%) when she is perfectly opaque down to 0 (0%) when she is completely transparent (invisible), although the object is still present. All values between 0 and 1 are possible.

To set the value of Alice's opacity property during runtime, select aliceLiddell, then under the properties tab of Alice's details, select the opacity property, drag it into the coding window, and set a value. Suppose you set her opacity to be 0.5, so she's half transparent. Your statement would appear as

```
aliceLiddell set opacity to 0.5
```

It helps to understand what you can control. This statement has the form:

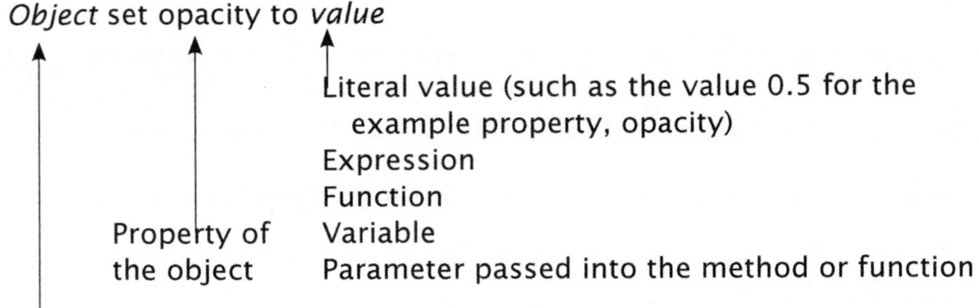

DISABLING AND ENABLING STATEMENTS

Once statements have been coded, if you wish them not to execute, you can simply delete them or copy them to some inactive (not called) method. In Alice, it's cumbersome to convert them into actual comments as is possible in many computer languages.

A simple way to disable a statement is to right-click on the statement and select *disable*. Later, if you wish, you can right-click again and select *enable*.

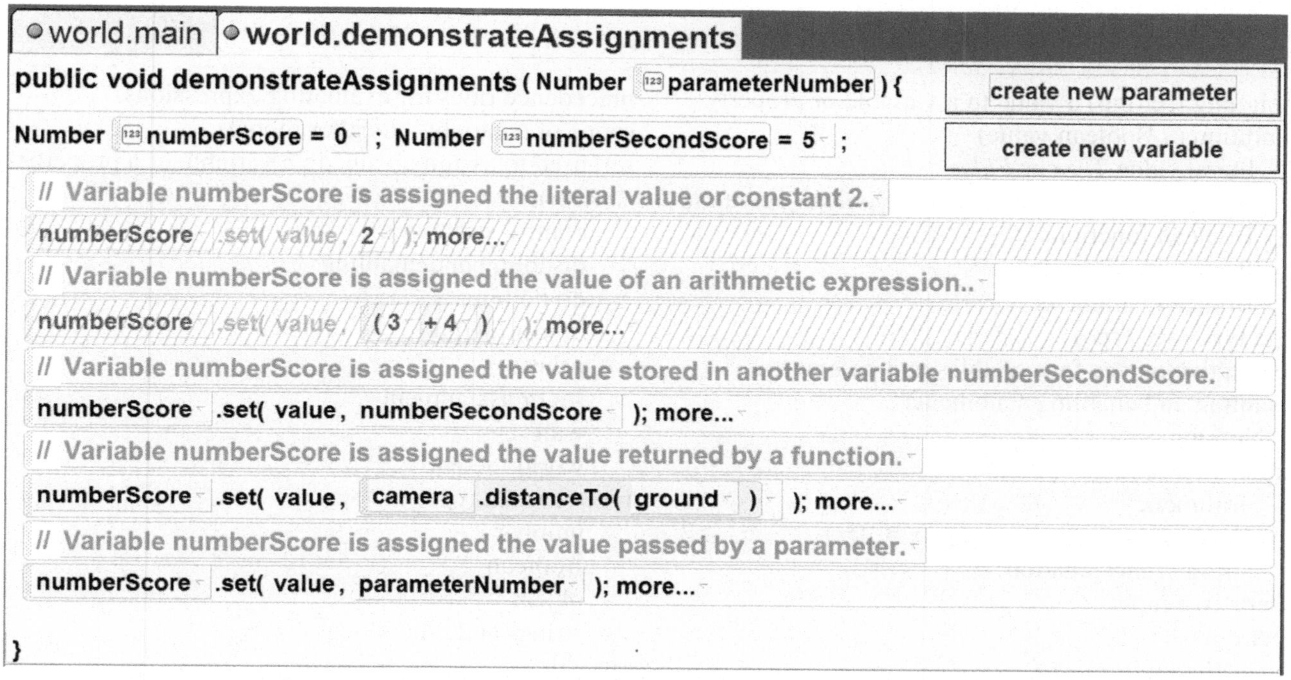

```
world.main | world.demonstrateAssignments
public void demonstrateAssignments ( Number parameterNumber ) {        create new parameter
Number numberScore = 0 ; Number numberSecondScore = 5 ;               create new variable
  // Variable numberScore is assigned the literal value or constant 2.
  numberScore .set( value, 2 ); more...
  // Variable numberScore is assigned the value of an arithmetic expression..
  numberScore .set( value, (3 + 4) ); more...
  // Variable numberScore is assigned the value stored in another variable numberSecondScore.
  numberScore .set( value, numberSecondScore ); more...
  // Variable numberScore is assigned the value returned by a function.
  numberScore .set( value, camera .distanceTo( ground ) ); more...
  // Variable numberScore is assigned the value passed by a parameter.
  numberScore .set( value, parameterNumber ); more...
}
```

Here, the top two statements (after the variables have been declared) have been disabled. Because they are disabled, they won't execute when the program runs. The lower four statements are enabled and will run.

SAVING AN OBJECT ALONG WITH ITS NEW USER-GENERATED METHODS AND NEW PROPERTIES AS A NEW CLASS (FILE WITH EXTENSION a2c)

Suppose in a program you've labored long and hard to create and test methods, functions, and/or new property variables for an object, and you'd like to use this "upgraded" object in another program. The procedure to save a class with new capabilities and features is as follows:

(1) Rename the object that you want to save as a new class so it will have a unique name that does not conflict with existing classes of objects.

(2) Save the new class by

   (a) right-clicking on the object in the object tree and selecting *save object*.

   (b) using **save as** to save it as a file with extension a2c (which stands for Alice version 2 **class**). As you create and save new classes, you'll need to save them where you have permission to write and permission to read (if you need to import the saved class). And you'll need to keep them organized so you can find them.

(3) To use this new class in another world that has been opened, use File:Import, then browse to find the object. After finding the .a2c file, select *Import*. An instance of that saved class will be created, and it will include the user-generated methods and properties in that class. This is an example of **inheritance**, where a new class **inherits** the previous methods, functions, and property variables, and includes any new ones.

KEY WORDS FOR THE CHAPTER

- assigning (setting) a value to a variable or property
- condition (a Boolean value)
  - literal value *True* or *False*
  - Boolean expressions and their Boolean operators
  - Boolean functions
  - Boolean variables
  - Boolean parameters
- data type (see type)
- descriptive names for variables and parameters
- disabling and enabling statements
- do Nothing
- expression (and its operators)
  - arithmetic (+ – * /)
  - Boolean (==, <, <=, >, >=, !=)
  - string (concatenation)
- interactive input
- operators
  - arithmetic: + – * /
  - Boolean: ==, <, >, <=, >=, !=
  - string: concatenation
- parameter
  - name
  - type (or data type)
  - using descriptive names
- precedence rules for evaluating expressions
- scope of a variable (local or global)
- set, used to assign a value to a variable or a property
- statement
  - control structures
  - disabling and enabling
  - do nothing
  - object.method
  - print
  - set or assignment
  - wait
  - world.method
- type (or data type)
  - number
  - Boolean
  - object
  - string (and others)
- variable
  - declaring name (use a descriptive name)
  - initial value
  - local variable or method variable
  - property variable (with a global scope)
  - type (or data type)
  - using set to change its value

CHAPTER 6 PROJECT: USER-GENERATED METHODS

Due ______________________________

- ☐ Study Chapter 5 on **If control statements** and the **Loop control** and Chapter 6 on **parameters**.
- ☐ From Alice, open your project from Chapter 4 and immediately Save As . . . a new file named *CourseNumber_ProjectNumber_SectionNumber_LastName_FirstName.a2w*, where *LastName* and *FirstName* are your names, or use a filename that your professor wants you to use. Edit the comment with your filename to show your new filename for this project. Correct any problems with earlier projects. Keep your user story (scenario), outline (pseudocode), and code from earlier projects to document and animate your program, but you may need to move some comments and related code into new methods.
- ☐ Plan how you can make a person object **take one step** (including arm swings) starting from a standing position with arms down. Hints: sketch on paper the positions of the legs at various times in the cycle, then write pseudocode to plan what your code will do. Also see the Alice program *Demonstrates object-level method for stepping soldier.a2w* in the folder of Alice programming examples. A stiff-legged step without bending the knees and elbows is OK.
- ☐ Create an object-level method named **stepOne** for a person to take one full step, which you planned above. Include pseudocode that breaks a full step into separate actions that can be coded. Test your stepOne method.
- ☐ Create another object-level method named **stepMany** with a **parameter** (data type *number*) to control how many steps the person takes. Chapter 6 describes parameters. In this method, set up a loop that uses the parameter to control the number of repetitions (the number of full steps). In the body of the loop, include your stepOne method. Using this **stepMany** method, the person will take as many whole steps as your parameter indicates. Use the **stepMany** method in your story where the person walks.
- ☐ Break up the long, stringy program that you probably coded in the Chapter 5 project into smaller methods, either world-level or object-level methods. Move code from your old *main* method (or *my First Method*) into your new methods using the clipboard. You can move only one tile onto a clipboard at once, but the tile can be one that includes many statements, such as a *doInOrder*, *doTogether*, *Loop*, and so forth. You could break your original stringy method into scenes or groups of statements that complete some part of your story. For example, if a person stands up or sits down, you could create *stand* and *sit* methods, and you can also break your program into scenes and shots. Once you program a method, you'll have to drag its tile into *main* or another method so it executes.
- ☐ **Extra credit of 15/100:** Plan and code the process of picking up the baseball or other ball that you placed on your tabletop and throwing a ball into two or more methods: (1) a method named **pickUpBall** that moves a person near enough to pick up the ball and the person picks it up, and (2) a method named **throwBall** so the person throws the ball either underhand or overhand. This method has a parameter named **speedOfBall** that controls how fast the ball travels. (The baseball has a method *move at speed*, or *move* has a duration that you could use to control speed.) After your person first throws the ball slowly, then magically move the ball back to the table, pick it up, and throw it fast. Letting the person's hand be the vehicle from the moment of picking up the ball to the moment of releasing the ball will be useful. That will keep the ball attached to the hand while the person is throwing it. At the point of releasing the ball, the ball's vehicle can be changed back to the world.
- ☐ **Extra credit of 5/100**: Add up to five additional and different events as described in Chapter 7. Different events are the different categories of events that appear when you click the Create new event button in the Events window.
- ☐ At the top of your *main* method before the scenario, include a comment that says **which object walks**. If you do the extra credit, include a comment that says **which object throws the ball**.
- ☐ Submit your project as directed by your professor.

CHAPTER 6 PROJECT: GRADING SHEET FOR USER-GENERATED METHODS

Lastname ______________________ Firstname ______________________ Section ______________________

☐ Project not submitted or submitted after the deadline (**No credit**).

☐ (–3) Filename should have the form *CourseNumber_ProjectNumber_SectionNumber_LastName_FirstName.a2w* with a _B or _C just after *FirstName* if you submitted several versions.

☐ (–2) Omitted comment with your filename for this project in the editing window.

☐ _____ **This project did not meet all specifications for the Chapter 2 project:** a land or water vehicle, an aerial vehicle, a building, five people, three nonflying animals, two flying birds or pterodactyls, table and four chairs, four kitchen things on the table, a ball on the table, 3D text with your names.

☐ Objects have positioning or angular errors.

☐ **This project did not meet all specifications for the Chapter 3 project:**

_____ A **user story** as a paragraph in English. This remains in the project as documentation.

_____ **Pseudocode** needs to be broken into finer steps with the objective of finally having a line of pseudocode that can be coded with one statement. Missing two or more camera positions (you have one). Story is short. You need a minimum of 30 actions (not including the control structures).

☐ **This project did not meet all specifications for the Chapter 5 project:**

_____ **Executable code for at least 30 actions and three camera positions** appears just after the pseudocode that describes the code. Program has groups of pseudocode comments followed by groups of actual code. Intermingle the pseudocode and actual code so someone reading the program will have plain-English sentences describing the action, followed on the next line by the actual code. Logic in the doInOrder, doTogether, or other control structures can be simplified.

☐ _____ You have a doTogether with one statement.

☐ _____ When you were already in a doInOrder, you began another unnecessary doInOrder.

☐ _____ Sometimes you used a doInOrder tile, then shifted to not using it (or the opposite).

New tasks

☐ _____ *Main* method not broken into specialized or focused methods such as standing up, flying, fights, or arguments, or the *main* method hasn't been broken into smaller methods such as a new method for each shot (each camera position).

☐ _____ stepOne doesn't cause the person to take one step.

☐ _____ Missing pseudocode in your walking methods.

☐ _____ stepMany has no parameter, numberOfSteps, to control the number of steps that the person takes, or stepMany does not use the parameter in the loop. The person always takes the same number of steps.

Extra credit

☐ _____ **pickUp and throwBall methods (+15)** don't have or don't use a parameter to control the speed of the ball. Requires two throws with slow and fast speeds. Use your pickUp and throwBall methods twice.

☐ ____Did not say in a comment who picks up and throws the ball.

☐ _____ **Five new, different events (+5 max; 1 point for each new, different event). This extra-credit task is based on Chapter 7.**

_____ **Did not describe how or when to use the events.**

Other comments:

Score _______ **out of 100.** Keep this sheet as evidence of your score. See your professor if you think there were grading errors.

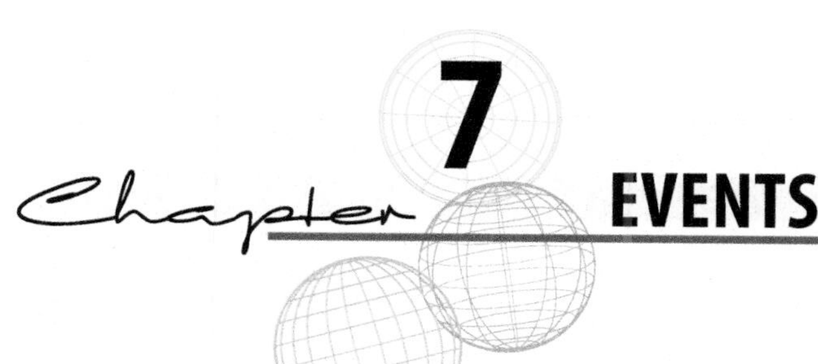

EVENTS

Contents

INTRODUCTION TO EVENTS

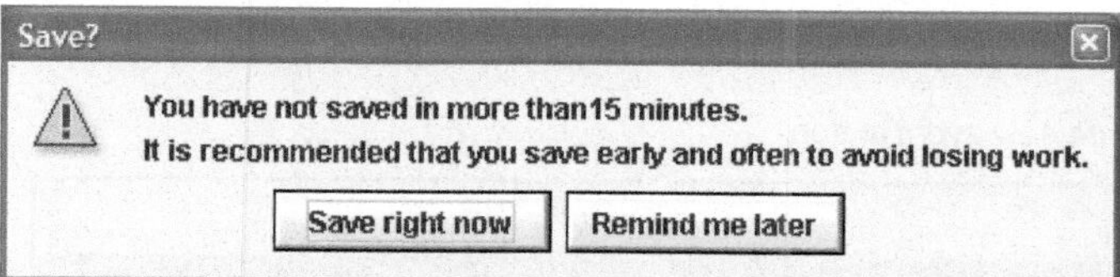

Windows like the above can be found throughout operating systems and application programs with graphical user interfaces (GUIs) when the languages used are event driven. Behind each button is a *when-button-is-clicked* event, which is linked to a specific program or set of instructions that is executed when the event occurs (when the button is clicked with the left mouse button here). The operating system keeps track of your cursor's position on the screen, and also knows the positions of the button's boundaries. So if you left-click on the button, the program knows that you've clicked on that button, and that event triggers some other action or program to execute.

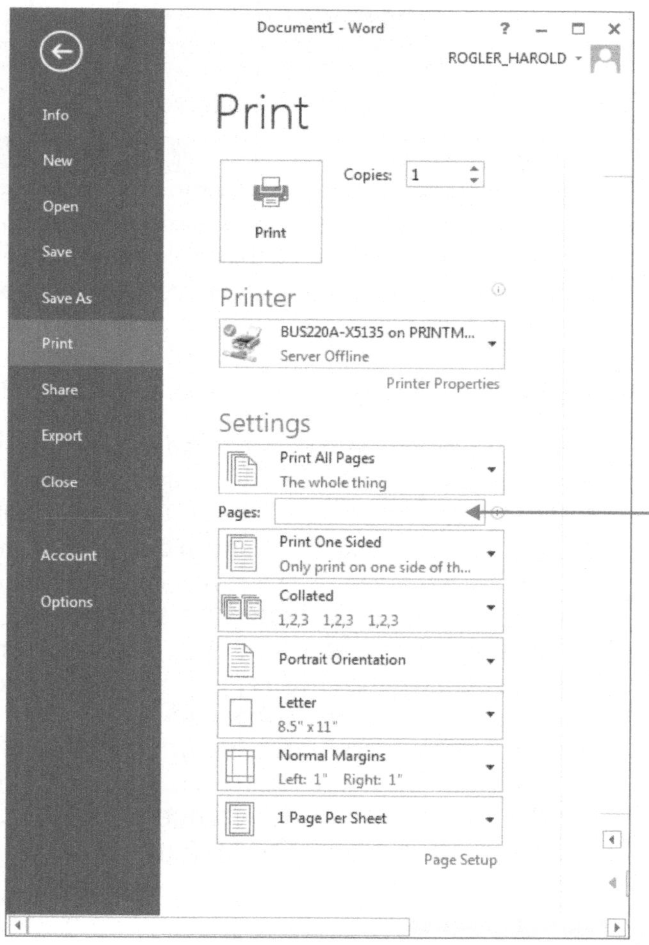

When you print, a window similar to this appears with several places where you can type data, such as the pages that you want to print. As you move your cursor into a textbox, the program triggers an event that your cursor is in that specific textbox. With the cursor there, you left-click, and an event associated with your left mouse button is triggered, causing the cursor to position itself left justified in the textbox and flash. The program will receive the numbers you type there. Other textboxes here have drop-down lists that appear when you click in those textboxes.

EVENTS IN ALICE AND CREATING NEW EVENTS

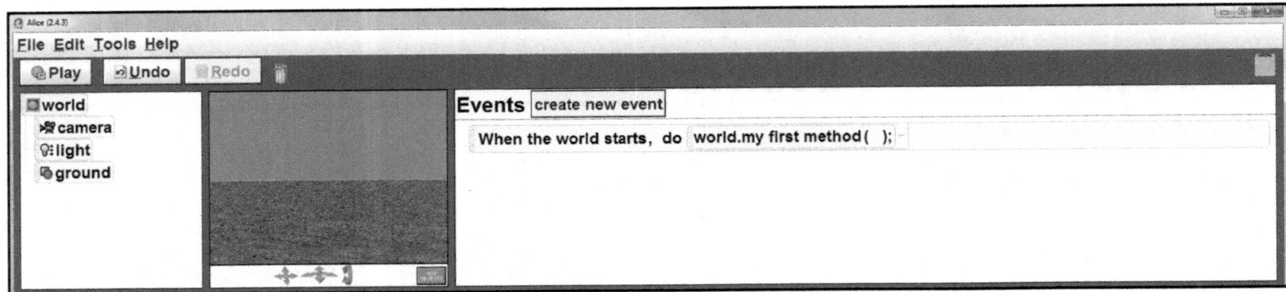

When Alice begins running a new project, it's set up to run the method named *my first method*, which initially only has a *do Nothing* tile. As you code that method and click *Play,* that code will execute because the event *When the world starts* has been triggered and an instruction appears in the Events window that when the world starts, method *my first method* is to be executed.

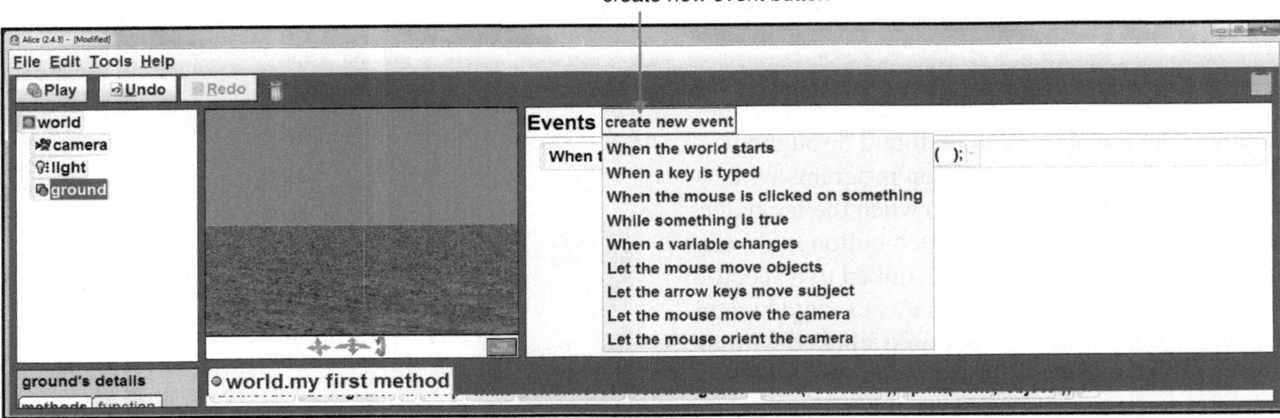

You can code other events that appear on the dropdown list after you click *create new event.* Many events allow the user to interact with the program while it is running. For example, clicking the mouse on some object or pressing keys (arrow keys, space bar, <Enter>, any letter or number) can cause programs to run. Other events are triggered when a variable changes or when something is *True.*

The choice of events appearing on the dropdown list above after clicking the *create new event* button are:

- `When the world starts` (triggered by clicking the *Play* button)
- `When a key is typed` (event is triggered when the finger is raised from the key and the circuit opens)
- `When a key is pressed` (event is triggered when the finger has pressed the key down to the bottom of the keystroke and the electrical circuit closes)
  To use the *key press* event, first choose *When a key is typed*, then right-click and alter the event.
- `When the mouse is clicked on something`
- `While something is true` } These two events execute methods or other statements while some condition is *True* or when the value stored in a variable is changed.
- `When a variable changes` }
- `Let the mouse move <objects>`
- `Let the arrow keys move <subject>` The movements caused by the arrow keys are forward (↑), backward (↓), turn right (→), and turn left (←).
- `Let the mouse move the camera`
- `Let the mouse orient the camera`

Responding to an event by executing a statement is called **handling the event**. The statement that executes and thereby handles or accomplishes some task when an event occurs is called the **event handler**. Although Alice doesn't show the period (dot) that separates the event and the method, essentially you have

*Event.*world*.method* (For example, **When the world starts, do world.main( );**)
Event.object.method (for example, **When F is typed, do frog.flip( );**)

Although these two are commonly used with events, as we've defined a statement in this book, a simpler and more general way is

Event.statement

The statement can be a method (world-level or object-level), any control statement (DoInOrder, doTogether, If, For loop, or While loop), or an assignment statement to assign a value to a variable or a property of an object. Any of these statements associated with an event would be the **event handler**.

This means that, besides the choices of *world.method* and *object.method* as event handlers, you have two more choices:

Event.control statement (any of the *doInOrder*, *doTogether*, *If*, *Loop*, or *While loop* control statements)
Event.assignment statement (store a value in a variable or set a value for a property of the world or an object)
For example to make the frog invisible, **When mouse is clicked on frog, do frog.set(opacity, 0(0%));**

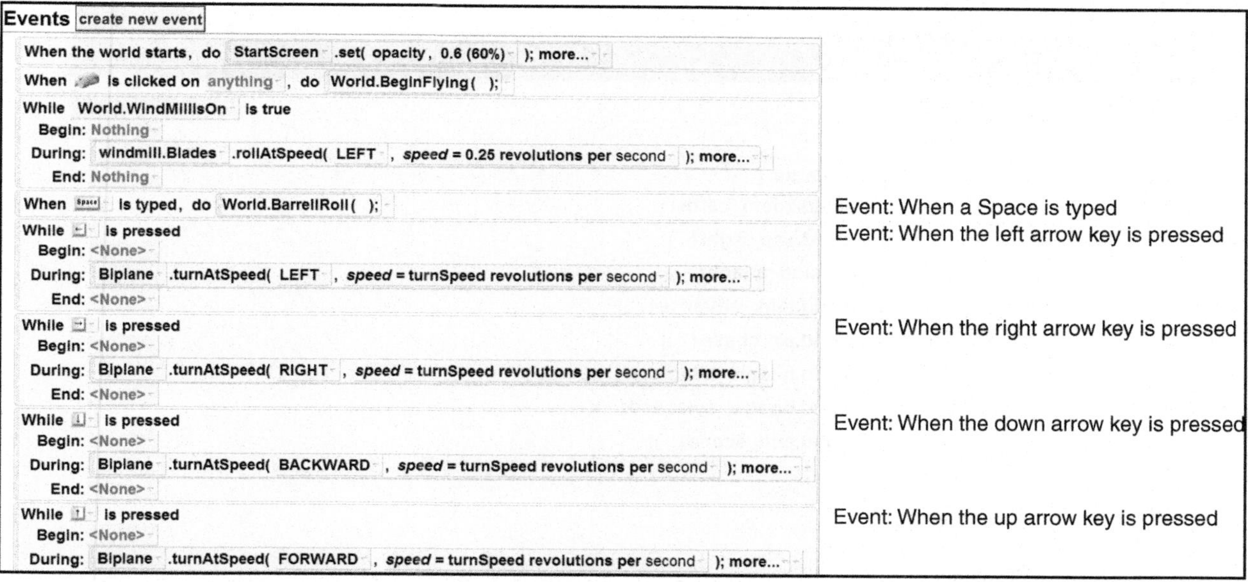

The events for the biplane flight simulator programmed in Alice and available from Help: Example worlds: flightSimulator. Arrow keys are pressed to continually turn the biplane left and continually right and cause it to ascend and descend. The first event handler assigns a value to a property variable. The other event handlers are world- and object-level methods.

MULTIPLE USES OF AN EVENT

If several methods are event handlers for the event *When the world starts*, they behave as if they are part of a doTogether block and all will begin execution when the world starts.

```
When the world starts, do World.skyrideAnimation( );
When the world starts, do World.teacupBaseAnimationLoop( );
When the world starts, do World.ferrisAnimation( );
When the world starts, do World.carouselAnimationLoop( );
When the world starts, do World.octoAnimationLoop( );
When the world starts, do World.swingsAnimation( );
```

Some of the events for the example world *amusementPark* available from Help: Example worlds. This illustrates one way to handle the execution of several handlers that all execute with one event. The event here is *when the world starts*, but this style could also be used with other events that each have several handlers. The handlers here are world-level methods.

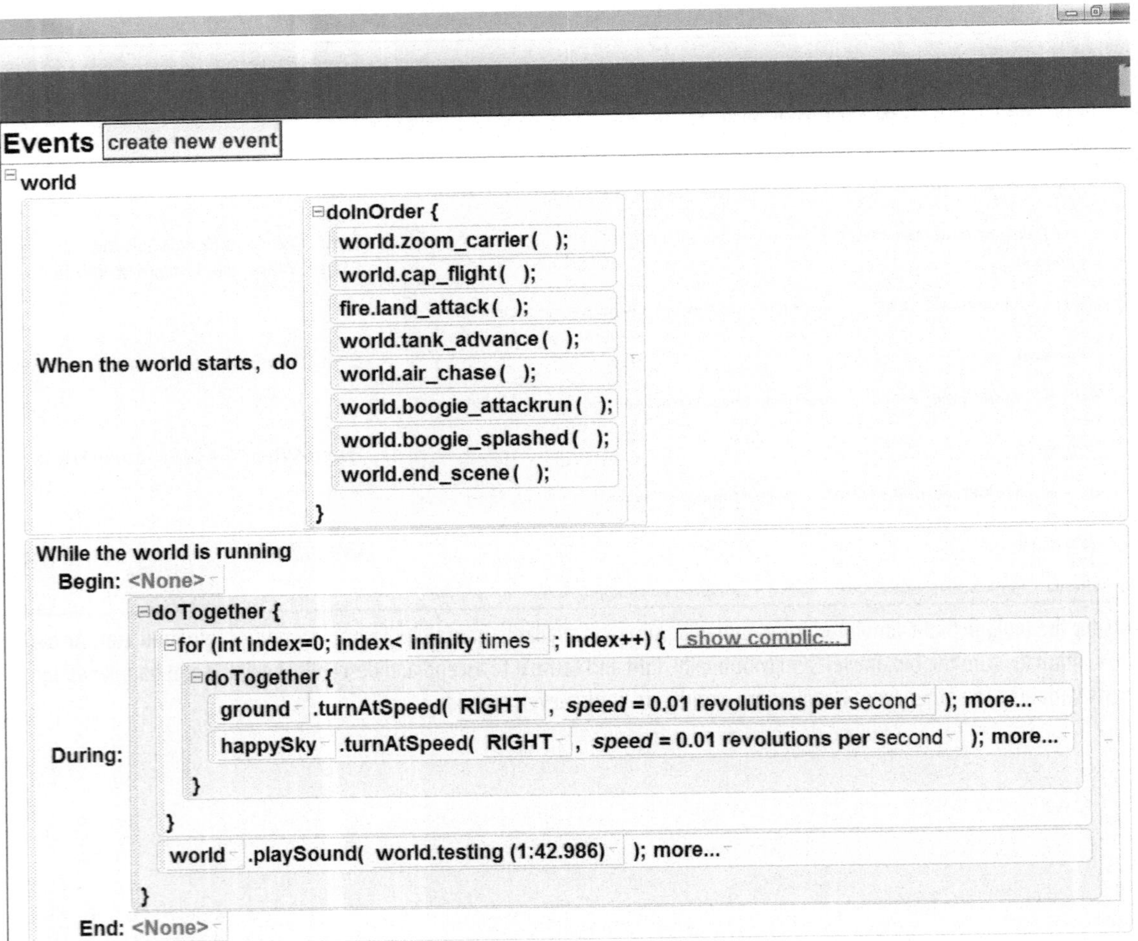

For this set of events, the handlers were doInOrder and doTogether control statements. A sequence of methods run when the world starts. While the world is running, two thing happen simultaneously in the doTogether statement: a loop and playing a sound. These events are from the world TOP NOOB by Joseph Twu in the Alice Examples folder.

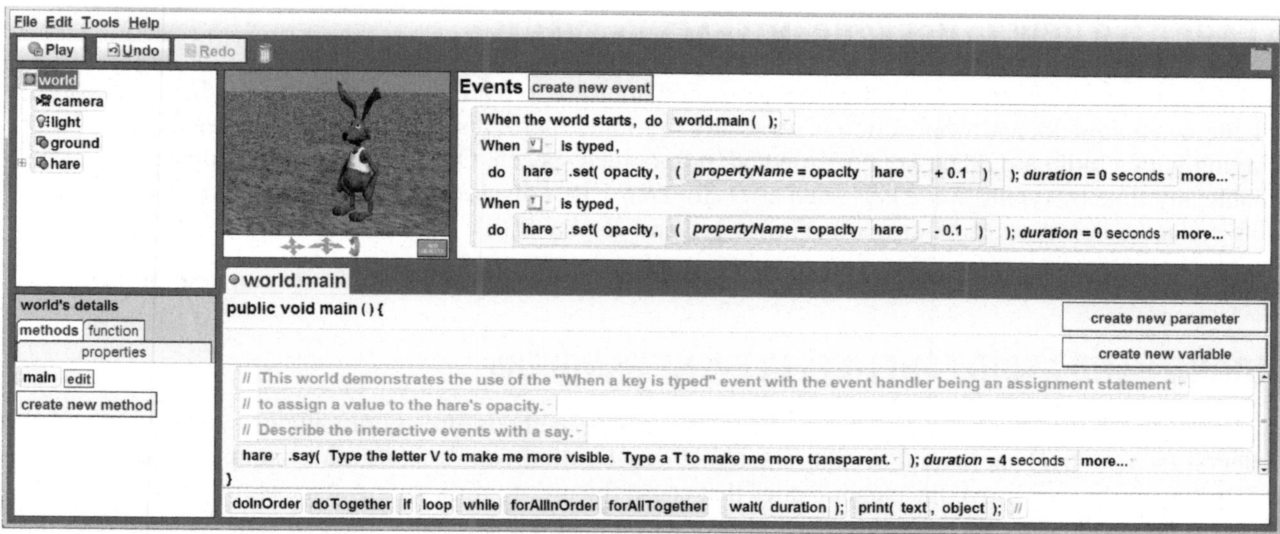

This event handler allows the user to gradually make the hare more visible by repeatedly typing the letter V. Each time you type a V, the event gets the present value of the opacity, adds 0.1 to it, and sets the opacity property to have this increased opacity. By typing the letter T, the user can make the hare more transparent by getting the present value of the opacity, subtracting 0.1 from it, and setting the opacity to have this diminished value. These are examples of using an event to set the value of a property. These could be changed to a key press event, and you could take the previous value of the opacity and multiply by 1.1 (rather than add 0.1) and set the property to have this new value to increase the opacity. These use assignment statements as event handlers.

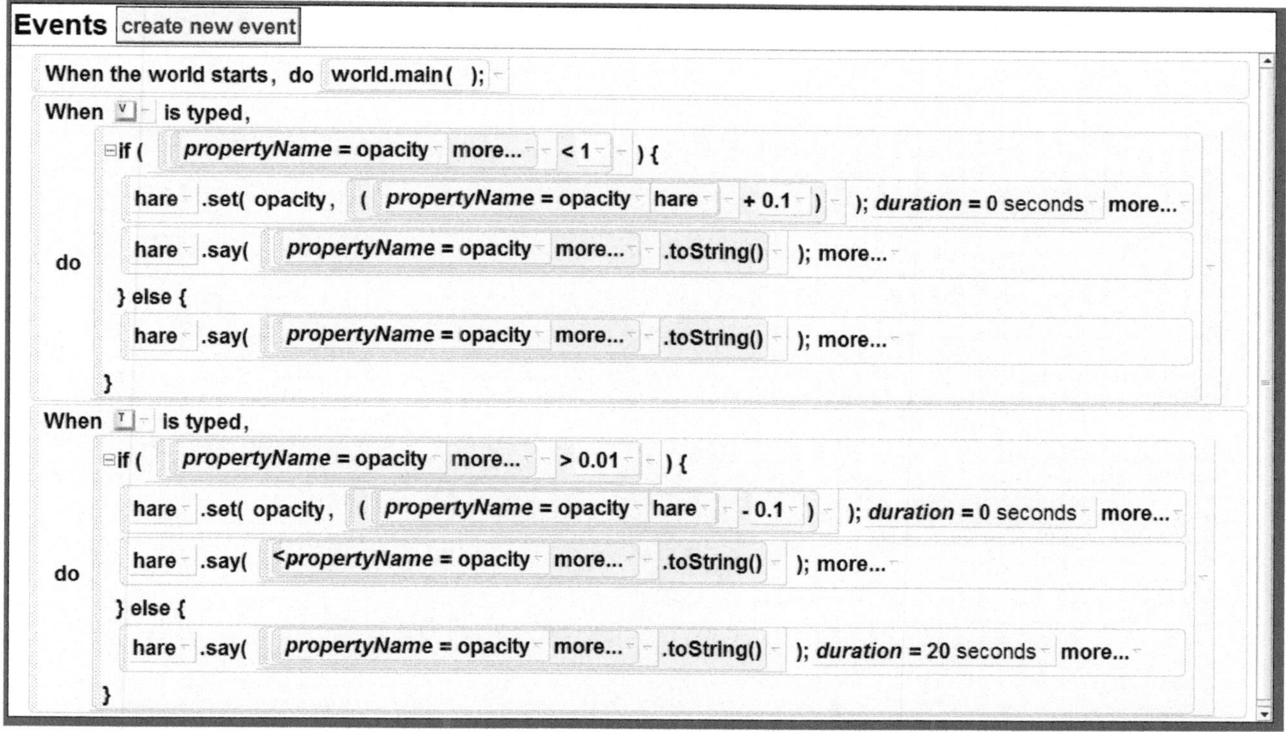

The events to make the hare less or more visible shown earlier have the weakness of making the opacity either less than zero or greater than one, instead of limiting the range from 0 to 1. The above corrects that problem by using if statements as event handlers. It also outputs the value of the opacity after the subtraction or addition. Beginning with opacity exactly 1 and typing the letter T ten times, with 0.1 subtracted from the opacity 10 times, with exact arithmetic the opacity would be zero. The actual value calculated by Alice after typing T ten times is about 1.39 (10-16) or 0.000000000000000139 and had the condition in the last IF statement been **opacity > 0**, it would test True and the opacity would have become about -0.1, outside of the allowable range. The limit was changed so 1.39 (10-16) > 0.09 is False and another subtraction never takes place. This illustrates the importance of testing your program and recognizing that arithmetic may not be carried out exactly because of roundoff errors.

TELL THE USER HOW TO USE YOUR INTERACTIVE EVENTS

If you program some interactive events, the user should not have to read your code to know what events are available, what they do, and what action is necessary to trigger them. Instructions could be displayed in the beginning with a billboard, 3D text, a *say* method, or recorded speech. Or the instructions could be made available any time by typing some key, such as *H* (for *Help*), that displays instructions on a billboard, in the bubble created by a *say* method, or in other ways you can display text.

Rather than using text, you may think of animations or audio that could describe how to run your program.

RECOGNIZE AND AVOID CONFLICTS IN EVENT HANDLERS

The handler for an event, when triggered, could interfere with methods already running or interfere with other handlers if the user triggers several events. The effect may be what you want, or it may simply mess up everything. If you let the user move the camera, does that cause the user to miss seeing some significant action? If you allow the user to move or turn the frog, and another method will later also move or turn the frog, does the interactive event then mess up the later actions because the initial orientation of the frog has been changed? Have you created two or more events that conflict, such has two playSounds taking place at the same time?

KEY WORDS FOR THE CHAPTER

conflicts between events
distinction between typing and pressing a key event
event
event-driven programs and computer languages
event handler

Appendix A SOFTWARE DEVELOPMENT LIFE CYCLE

1. **Analyzing. Analysis is the *dissection* of a task, a critical tearing apart of existing computer programs to identify their characteristics**. The analysis of a chair would include weighing and measuring it; identifying its materials, strength, and who would use it for what purposes; and determining whether it is stackable or folding, has a pleasing appearance, its lifetime, and other characteristics. A chair analyst may analyze many existing or proposed chairs.
2. **Designing.** In contrast, **design is a *synthesis***, a bringing together of choices. Of possible materials, shapes, costs to manufacture, and so on, the designer picks one of the possible choices from each category that "best" meets the overall purpose of the chair. In Alice, our design includes a user story (a scenario) and a step-by-step outline (pseudocode) of that story. But design also may include storyboards (sketches of the various shots in each scene). It may include flow charts or graphical forms of the outline that show how tasks are broken into subtasks. It may include sketches of stick figures, for example, to help plan the motions of legs and arms while a person walks, or to help pick up an object, or to help a person sit down.
3. **Implementing or coding the program.** This involves selecting and dragging tiles, typing code, and other ways to create executable statements and organize them into a program.
4. **Testing (every possible path through) the program.** Styles vary for different programmers in the testing stage. Some programmers test frequently—right after enough new code has been entered to test. Other programmers begin to test only after they've completely finished some method or function or some other chunk of code.
5. **Documenting the program.** Some documentation is internal (through **comments** that appear in your source code and through your **descriptive naming of objects, methods, functions, variables, parameters, and other things**). Other documentation includes help messages in the program, and printed and online operating manuals. The overall design of the program may require separate documentation for program testers and programmers who will later upgrade the program or remove bugs.
6. **Distributing, installing, and maintaining the program.** This stage involves collecting and compiling comments to help design upgrades to the program, eliminating bugs found later, and training of program users.

The development of software doesn't always follow this order. You may first analyze, then design. But when you design, you may recognize that further analysis is necessary, and thus you do some further analysis. While coding, you may do some redesign, but if too much redesign is necessary, you probably didn't design it adequately in the first place.

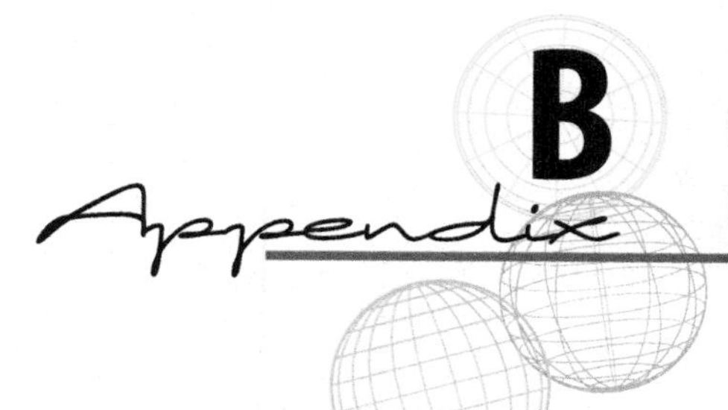

PRECEDENCE RULES CONTROL THE ORDER IN WHICH OPERATIONS ARE CARRIED OUT IN AN EXPRESSION

Expressions can include

arithmetic operations (multiplication, division, addition, and subtraction using the operators +, –, *, /)
relational Boolean operations (the six relational operators that compare two values with the operators ==, <, <=, >, >=, and !=)
compound or logical Boolean operations using NOT, AND, OR (in Alice style) or using !, &&, and || (in Java style)

The precedence rules must be followed to insure that the expressions are evaluated properly.

Highest priority in the precedence rules for computer languages is to first evaluate the expressions within parentheses. If parentheses appear within parentheses, evaluate them inside out (do the innermost ones first, followed by the next outer ones, and so forth).

Fortunately in Alice programming, parentheses are automatically included as you drag the tiles for arithmetic and Boolean expressions into your code. Except for (! a), the groupings are always in pairs.

```
(a + b)     (a == b)    (! a)
(a – b)     (a  != b)   (a && b)
(a * b)     (a   < b)   (a || b)
(a /  b)    (a <= b)
            (a   > b)
            (a >= b)
```

So in combinations of these expressions where more than two operations appear, the above precedence rule is the only one you need to apply.

For example, to evaluate the (1 – (2 * 3)), evaluate the innermost 2 * 3 first, then the outer one reduces to (1 – 6) which is –5.

For another example, to evaluate ((1 < 2) OR (6 > 7)) requires that you first evaluate (1 < 2) as True and evaluate (6 > 7) as False. Then you can evaluate the compound expression (True OR False) as True. Again, Alice's automatic use of parentheses will help.

In Alice code, recognize that parentheses are used to surround more than just expressions.

Parentheses are included in methods to surround the values of arguments that influence the method such as

```
frog.move( FORWARD, 5 meters ) more; ...
```

Parentheses are included in functions such as

Math.sqrt(4) for the square root of 4
Math.pow(2, 3) for 2 raised to the 3rd power, $2^3 = 8$
Frog.getHeight() which has no additional arguments upon which the frog's height depends

Parentheses are included in control statements to surround the condition

```
if ( true )
   frog.move
else
   frog.turn
```

```
While ( true )
   doTogether
      frog.move
      frog.turn
```

So if you pay attention to the use of parentheses and what's being grouped, you'll be able to evaluate expressions in the same way that Alice will do them when your program runs.

Optional note: In many other computer languages where you type the code rather than dragging tiles into your coding pane, the precedence rules are

First evaluate the expressions within parentheses. If parentheses appear within parentheses, evaluate them inside out. This is the same as for Alice.

Evaluate exponentiation. One of the several forms of this is to code two cubed (2*2*2) as 2**3.

Evaluate multiplication and division operations. Multiplication and division have equal priority. If more than one appear, do them left to right.

Evaluate addition and subtraction operations. Addition and subtraction have equal priority. If more than one appear, do them left to right.

Evaluate the relational Boolean expressions that use the operators ==, <, <=, >, >=, !=. The values being compared must be comparable, which ordinarily means that the data types must be the same. The programmer must supply values that can be compared, perhaps by using a function. If the language can implicitly convert a value with one data type into a value with another, then the data on the right side is converted into the data type on the left side of the comparison.

Evaluate compound or logical operations that use the operators AND, OR, and NOT.

REFERENCES

1. Adams, Joel, *Alice in action: Computing through animation*, Thomson Course Technology (2007) ISBN-13: 978-1-4188-3771-b, ISBN-10: 1-4188-3771-7.
2. Dick Baldwin, On-line tutorials for Alice programming: www.dickbaldwin.com/tocalice.htm.
3. Alice website: www.Alice.Org, maintained by Carnegie Mellon University.
4. Wanda P. Dann, Stephen Cooper, and Randy Pausch, *Learning to program with Alice*, Pearson/Prentice Hall (2006) ISBN-10: 0-13-187289-3.
5. Tony Gaddis, *Starting out with Alice—A visual introduction to programming*, Pearson/Addison Wesley (2006) ISBN-13: 978-0-321-47515-2; ISBN-10: 0-321-47515-1.
6. John Lewis and Peter Depasquale, *Programming with Alice & Java*, Pearson/Addison Wesley (2009) ISBN-13: 978-0-321-51209-3; ISBN-10: 0-321-51209-X.

INDEX

CPSIA information can be obtained
at www.ICGtesting.com
Printed in the USA
LVOW02s0545280616
494353LV00001B/3/P